Fifty Years in the East
The Memoirs of Wladimir Ivanow

Farhad Daftary is the Co-Director of The Institute of Ismaili Studies, London, and Head of the Institute's Department of Academic Research and Publications. Since the mid-1960s, when he was completing his doctoral studies at the University of California, Berkeley, he has cultivated his interest in Shiʿi studies, with special reference to its Ismaili tradition, on which he is an authority. As well as serving on various editorial boards, Dr Daftary is a consulting editor of *Encyclopaedia Iranica*, co-editor (with W. Madelung) of *Encyclopaedia Islamica*, and the general editor of the 'Ismaili Heritage Series', the 'Ismaili Texts and Translations Series' and the 'Shiʿi Heritage Series'. He is the author and editor of numerous publications, including *The Ismāʿīlīs* (1990; 2nd ed., 2007), *The Assassin Legends* (1994), *A Short History of the Ismailis* (1998), *Intellectual Traditions in Islam* (2000), *Ismaili Literature* (2004), *A Modern History of the Ismailis* (2011), *Historical Dictionary of the Ismailis* (2012), *A History of Shiʿi Islam* (2013), as well as many articles and encyclopaedia entries. Dr Daftary's books have been translated into Arabic, Persian, Turkish, Urdu, Gujarati, Chinese and various European languages.

Wladimir Ivanow

Fifty Years in the East
The Memoirs of Wladimir Ivanow

Edited with Annotations

by

Farhad Daftary

I.B.Tauris *Publishers*
LONDON • NEW YORK
in association with
The Institute of Ismaili Studies
LONDON, 2015

Published in 2015 by I.B.Tauris & Co. Ltd
6 Salem Road, London W2 4BU
175 Fifth Avenue, New York NY 10010
www.ibtauris.com

in association with The Institute of Ismaili Studies
210 Euston Road, London NW1 2DA
www.iis.ac.uk

Distributed in the United States and Canada Exclusively by Palgrave Macmillan, 175 Fifth Avenue, New York NY 10010

Copyright © Islamic Publications Ltd, 2015

All rights reserved. Except for brief quotations in a review, this book, or any part thereof, may not be reproduced, stored in or introduced into a retrieval system, or transmitted, in any form or by any means, electronic, mechanical, photocopying, recording or otherwise, without the prior written permission of the publisher.

Every attempt has been made to gain permission for the use of the images in this book. Any omissions will be rectified in future editions.

ISBN: 978 1 78076 841 0
eISBN: 978 0 85773 850 9

A full CIP record for this book is available from the British Library
A full CIP record is available from the Library of Congress

Library of Congress Catalog Card Number: available

Typeset in Minion Tra for The Institute of Ismaili Studies

Printed and bound in Great Britain by T.J. International, Padstow, Cornwall

The Institute of Ismaili Studies

The Institute of Ismaili Studies was established in 1977 with the object of promoting scholarship and learning on Islam, in the historical as well as contemporary contexts, and a better understanding of its relationship with other societies and faiths.

The Institute's programmes encourage a perspective which is not confined to the theological and religious heritage of Islam, but seeks to explore the relationship of religious ideas to broader dimensions of society and culture. The programmes thus encourage an interdisciplinary approach to the materials of Islamic history and thought. Particular attention is also given to issues of modernity that arise as Muslims seek to relate their heritage to the contemporary situation.

Within the Islamic tradition, the Institute's programmes promote research on those areas which have, to date, received relatively little attention from scholars. These include the intellectual and literary expressions of Shi'ism in general, and Ismailism in particular.

In the context of Islamic societies, the Institute's programmes are informed by the full range and diversity of cultures in which Islam is practised today, from the Middle East, South and Central Asia, and Africa to the industrialised societies of the West, thus taking into consideration the variety of contexts that shape the ideals, beliefs and practices of the faith.

These objectives are realised through concrete programmes and activities organised and implemented by various departments of the Institute. The Institute also collaborates periodically, on a programme-specific basis, with other institutions of learning in the United Kingdom and abroad.

The Institute's academic publications fall into a number of interrelated categories:

1. Occasional papers or essays addressing broad themes of the relationship between religion and society, with special reference to Islam.
2. Works exploring specific aspects of Islamic faith and culture, or the contributions of individual Muslim thinkers or writers.
3. Editions or translations of significant primary or secondary texts.
4. Translations of poetic or literary texts that illustrate the rich heritage of spiritual, devotional and symbolic expressions in Muslim history.
5. Works on Ismaili history and thought, and the relationship of the Ismailis to other traditions, communities and schools of thought in Islam.
6. Proceedings of conferences and seminars sponsored by the Institute.
7. Bibliographical works and catalogues that document manuscripts, printed texts and other source materials.

This book falls into category two listed above.

In facilitating these and other publications, the Institute's sole aim is to encourage original research and analysis of relevant issues. While every effort is made to ensure that the publications are of a high academic standard, there is naturally bound to be a diversity of views, ideas and interpretations. As such, the opinions expressed in these publications must be understood as belonging to their authors alone.

Table of Contents

List of Illustrations	XI
Preface by W. Ivanow	XV
1: Introduction by F. Daftary	1
2: Modern Ismaili Studies and W. Ivanow's Contributions by F. Daftary	9
3: Autobiography	39
My Family and Childhood	39
University	41
The Asiatic Museum	47
Service in the Bank	54
Journey to India	56
Military Service	60
Persia Again	63
Service in the British Indian Forces	67
Calcutta Again	70
Naturalisation as a British Subject	79
Bombay	80
4: Impressions and Experiences	97
Persia	97
Bukhara	114
Iraq	121
Egypt	126
Syria	131
India	140
Eastern India	146
Northern India	153
North-western India	158
Western India	165
An Accident in the Jungle	176

Appendices by F. Daftary	183
Appendix 1: Bibliography of the Works of Wladimir Ivanow	185
Appendix 2: Publications of the Islamic Research Association	209
Appendix 3: Publications of the Ismaili Society	211
Bibliography	215
Index	235

List of Illustrations

Unless otherwise indicated, all images are from private collections or in the public domain

Cover and frontispiece / Wladimir Ivanow, courtesy of the Institute of Oriental Manuscripts, Russian Academy of Sciences, St Petersburg IV
Wladimir Ivanow 4
Map of Near East, Central and South Asia, early 1940s 8
Louis Massignon 21
Asaf A. A. Fyzee, courtesy of Photo Division, Ministry of Information and Broadcasting, Government of India 22
Title page of *A Guide to Ismaili Literature*, courtesy of the Library of the Institute of Ismaili Studies, London 23
Title page of *Diwan of Khaki Khorasani*, courtesy of the Library of the Institute of Ismaili Studies, London 24
Husayn F. al-Hamdani, courtesy of Professor A. Hamdani 25
Zahid Ali 26
Title page of *The Alleged Founder of Ismailism*, courtesy of the Library of the Institute of Ismaili Studies, London 28
Opening page of a manuscript of the *Pandiyat-i jawanmardi*, Ismaili Society of Bombay, courtesy of the Library of the Institute of Ismaili Studies, London 30
A page from Aga Khan I's *Ibrat Afza* copied in Ivanow's own handwriting, courtesy of the Library of the Institute of Ismaili Studies, London 31
Henry Corbin 33
Muhammad Kamil Husayn, courtesy of Ms Hala Kamil, Cairo 33
Rudolf Strothmann, courtesy of Professor W. Madelung 34
Prince Karim Aga Khan IV, courtesy of the Aga Khan Development Network 35

The rock of Alamut, photographed by W. Ivanow, reproduced
  from W. Ivanow, *Alamut and Lamasar*, Tehran, 1960 37
The rock of Alamut, photographed in 2014 by Dr Janis Esots 38
Fedor Ippolitovich Shcherbatskoi, courtesy of the Institute of
  Oriental Manuscripts, Russian Academy of Sciences,
  St Petersburg 43
Vasilii Vladimirovich Barthold, courtesy of the Institute of
  Oriental Manuscripts, Russian Academy of Sciences,
  St Petersburg 45
Karl Germanovich Zaleman, courtesy of the Institute of
  Oriental Manuscripts, Russian Academy of Sciences,
  St Petersburg 45
Victor Romanovich Rozen, courtesy of the Institute of
  Oriental Manuscripts, Russian Academy of Sciences,
  St Petersburg 45
Valentin Alekseevich Zhukovskii, courtesy of the Institute of
  Oriental Manuscripts, Russian Academy of Sciences,
  St Petersburg 46
Ch. D. Fraehn, courtesy of the Institute of Oriental
  Manuscripts, Russian Academy of Sciences, St Petersburg 48
Institute of Oriental Manuscripts of the Russian Academy of
  Sciences, St Petersburg, courtesy of the Institute of Oriental
  Manuscripts, Russian Academy of Sciences, St Petersburg 49
Asiatic Museum, exterior, courtesy of the Institute of Oriental
  Manuscripts, Russian Academy of Sciences, St Petersburg 50
Asiatic Museum, interior, courtesy of the Institute of Oriental
  Manuscripts, Russian Academy of Sciences, St Petersburg 50
Fedor Aleksandrovich Rozenberg, courtesy of the Institute of
  Oriental Manuscripts, Russian Academy of Sciences,
  St Petersburg 51
Bombay, 1921, press photograph, courtesy of the Bibliothèque
  nationale de France 57
Vasilii Vasil'evich Radlov, courtesy of the Institute of Oriental
  Manuscripts, Russian Academy of Sciences, St Petersburg 60
Sergei Federovich Oldenburg, courtesy of the Institute of
  Oriental Manuscripts, Russian Academy of Sciences,
  St Petersburg 61

List of Illustrations

Dervish by Antoin Sevruguin (ca. 1837–1933), courtesy of the
    V&A Museum, London 65
A Russian letter in Ivanow's own handwriting on the subject
    of dervishes, courtesy of the Institute of Oriental
    Manuscripts, Russian Academy of Sciences, St Petersburg 66
Sir Ashutosh Mukherjee 70
Calcutta, 1922, press photograph, courtesy of Library of
    Congress, Washington, DC 71
Sir E. Denison Ross, courtesy of the School of Oriental and
    African Studies, University of London 72
Sir Aurel Stein, courtesy of the National Portrait Gallery,
    London 75
Sir Akbar Hydari, courtesy of the National Portrait Gallery,
    London 76
The Nizam of Hyderabad, from *Indian Princes and the Crown:
    A brief historical record of the Indian Princes who attended
    the Imperial Durbar at Delhi in 1911*, Bombay, 1912 77
Sir Sultan Muhammad (Mahomed) Shah, Aga Khan III 84
Hasan Ali Shah, Aga Khan I, courtesy of F. Daftary 87
Aleksandr Aleksandrovich Semenov, courtesy of the Semenov
    Museum, Academy of Sciences of the Republic of Tajikistan 89
Doroshke, Tehran, 1909, from Henry-René d'Allemagne, *Du
    Khorassan au pays des Backhtiaris: Trois mois de voyage en
    Perse*, Paris, 1911 98
Qahwa-khana, Isfahan, ca. 1910, courtesy of F. Daftary 99
Khaju Bridge, Isfahan, ca. 1911, from d'Allemagne, op. cit. 101
Tup-khane Square, Tehran, early 1930s, courtesy of F. Daftary ... 107
Tup-khane Gate, Tehran, ca. 1910, from d'Allemagne, op. cit. 108
Shams al-Imare, Tehran, ca. 1911, from d'Allemagne, op. cit. 109
The shrine of Imam Reza, Meshhed, ca. 1911, from
    d'Allemagne, op. cit. 111
The shrine of Imam Ali b. Abi Talib, Najaf, ca. 1948, from
    *An Introduction to the past and present of the Kingdom of
    Iraq by a Committee of Officials*, Baghdad, 1946 112
Bazar in Bukhara, ca. 1898, from J. T. Woolrich Perowne,
    Russian Hosts and English Guests in Central Asia,
    London, 1898 116
Paul Kraus 126

Dr Taha Husayn 127
Umm Kulthum in concert 129
Merje Square, Damascus, ca. 1920 131
M. Kurd Ali 132
The castle of Masyaf, photograph by Gary Otte, copyright Aga
 Khan Historic Cities Programme 135
Karbala, ca. 1948, from *An Introduction to the past and present
 of the Kingdom of Iraq by a Committee of Officials*, Baghdad,
 1946 139
Wladimir Ivanow in India, courtesy of the Institute of Oriental
 Manuscripts, Russian Academy of Sciences, St Petersburg 141
Benares, the *ghat*s on the River Ganges, late 19th century,
 photograph by Samuel Bourne, courtesy of the Bibliothèque
 nationale de France 154
Agra, early 20th century, photograph by Charles Mangin,
 courtesy of the Bibliothèque nationale de France 158
A page from the Khojki manuscript *Kalam-e Mawla* (KH 21,
 f. 33v), courtesy of the Library of the Institute of Ismaili
 Studies, London 167

Preface

The circumstances of my life have unfolded in such a way that I have spent fifty years, virtually continuously, as a researcher in the field of Iranian studies (Persian dialects) and Ismaili studies. This period coincided with one of the most tragic eras in the history of mankind, one of radical change and enormous shifts in lifestyles, worldviews and of social and political changes in the life of nations, including the peoples of the East. Over such a long period of time I have accumulated a wealth of information, personal observations, experiences, feelings and impressions. Thus, some of this collected material may prove to be of academic interest and to have some value as an eyewitness testimony.

My friends and acquaintances of different nationalities and professions often advised me to publish at least some of this material, and perhaps I should have done so. It was invariably recommended that I should present it in the form of an autobiography rather than as a narrative of my travels, which would have been an easier task. Yet my advisors have sought to convince me that the inclusion of an autobiographical element would be most useful for a correct understanding of my approach to this subject matter and its interpretation. Even though I did not agree with their views completely, they have insisted and thus, as a compromise, I have agreed to provide a short biography along with examples of my observations, impressions and the most essential and characteristic experiences. I have tried my best to avoid giving excessive detail and tedious descriptions, while also not being too curt. One of the features of human memory is its capacity to remember events from the distant past and its comparative inability to recall the most recent experiences.

As I write this at the age of eighty-two, I am a novice in this genre as I have never written memoirs that could be readily classified as 'easy reading'. As my guide, I have taken a 500-year-old book of travels,

Khozhdenie za tri moria 1466–1472 (A Journey Beyond Three Seas), by the Russian merchant from Tver, Afanasii Nikitin, who, like me, also travelled through Persia to India.

W. Ivanow

March 1968

1

Introduction

F. Daftary

Wladimir Ivanow,[1] the Russian author of the *Memoirs* published here for the first time, was destined to spend the bulk of his days in exile. In the wake of the Russian Revolution of 1917, Ivanow abandoned his secure life and a guaranteed academic career in his native St Petersburg and embarked on a journey that would last more than half a century, until the end of his life. He never returned to Russia, not even for a brief visit. Ivanow led a lonely life. He had a chequered career and a generous share of unintended adventures during the fifty years he spent in the East, or *vostok* in his native tongue, which are so vividly described in these *Memoirs*.

Outside Russia, Ivanow experienced a variety of jobs, having stints as a bank official, language teacher and cataloguer of Persian manuscripts, before being formally commissioned by the Nizari Ismailis' contemporary spiritual guide or Imam, Sultan Muhammad Shah Aga Khan III (1877–1957), to study the history, literature and thought of that hitherto grossly misrepresented Shi'i Muslim community. As we shall see in the next chapter, it was in that capacity that Ivanow made his invaluable contributions to modern scholarship in Ismaili studies. He retained his unofficial status as the historian of the Nizari Ismaili community when leadership of the community passed in 1957 to Aga Khan III's grandson, Prince Karim Aga Khan IV, the 49th and present hereditary Imam of the Nizari Ismailis. Ivanow's work was indeed his life and, despite incessant hardship and vicissitudes, he never wavered in pursuing his academic goals.

---

[1] His full name in Russia was Vladimir Alekseevich Ivanov, which he changed to Wladimir Ivanow when he was outside Russia.

He devoted himself indefatigably to discovering and studying Ismaili textual sources until the very end of his life.

From early on Ivanow entertained an interest in Oriental studies, being the first member of his family to do so. Enrolled in the Faculty of Oriental Languages of St Petersburg University, he studied Persian language, literature and folklore, as well as Sufism – which he later denigrated – under a number of eminent Russian scholars. Upon his graduation in 1911, Ivanow unexpectedly accepted totally unrelated employment in a branch of the Russian bank in Persia, simply in order to obtain suitable opportunities to carry on field research there. He spent some three years in the country, collecting specimens of Khorasani and other local dialects and also studying the Persian gypsies who were by then rapidly disappearing. These materials, meticulously collected, catalogued and analysed, provided the bases of Ivanow's earliest linguistic and ethnographic publications, which are still valuable for scholars of Iranian languages and dialects. It was also in the course of these early fieldworks that Ivanow acquired a lifelong love for Oriental manuscripts.

By 1915, with the outbreak of World War I, Ivanow had returned to St Petersburg in the expectation of launching his academic career in a more structured manner. The right opportunity soon presented itself: he was offered the position of Assistant Keeper in the Asiatic Museum of the Russian Academy of Sciences, where he had earlier conducted some research in his student days. Shortly afterwards, the Museum's director, Karl Zaleman, dispatched Ivanow to Bukhara to collect manuscripts. Ivanow accomplished this mission admirably and enriched the Asiatic Museum's manuscript holdings by the so-called Bukharan Collection of some 1,057 items, all carefully listed and described, including dates of acquisition and purchase prices for every manuscript. In the spring of 1918, Ivanow was sent to Bukhara for a second time to collect Arabic and Persian manuscripts for the Asiatic Museum. He would never return to St Petersburg, then witnessing revolutionary upheavals following the demise of the Romanovs and the establishment of Bolshevik rule.

The Soviet era of Russian history had just commenced when Ivanow found himself stranded in Central Asia. The circumstances of Ivanow's life had now changed drastically. With little money and no obvious job prospects, he decided not to return to Russia, abandoning himself to what fate might have in store for him. It was under such bleak circumstances that he travelled from Bukhara, then in the grip of an anti-Russian Basmachi revolt, to Mashhad (written as Meshhed in his *Memoirs*), the capital of the north-eastern province of Khorasan in Persia. The next couple of years in Ivanow's life, as recounted in the *Memoirs*, were filled by constant anxiety, worsened by the deplorable circumstances afflicting Russian diplomats of the *ancien régime* in Persia. Ivanow turned out to be one of the more fortunate Russian émigrés, however, as he succeeded in attaching himself, as a Persian translator, to an Anglo-Indian force, the Malmisa Force, then stationed in eastern Persia in the aftermath of World War I. At the time, this force had been charged with patrolling the Persian–Afghan border region, through which German and Turkish agents penetrated into Afghanistan. Strangely enough, our young Russian scholar was then also made responsible for a large number of camels and horses, all serving in the force. Destiny next landed Ivanow in India in 1920, when the force was disbanded on its return to Quetta. Ivanow was once again out of a job, but he was permitted to stay in India and seek employment there.

Soon after his arrival in India, Ivanow went to Calcutta and found employment at the Asiatic Society of Bengal. He was commissioned to catalogue the large collection of Persian manuscripts in the Society's library. Constantly annoyed by the petty rivalries and draconian bureaucratic procedures he witnessed at the Asiatic Society, Ivanow completed the task assigned to him in four catalogues, published during 1924–1928 in the well-known Bibliotheca Indica Series. In the meantime, he collected 1,500 Arabic and Persian manuscripts for the Society. In addition, unknown to the scholarly world and omitted from his *Memoirs*, he also acquired, during 1926–1927, a collection of 238 manuscripts, on the science of medicine, and to a lesser extent on general literature, at the request of McGill University in Montreal.[2] In 1930, Ivanow suffered the consequences of Hindu–Muslim rivalries in

---

[2] These manuscripts were, in due course, donated to McGill University by Dr Casey A. Wood (1856–1942), an ophthalmologist; they are currently kept there in the Blacker–Wood Library. Ivanow himself provided a handwritten list of this collection: 'Annotated Catalogue of the Casey A. Wood Collection of Persian, Arabic and Hindustani Manuscripts', which remains unpublished. In 1994, this editor had the opportunity of seeing Ivanow's handwritten letters and other archival materials

India and within the Asiatic Society, and lost his cataloguing post because the management of the Society had then decided to terminate such 'Islamic' projects as Ivanow had been involved in. The catalogue of the Society's Arabic manuscripts, on which Ivanow was then working, was thus left unfinished for several years.

Ivanow, once again, found himself looking for a suitable job. A couple of prospective cataloguing projects, including one for the Nizam of Hyderabad, failed to materialise, however, leaving him utterly despondent. At this juncture in his *Memoirs*, he complains bitterly about the circumstances of his life, characterised for the most part by financial insecurity and lack of appreciation for his talents; he remained without any academic affiliation throughout his life. Henceforth, Ivanow appears as a lonely man, his loneliness made all the more acute by the fact that he never married and did not start a family of his own. For the greater part of his subsequent three decades of residence in Bombay, Ivanow was looked after by an Indian female servant. His later harsh, and at times blatantly biased, judgement of his peers may not be fully understood except within terms of the sad realities of his own life.[3]

Wladimir Ivanow

Ivanow first encountered some Persian Ismailis in 1912, when he was engaged in fieldwork in Qa'in and Birjand, in southern Khorasan. Subsequently, he published some notes on them.[4] More importantly, in 1928 he established contacts with certain

---

related to this collection at McGill University. See Adam Gacek, *Arabic Manuscripts in the Libraries of McGill University. Union Catalogue* (Montreal, 1991), pp. vii–viii, x.

[3] Note, for instance, Ivanow's demurral about the scholarship of Marshall Hodgson (1922–1968), amongst other scholars of Islamic studies, as expressed in his letters to Henry Corbin; see *Correspondance Corbin-Ivanow. Lettres échangées entre Henry Corbin et Vladimir Ivanow de 1947 à 1966*, ed. S. Schmidtke (Paris and Louvain, 1999), especially pp. 141–144; see also University of Chicago Library, 'Marshall G. S. Hodgson Papers 1940–1971', series II, box 2, folders 10–11.

[4] See W. Ivanow, 'Notes on the Ismailis in Persia', in his *Ismailitica*, in *Memoirs of the Asiatic Society of Bengal*, 8 (1922), pp. 50–76.

'enlightened' leading members of the Nizari Ismaili (Khoja) community in Bombay. And in 1930, while seeking employment, he offered his scholarly services to them. Ivanow's proposal was duly brought before Aga Khan III, whose approval was required. The Ismaili Imam gave his consent; and in January 1931 Ivanow was formally recruited to study the literature and intellectual contributions of the Ismailis. Thus commenced, in a sense coincidentally, Ivanow's distinguished career in Ismaili studies.

Ivanow remained in Bombay for about three decades, establishing an extensive network of contacts with the Ismailis of various branches and regions. He systematically collected Ismaili manuscript sources, and produced his Ismaili publications. In 1959, he transferred his residence to Tehran, where the climate suited him better. He was offered complementary lodgings at the 'university club' (Bashgah-i Danishgah) of Tehran University, on Shah Reza Avenue, never relenting his study of the manuscripts that were regularly sent to him from India. It was also in the final years of his life, in Tehran, that Ivanow compiled his *Memoirs*, drawing selectively on diaries, or perhaps notes, that he had evidently kept throughout his life. He completed the *Memoirs*, which were destined to be his last work, in March 1968. His retirement was formally accepted early in 1970, shortly before his death. He died on 19 June 1970, at the age of eighty-three, and was buried in the Russian cemetery outside Tehran.

Having completed the *Memoirs* in Russian, he very much wished to publish the work in his native land. As a result, he sent a copy to Yuri Vladimirovich Gankovskii, the then deputy-director of the Institute of Oriental Studies of the Academy of Sciences USSR in Moscow. Ivanow had evidently met Mr Gankovskii in Tehran earlier in 1968. The typescript of Ivanow's *Memoirs* was, in due course, forwarded to the chief editor of the 'Vostochnaia Literatura' (Eastern Literature) section of Nauka Publishers in Moscow. By July 1968, Nauka Publishers had conveyed the sad news to Ivanow that they could not consider such an autobiographical genre of work for publication, since they functioned as an academic outfit. Meanwhile, Prince Karim Aga Khan IV had expressed his own interest in the *Memoirs*, and had asked Ivanow to prepare an English translation of the work. Ivanow apparently never accomplished this task. The present editor obtained the above details from Professor Oleg Fedorovich Akimushkin (1929–2010), a Russian scholar of Islamic studies and noted cataloguer of Persian manuscripts. The late Professor Akimushkin was a friend of mine and kindly edited several of the Russian translations of my own works.

Another copy of the Russian original of Ivanow's *Memoirs* had been given by the author himself to Kamol Ayni (1928–2010), who had first met Ivanow in 1966 in Tehran on the occasion of the First World Congress of Iranologists. Much earlier, Ivanow had met, in Bukhara, Kamol's father, Sadr al-Din Ayni (1878–1954),[5] a poet, novelist and the leading figure of Soviet Tajik literature. The Ayni family hailed from Samarkand but settled in Tajikistan. Educated at the Faculty of Oriental Studies of Leningrad State University, Kamol Ayni had started his own career as the first head of the Manuscripts Department of the Academy of Sciences of Tajikistan; and, subsequently, he served in other sections of the Academy, including its Iran Division. Kamol Ayni was also one of the few Tajik scholars of the Soviet era who was permitted to visit Iran. He did, in fact, spend some time in Tehran collaborating with a number of Iranian scholars, and several of his works, too, were published in Tehran.

The present writer was introduced to Kamol Ayni in Dushanbe in 1995, on the occasion of Aga Khan IV's first historic visit to Tajikistan. The large Nizari Ismaili community of Tajikistan, concentrated in the mountain region of Badakhshan, were now seeing their Imam for the first time. Kamol Ayni must have been informed about Ivanow's unsuccessful attempt to publish his *Memoirs* in Russia. At any event, knowing about this editor's affiliation to The Institute of Ismaili Studies, Kamol Ayni gave me a copy of W. Ivanow's *Memoirs* (in Russian), and expressed his interest in seeing it published. Many other commitments have prevented me from taking up this project until now, almost twenty years later.

I have had my own keen interests in this important work. After all, it was mainly through reading Ivanow's numerous publications in the Central Library of the University of California, Berkeley, in the 1960s that I had started to develop a passion for Ismaili studies and so corresponded with Ivanow towards the very end of his life. And some three decades later, in recognition of his contributions, I collected and published in 1996 a volume of essays on Ismaili studies in memory of

---

[5] See K. Hitchins, 'Ayni', *EIR*, vol. 3, pp. 144–149.

W. Ivanow,[6] who had never had a *Festschrift* produced in his honour. Also, in 2011, The Institute of Ismaili Studies and the Institute of Oriental Manuscripts of the Russian Academy of Sciences jointly organised a conference in St Petersburg devoted to Russian scholarship on Ismailism; this conference and its Proceedings were dedicated to the 125th anniversary of W. Ivanow's birth.[7]

The Russian text of these *Memoirs*, typed by Ivanow himself, was originally translated into English, in the late 1990s, by Dr Sergei Andreyev, who was then a Research Fellow at The Institute of Ismaili Studies in London. The original translation has now been substantially revised and edited. We have remained faithful to Ivanow's choice for the main title of the work, *Piat'desiat Let na Vostoki*, translating it as *Fifty Years in the East*. In editing these *Memoirs*, we have constantly striven to retain the flavour of the author's prose as well as his personal 'humour'. Annotations have been provided to describe and contextualise many of the personalities, events, places or terms mentioned by Ivanow.

In preparing Ivanow's *Memoirs* for publication I have received the assistance of several individuals at The Institute of Ismaili Studies; it is my pleasant duty to thank all of them. Sergei Andreyev did an admirable job of producing the first draft of the English translation of the work. More recently, Sultonbek Aksakolov checked the translation against the text of the original Russian, provided additional passages, and also assisted with Russian sources, terms and annotations in collaboration with Russell Harris and Najam Abbas. Wafi Momen kindly helped with a number of Hindustani terms. Nadia Holmes patiently prepared various drafts of the work, and Isabel Miller copyedited the final draft. In identifying, assembling and preparing the images that appear in the publication I have been variously assisted by Hakim Elnazarov, Patricia Salazar and Russell Harris. I owe a deep debt of gratitude to all these colleagues at The Institute of Ismaili Studies.

---

[6] F. Daftary, ed., *Mediaeval Ismaʿili History and Thought* (Cambridge, 1996).

[7] See S. Prozorov and H. Elnazarov, ed., *Russkie uchënye ob Ismailisme/Russian Scholars on Ismailism* (St Petersburg, 2014).

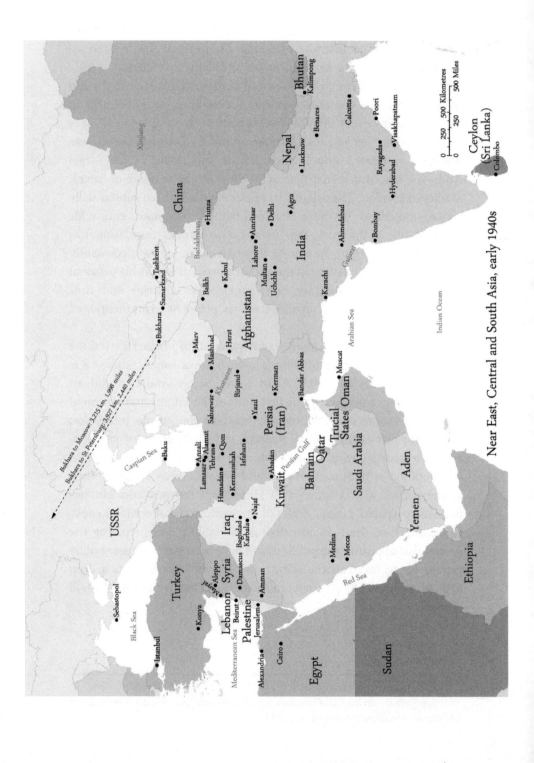
Near East, Central and South Asia, early 1940s

2

Modern Ismaili Studies and W. Ivanow's Contributions

F. Daftary

Few fields of Islamic studies have witnessed as much progress in modern times as Ismaili studies. And in even fewer areas has the role of a single scholar been as pivotal in initiating change as that of W. Ivanow in his chosen field of research. Indeed, Ismaili studies have undergone nothing short of a revolution since the 1930s. The breakthrough in modern Ismaili studies occurred mainly as a result of the recovery and study of a large number of genuine Ismaili texts, which had not been available to the orientalists of the 19th century or the earlier generations of scholars interested variously in investigating this often misrepresented Shiʿi Muslim community. The Ismaili manuscript sources, reflecting a diversity of intellectual and literary traditions, had been preserved secretly in numerous collections in Yemen, Syria, Persia, Afghanistan, Central Asia and South Asia. Ivanow, as the foremost pioneer of Ismaili studies, played a key role, both directly and indirectly, in initiating an entirely new phase in the study of the Ismailis and their heritage.

The Ismailis have had an eventful history dating back to the middle of the 8th century, when the main Shiʿi communities were beginning to be organised with distinct doctrinal identities. The Ismailis separated from the rest of the Imami Shiʿis, who eventually became known as the Twelver (or Ithnaʿashari) Shiʿis. From early on, the Shiʿi Ismailis under the leadership of their spiritual leaders or Imams organised a dynamic, revolutionary movement for uprooting the Abbasids, who served as the spiritual spokesmen of Sunni Islam. The religio-political message of the Ismailis was disseminated by their network of theologically trained propagandists or *daʿi*s throughout the Islamic world, from Central Asia to North Africa.

By 909, the Ismailis had, in fact, succeeded in establishing their own state, the Fatimid caliphate, in North Africa, under the leadership of their Imam. The Fatimid state soon evolved into a flourishing empire, especially after the Fatimids transferred their seat of power to Cairo in 973, their newly founded capital city in Egypt. The Fatimids were challenged from early on by a variety of adversaries, including the Abbasids, the Umayyads of Spain and the Byzantines, as well as some regional Berber tribal confederations. In later times, Fatimid rule was undermined by the Zangids of Syria and the Crusaders, who arrived in the Near East in 1099 under the pretext of liberating their co-religionists. Nevertheless, the Fatimids survived precariously as a regional power until 1171, when Salah al-Din Ayyubi (Saladin of the Crusader sources) ended Fatimid rule and restored Sunni Islam to Egypt.[1]

The Fatimid period represents the 'golden age' of Ismaili history, when Ismaili thought and literature also attained their summit. The Ismaili *daʿi*s of this period, who were also the scholars of their community, produced the classical texts of Ismaili literature, reflecting a diversity of intellectual traditions. At the same time, the learned *daʿi*s of the Iranian lands, such as Abu Yaʿqub al-Sijistani, Hamid al-Din al-Kirmani, and the famous poet and traveller Nasir-i Khusraw, amalgamated their expositions of Ismaili theology with a variety of philosophical traditions, which resulted in the distinctive Ismaili intellectual tradition of 'philosophical theology'.[2]

---

[1] For a brief survey of the Fatimid period in Ismaili history, see F. Daftary, *A Short History of the Ismailis: Traditions of a Muslim Community* (Edinburgh, 1998), pp. 63–119, and his 'Fatimids', in *Medieval Islamic Civilization: An Encyclopedia*, ed. Josef W. Meri (New York, 2006), vol. 1, pp. 250–253.

[2] See Paul E. Walker, *Abu Yaʿqub al-Sijistani: Intellectual Missionary* (London, 1996); his *Hamid al-Din al-Kirmani: Ismaili Thought in the Age of al-Hakim* (London, 1999), and Alice C. Hunsberger, *Nasir Khusraw, The Ruby of Badakhshan: A Portrait of the Persian Poet, Traveller and Philosopher* (London, 2000). See also H. Halm, *The Fatimids and their Traditions of Learning* (London, 1997), and Paul E. Walker, 'Fatimid Institutions of Learning', *Journal of the American Research Center in Egypt*, 34 (1997), pp. 179–200; reprinted in his *Fatimid History and Ismaili Doctrine* (Aldershot, 2008), article I.

Subsequently, Ismailism survived in its Nizari and Tayyibi Mustaʿlian forms. These divisions were rooted in a dispute over the succession to the eighth Fatimid Imam-caliph, al-Mustansir, who died in 1094. The two major branches of Ismailism were designated after Nizar and al-Mustaʿli, sons of al-Mustansir who had both claimed his heritage. The Tayyibi Mustaʿlian Ismailis found their permanent stronghold in Yemen, and later in India, where they became known as Bohras.[3] They also preserved a substantial portion of the Arabic Ismaili literature of the Fatimid and later times. However the Nizari Ismailis, under the initial leadership of Hasan-i Sabbah (d. 1124), founded a state in Persia, with a subsidiary in Syria, centred at the mountain fortress of Alamut in northern Persia.[4] The Nizari state in Persia, comprised of a network of fortresses and a number of towns in several scattered territories, survived until 1256, despite the incessant hostilities launched by the ardently Sunni Saljuqs and their successors in the Iranian world. The Syrian Nizaris, too, succeeded in maintaining their coherence despite sporadic conflicts with the Sunni Ayyubids and the Christian Crusaders.

The Nizari state was eventually uprooted in Persia by the all-conquering Mongols. Subsequently, the Nizaris, devoid of any political prominence, survived precariously as religious minorities in several regions, notably Syria, Persia, Afghanistan, Central Asia, and South Asia, where they became designated as Khojas. The Nizari Ismailis elaborated their own intellectual and literary traditions using mainly Persian and a variety of Indic languages, while the Nizaris of Syria produced their literature in Arabic. In modern times, the Nizari Ismailis have emerged as a progressive Muslim community, with high

---

[3] See Sh. T. Lokhandwalla, 'The Bohras, a Muslim Community of Gujarat', *Studia Islamica*, 3 (1955), pp. 117–135, and T. Qutbuddin, 'The Daʾudi Bohra Tayyibis: Ideology, Literature, Learning and Social Practice', in F. Daftary, ed., *A Modern History of the Ismailis* (London, 2011), pp. 331–354.

[4] See Marshall G. S. Hodgson, 'The Ismaʿili State', in *The Cambridge History of Iran*: Volume 5, *The Saljuq and Mongol Periods*, ed. John A. Boyle (Cambridge, 1968), pp. 422–482; F. Daftary, 'Hasan-i Sabbah and the Origins of the Nizari Ismaʿili Movement', in Daftary, ed., *Mediaeval Ismaʿili History and Thought*, pp. 181–204; reprinted in his *Ismailis in Medieval Muslim Societies* (London, 2005), pp. 124–148, and his *A Short History of the Ismailis*, pp. 120–158.

standards of education, under the leadership of their Imams who are internationally known as the Aga Khans.[5]

Before modern scholarship in the field, the Ismailis were almost exclusively studied and judged by their medieval observers, as well as orientalists, on the basis of evidence collected, or fabricated, by their detractors. As a result, a multitude of myths and legends circulated about their teaching and 'secret' practices. Ismaili historiography and the medieval perceptions of the Ismailis by 'others' in both Muslim and Christian contexts have had their own fascinating trajectory. Here we can cover only highlights of the story as background material for a better appreciation of modern scholarship in Ismaili studies and W. Ivanow's contributions to it.

As the most revolutionary faction of Shi'i Islam, with a religio-political agenda that aimed to uproot the Sunni Abbasids and restore the caliphate to a line of Alid Imams, descended from the Prophet Muhammad's cousin and son-in-law Ali b. Abi Talib (d. 661), the first Shi'i Imam and the fourth of the early caliphs, the Ismailis from early on aroused the hostility of the Sunni establishment of the Muslim majority. Upon the foundation of the Fatimid state in 909, the Ismaili potential challenge to the established order had become actualised, and thereupon the Abbasid caliphs and the Sunni *ulama* or religious scholars launched what amounted to a widespread and official anti-Ismaili campaign. The overriding objective of this prolonged campaign was to discredit the entire Ismaili movement from its origins so that the Ismailis could be readily condemned and refuted as *malahida*, 'heretics' or 'deviators' from the true religious path.

Several generations of Sunni polemicists, starting with Ibn Rizam who lived in Baghdad during the first half of the 10th century, contributed to the campaign of fabricating evidence that lent support to the condemnation of the Ismailis on specific doctrinal grounds. They cleverly concocted detailed accounts of the purportedly sinister teachings and practices of the Ismailis, while refuting the Alid genealogy of their Imams. Anti-Ismaili polemical writings provided a major source of information for Sunni heresiographers, such as

---

[5] See Daftary, *A Short History of the Ismailis*, pp. 159–185, 193–216, and M. Ruthven, 'The Aga Khan Development Network', in Daftary, ed., *A Modern History of the Ismailis*, pp. 189–220.

al-Baghdadi (d. 1037),[6] who generated another important category of anti-Ismaili source material. A number of polemicists also fabricated travesties in which they attributed a variety of shocking beliefs and practices to the Ismailis. Circulating as authentic Ismaili treatises, these forgeries proved to have a great effect and they were used as primary sources by subsequent generations of polemicists and heresiographers. One of these forged texts, which has survived only fragmentarily in later Sunni sources, reportedly expounded the procedures used by the Ismaili daʿis for winning new converts and instructing them through some seven stages of initiation, leading ultimately to unbelief and atheism.[7] The anti-Ismaili polemical and heresiographical works, in turn, influenced the Muslim historians, theologians and jurists who sought to say something about the Ismailis.

By spreading defamations and fictitious accounts, the anti-Ismaili authors produced a 'black legend', depicting Ismailism as the arch-heresy of Islam. This heresy, it was alleged, had been carefully designed by a certain mischievous character called Abd Allah b. Maymun al-Qaddah, or some other non-Alid impostor, or possibly even a Jewish magician disguised as a Muslim, who aimed to destroy Islam from within. By the 11th century, this fiction, with its elaborate details and stages of initiation, had been accepted as an accurate and reliable description of Ismaili motives, beliefs and practices, leading to further anti-Ismaili polemics as well as intensifying the animosity of other Muslim communities towards the Ismailis.

The struggles of the Persian Ismailis, led by Hasan-i Sabbah, against the Saljuq Turks, the new overlords of the Abbasids, called forth another vigorous Sunni reaction against the Ismailis in general and the Nizari Ismailis of Persia and Syria in particular. The new literary campaign, accompanied by sustained military offensives against Alamut and other Nizari strongholds in Persia, was initiated by Nizam al-Mulk (d. 1092), the powerful Saljuq vizier and virtual master of their dominions for more than two decades. Nizam al-Mulk himself

---

[6] See Abd al-Qahir b. Tahir al-Baghdadi, *al-Farq bayn al-firaq*, ed. M. Badr (Cairo, 1910), pp. 265–299; English trans., *Moslem Schisms and Sects*, part II, tr. A. S. Halkin (Tel Aviv, 1935), pp. 107–157.

[7] See S. M. Stern, 'The "Book of the Highest Initiation" and Other Anti-Ismaʿili Travesties', in his *Studies in Early Ismaʿilism* (Jerusalem and Leiden, 1983), pp. 56–83.

devoted a long chapter in his *Siyasat-nama* (Book of Government) to the condemnation of the Ismailis.[8] However, the earliest polemical treatise against the Persian Ismailis was written by al-Ghazali (d. 1111), the most renowned contemporary Sunni theologian and jurist. He was, in fact, commissioned by the Abbasid caliph al-Mustazhir (1094–1118) to write a major treatise in refutation of the Batinis, or Esotericists – another designation coined for the Ismailis by their adversaries, who accused the Ismailis of dispensing with the commandments and prohibitions of Islamic law (*shariʿa*) because they claimed to have found access to its *batin*, or the inner meaning of the Islamic message. In this widely circulated book, known as *al-Mustazhiri*, al-Ghazali fabricated an elaborate and gradual 'Ismaili' system of initiation leading in the final stage to atheism.[9] Influenced by al-Ghazali, other Sunni authors, including Saljuq chroniclers, participated actively in the renewed literary campaign against the Ismailis, while the Saljuq armies failed to dislodge the Nizari Ismailis from their mountain fortresses in Persia.

The Ismailis soon found a new enemy in the Christian Crusaders, who had arrived in the Near East to liberate their co-religionists. The Crusaders seized Jerusalem, their primary target, in 1099, and then founded four principalities in the Near East. The Crusaders had extensive military and diplomatic encounters with the Fatimids in Egypt and the Nizari Ismailis in Syria, with lasting consequences in terms of the distorted image of the Nizaris that became established in medieval Europe.

The Syrian Nizaris attained the peak of their power and fame under the leadership of Rashid al-Din Sinan, who was their chief *daʿi* for some three decades until his death in 1193.[10] It was in the time of Sinan, the original 'Old Man of the Mountain' of the Crusader sources,

---

[8] Nizam al-Mulk, *The Book of Government or Rules for Kings*, tr. H. Darke (2nd ed., London, 1978), pp. 208–231.

[9] Abu Hamid Muhammad al-Ghazali, *Fadaʾih al-Batiniyya*, ed. A. Badawi (Cairo, 1964); partial English trans. in Richard J. McCarthy, *Freedom and Fulfillment* (Boston, 1980), pp. 175–286. See also W. Madelung, 'Ḡazali. vii. Ḡazali and the Batenis', *EIR*, vol. 10, pp. 376–377.

[10] F. Daftary, 'Sinan and the Nizari Ismailis of Syria', in Daniela Bredi et al., ed., *Scritti in onore di Biancamaria Scarcia Amoretti* (Rome, 2008), vol. 2, pp. 489–500, and his 'Rashid al-Din Sinan', *EI2*, vol. 8, pp. 442–443.

that occidental chroniclers of the Crusades and a number of European travellers and diplomatic emissaries began to write about the Nizari Ismailis, designated by them as the 'Assassins'. The very term Assassin, evidently based on the variants of the Arabic word *hashishi* (plural, *hashishiyya*) that was applied to the Nizari Ismailis in the derogatory sense of 'irreligious social outcasts' by other Muslims, was heard and picked up locally in the Levant by the Crusaders and their European observers. At the same time the Franks, being uninterested in collecting accurate information about Islam as a religion and its internal divisions despite their proximity to Muslims, remained completely ignorant of Islam in general and the Ismailis in particular. It was under such circumstances that the Crusaders themselves began to fabricate and circulate, both in the Latin Orient and in Europe, a number of tales about the secret practices of the Ismailis. Moreover, they now began to use *hashishi* in its literal sense of referring to a person taking hashish, a product of hemp. It is important to note that none of the variants of these tales are to be found in contemporary Muslim sources, not even the most hostile ones, produced during the 12th and 13th centuries.

The Crusaders were particularly impressed by the highly exaggerated reports and rumours of the Nizari-related assassinations and the daring behaviour of their *fidaʾis*, the self-sacrificing devotees who carried out selective missions in public places and normally lost their own lives in the process. It should be added that in the 12th century, almost any assassination of significance committed in the central Islamic lands was readily attributed to the daggers of the Nizari *fidaʾis*. This explains why these imaginative tales revolved around the recruitment and training of the *fidaʾis*, for the stories were meant to provide a satisfactory explanation for behaviour that would otherwise seem strange or irrational to the medieval European mind. These so-called Assassin legends, consisting of a number of interconnected tales, including the 'hashish legend' and the 'paradise legend', developed in stages and finally culminated in a synthesis popularised by Marco Polo (d. 1324).[11] The famous Venetian traveller added his own contribution in the form of a 'secret garden of paradise', where bodily pleasures

---

[11] For a survey of these legends, see F. Daftary, *The Assassin Legends: Myths of the Ismaʿilis* (London, 1994), especially pp. 88–127; see also his 'Assassins', in *The Oxford*

were supposedly procured for the would-be *fida'is* with the aid of hashish provided by their mischievous leader, the Old Man, as part of their indoctrination and training.[12]

Marco Polo's version of the Assassin legends, offered as a report obtained from reliable contemporary sources in Persia, was reiterated to various degrees by subsequent European writers as the standard description of the early Nizari Ismailis, or the 'Old Man of the Mountain and his Assassins'. Strangely, it did not occur to any European observer that Marco Polo may have actually heard the tales in Italy after returning to Venice in 1295 from his journeys to the East – tales that were by then widespread in Europe – not to mention the possibility that the Assassin legends found in Marco Polo's travelogue may have been entirely inserted, as a digressionary note, by Rustichello of Pisa, the Italian romance writer who was actually responsible for committing the account of Marco Polo's travels to writing. Be that as it may, by the 14th century the Assassin legends had acquired wide currency and were accepted as reliable descriptions of secret Nizari Ismaili practices, in much the same way as the earlier 'black legend' of the Sunni polemicists had been accepted as an accurate explanation of Ismaili motives, teachings and practices. Henceforth, the Nizari Ismailis were portrayed in medieval European sources as a sinister order of drugged assassins bent on indiscriminate and senseless murder.

Meanwhile, the word 'assassin', instead of signifying the abusive name applied to the Nizari community in Syria, had acquired a new meaning in European languages. It had become a common noun designating a professional murderer. With the advent of this usage, the origin of the term was soon forgotten in Europe, while the 'oriental sect' designated by it in the Crusader sources continued to arouse some interest among Europeans, mainly because of the enduring popularity of the Assassin legends, which had acquired an independent life of their own.

Encyclopedia of the Islamic World, ed. John L. Esposito (Oxford, 2009), vol. 1, pp. 227–229.

[12] Marco Polo, *The Book of Ser Marco Polo, the Venetian, Concerning the Kingdoms and Marvels of the East*, ed. and tr. H. Yule, 3rd ed. by H. Cordier (London, 1929), vol. 1, pp. 139–146.

By the beginning of the 19th century, Europeans still perceived the Ismailis in an utterly confused and fanciful manner.[13] The orientalists of the 19th century, led by A. I. Silvestre de Sacy (1758–1838), began their more scholarly study of Islam on the basis of the Arabic manuscripts which were written mainly by Sunni authors. As a result, they too studied Islam according to Sunni perspectives and, borrowing classifications from Christian contexts, treated Shi'i Islam as the 'heterodox' interpretation of Islam in contrast to Sunnism which was taken to represent 'orthodoxy'. It was mainly on this basis, as well as the continued attraction of the seminal Assassin legends, that the orientalists launched their own studies of the Ismailis.

It was left for Silvestre de Sacy to finally resolve the mystery of the name 'Assassin' in his scholarly *Memoir*, which he originally read before the Institut de France.[14] He examined and rejected a number of earlier etymologies, and showed that the term Assassin was connected to the Arabic word *hashish*; and he cited Arabic chronicles in which the Ismailis were called *hashishi*. Silvestre de Sacy also produced important studies on the early Ismailis as background materials for his major work on the Druze religion.[15] Although the orientalists had now correctly identified the Ismailis as a Shi'i Muslim community, they were still obliged to study them exclusively on the basis of the hostile Sunni sources and the fictitious occidental accounts of the Crusader

---

[13] See, for instance, Camille Falconet (1671–1762), 'Dissertation sur les Assassins, peuple d'Asie', in *Mémoires de Littérature, tirés des registres de l'Académie Royale des Inscriptions et Belles Lettres*, 17 (1751), pp. 127–170; English trans., 'A Dissertation on the Assassins, a People of Asia', as an appendix in John of Joinville (d. 1317), *Memoirs of John Lord de Joinville*, tr. T. Johnes (Hafod, 1807), vol. 2, pp. 287–328, and Simone Assemani (1752–1821), *Ragguaglio storico-critico sopra la setta Assissana, detta volgarmente degli Assassini* (Padua, 1806).

[14] A. I. Silvestre de Sacy, 'Mémoire sur la dynastie des Assassins, et sur l'étymologie de leur nom', *Mémoires de l'Institut Royal de France*, 4 (1818), pp. 1–84; reprinted in Bryan S. Turner, ed., *Orientalism: Early Sources*, Volume I, *Readings in Orientalism* (London, 2000), pp. 118–169; reprinted also in F. Daftary, *Légendes des Assassins*, tr. Z. Rajan-Badouraly (Paris, 2007), pp. 139–181; English trans., 'Memoir on the Dynasty of the Assassins, and on the Etymology of their Name', in Daftary, *Assassin Legends*, pp. 131–188.

[15] A. I. Silvestre de Sacy, *Exposé de la religion des Druzes* (Paris, 1838; reprinted, Paris and Amsterdam, 1964), 2 vols.

circles. Consequently, Silvestre de Sacy and other orientalists too, unwittingly and variously lent their own seal of approval to the anti-Ismaili 'black legend' of the medieval Sunni polemicists and the Assassin legends of the Crusaders rooted in their 'imaginative ignorance'.

In sum, Silvestre de Sacy's distorted evaluation of the Ismailis, though unintentionally so, set the frame within which other orientalists of the 19th century studied the medieval history of the Ismailis. The interest of the orientalists in the Ismailis had now, in fact, received a fresh impetus from the anti-Ismaili accounts of the then newly discovered Sunni chronicles which in a sense seemed to complement the Assassin legends contained in the medieval European sources familiar to them. It was under such circumstances that misrepresentation and plain fiction came to permeate the first Western book devoted exclusively to the Persian Nizari Ismailis and their state during the Alamut period (1090–1256). The author of this monograph was Joseph von Hammer-Purgstall (1774–1856), an Austrian orientalist-diplomat with many other publications on Muslim history and literature, including editions and translations of texts, to his name. Based on various chronicles of the Crusades and the Islamic manuscript sources then available in the Imperial Library, Vienna, as well as in his own private collection, von Hammer's book on the Nizari Ismailis was first published in German in 1818, but it soon achieved great success throughout Europe.[16] Endorsing Marco Polo's narrative in its entirety as well as all the defamations levelled against the Ismailis by their Sunni detractors, von Hammer's book continued to be treated as the standard work of reference on the early Nizari Ismailis until the 1930s. With rare exceptions, notably the French

---

[16] J. von Hammer-Purgstall, *Die Geschichte der Assassinen aus Morgenländischen Quellen* (Stuttgart and Tübingen, 1818); French trans., *Histoire de l'ordre des Assassins*, tr. J. J. Hellert and P. A. de la Nourais (Paris, 1833; reprinted, Paris, 1961); English trans., *The History of the Assassins, derived from Oriental Sources*, tr. O. C. Wood (London, 1835; reprinted, New York, 1968); Italian trans., *Origine, potenza e caduta degli Assassini*, tr. S. Romanini (Padua, 1838; reprinted, San Donato, 2006). On this work and its author, see further F. Daftary, 'The "Order of the Assassins": J. von Hammer and the Orientalist Misrepresentations of the Nizari Ismailis', *Iranian Studies*, 39 (2006), pp. 71–81, and J. T. P. de Bruijn, 'Hammer-Purgstall', *EIR*, vol. 11, pp. 644–646.

orientalist Charles F. Defrémery (1822–1883), who collected numerous references from Muslim chronicles related to the Nizari Ismailis of Persia and Syria,[17] the Ismailis continued to be misrepresented to various degrees by later orientalists.

Orientalism, thus, accorded a new lease of life to the centuries-old myths and misrepresentations surrounding the Ismailis. And, as we have seen, this deplorable state of Ismaili studies, reflecting the dearth of accurate knowledge on Ismaili history and thought, remained essentially unchanged until the 1930s. Even so eminent a scholar as Edward G. Browne (1862–1926), who devoted large sections of his magisterial survey of Persian literature to the Ismailis, could not resist repeating the orientalistic tales of his predecessors on the Ismailis.[18] Meanwhile, the Westerners continued to refer inappropriately to the Nizari Ismailis as the Assassins, a misnomer rooted in a medieval pejorative neologism.

The breakthrough in Ismaili studies still had to await the recovery and study of genuine Ismaili texts on a large scale, manuscript sources which had been preserved secretly throughout the centuries in numerous private collections. A few Ismaili manuscripts of Syrian provenance had already found their way to Paris during the 19th century, and some fragments of these texts were studied and published by Stanislas Guyard (1846–1884) and a few other orientalists.[19] More Ismaili manuscripts preserved in Yemen and Central Asia were recovered in the opening decades of the 20th century. In 1903, Giuseppe Caprotti (1869–1919), an Italian merchant who had spent some thirty years in Yemen, brought a collection of sixty Arabic texts from Sanaa to Italy; and between 1906 and 1909, he sold these and more than 1,500 other manuscripts of South Arabian origin to the Ambrosiana Library in Milan. On cataloguing the Caparotti

---

[17] See, for instance, C. F. Defrémery, 'Nouvelles recherches sur les Ismaéliens ou Bathiniens de Syrie, plus connus sous le nom d'Assassins', *Journal Asiatique*, 5 Series, 3 (1854), pp. 373–421 and 5 (1855), pp. 5–76.

[18] See, for instance, E. G. Browne, *A Literary History of Persia* (London and Cambridge, 1902–1924), vol. 1, pp. 391–415 and vol. 2, pp. 190–211, 453–460. See also the anonymous article 'Assassins', in *EI*, vol. 1, pp. 491–492.

[19] S. Guyard, ed. and tr., *Fragments relatifs à la doctrine des Ismaélîs*, in *Notices et Extraits des Manuscrits de la Bibliothèque Nationale*, 22 (1874), pp. 177–428.

Collection, the Italian orientalist Eugenio Griffini (1878–1925) discovered several works on Ismaili doctrine.[20]

Of greater importance were the efforts of some Russian scholars and officials who, having become aware of the existence of Ismaili communities within their own colonial domains in Central Asia, now made sporadic attempts to establish contact with them. The Central Asian Ismailis, it may be recalled, all belong to the Nizari branch and are concentrated mainly in the western Pamir districts in Badakhshan, an area lying north and east of the Panj River, a major upper headwater of the Oxus River (Amu Darya). From 1895, this region had come under the effective control of Russian military officials, although an Anglo-Russian boundary commission in that year had formally handed the region on the right bank of the Panj to the Emirate of Bukhara. For all practical purposes, from the 1860s, the Russians had secured a firm footing in Bukhara and other Central Asian khanates. At present, Badakhshan is divided by the Oxus River between Tajikistan and Afghanistan, with the Nizari Ismaili followers of the Aga Khan living in both regions. It is the Nizari Ismailis of Badakhshan who have preserved the bulk of the surviving Nizari literature of the Alamut and later periods, written in the Persian language.

It was under these circumstances that Russians travelled freely in the Upper Oxus region of Central Asia. Count Aleksey A. Bobrinskoy (1861–1938) was perhaps the earliest Russian scholar to have studied the Ismailis of the Wakhan and Ishkashim districts of western Pamir, which he visited in 1898. He published a couple of short studies based on his field research.[21] Subsequently, in 1914, Ivan I. Zarubin (1887–1964), the well-known Russian ethnologist and scholar of Iranian languages, visited Badakhshan and acquired a small collection of Ismaili manuscripts from that region's Shughnan and Rushan districts. In 1916, he presented these manuscripts to the Asiatic Museum of the Russian Academy of Sciences in St Petersburg. The Zarubin

---

[20] E. Griffini, 'Die jüngste ambrosianische Sammlung arabischer Handschriften', *Zeitschrift der Deutschen Morgenländischen Gesellschaft*, 69 (1915), especially pp. 80–88.

[21] See F. Daftary, *Ismaili Literature: A Bibliography of Sources and Studies* (London, 2004), p. 228.

Collection, catalogued by W. Ivanow,[22] also served coincidentally to introduce Ivanow to Ismaili literature, which would soon become his chosen field of research. In 1918, the Asiatic Museum came into possession of a second collection of Nizari Ismaili texts procured earlier, again from districts of western Pamir, by Aleksandr A. Semenov (1873–1958), a Russian pioneer in the study of the Central Asian Ismailis.[23] Semenov had already studied certain beliefs of the Badakhshani Ismailis, whom he had first visited in 1898 as part of Count Bobrinskoy's expedition to the region.[24] It is interesting to note that the small Zarubin and Semenov Collections of the Asiatic Museum, now part of the collections of the Russian Institute of Oriental Manuscripts in St Petersburg, then represented the most significant holding of Ismaili manuscripts in any European library.

The generally meagre number of Ismaili works known to orientalists and European libraries by 1922 is reflected in the first bibliography of (published and unpublished) Ismaili texts compiled and published in that year by Louis Massignon (1883–1962), the French pioneer in modern Shi'i studies.[25] Little further progress was made in Ismaili studies during the 1920s, apart from the publication of some of Nasir-i Khusraw's works by a

Louis Massignon

---

[22] V. A. Ivanov, 'Ismailitskie rukopisi Aziatskogo Muzeia. Sobranie I. Zarubina, 1916 g', *Izvestiia Rossiiskoi Akademii Nauk*, 6 Series, 11 (1917), pp. 359–386.

[23] A. A. Semenov, 'Opisanie ismailitskikh rukopisei, sobrannykh A. A. Semyonovym', *Izvestiia Rossiiskoi Akademii Nauk*, 6 Series, 12 (1918), pp. 2171–2202.

[24] For some of Semenov's Ismaili publications, see Daftary, *Ismaili Literature*, pp. 381–382.

[25] L. Massignon, 'Esquisse d'une bibliographie Qarmate', in Thomas W. Arnold and R. A. Nicholson, ed., *A Volume of Oriental Studies Presented to Edward G. Browne on his 60th Birthday (7 February 1922)* (Cambridge, 1922), pp. 329–338; reprinted in L. Massignon, *Opera Minora*, ed. Y. Moubarac (Paris, 1969), vol. 1, pp. 627–639. This bibliography did not include the then newly acquired Ismaili collections of the Asiatic Museum.

group of Persian scholars in Berlin.[26] It may be noted in passing here that Nasir-i Khusraw (d. after 1070) was the only daʿi-author of the Fatimid period who wrote all his works in Persian. At any rate, by 1927, when the article 'Ismaʿiliya', written by the French orientalist Clément Huart (1854–1926), appeared in the second volume of *The Encyclopaedia of Islam*, the Ismaili studies by European orientalists still displayed the misrepresentations of the Crusaders and the defamations of the medieval Sunni polemicists. Indeed, the Sunni-centric approach to the study of Islam, even when the orientalists had embarked on more academic studies, permeated the entries of this first major Western work of reference on Islam, published in four volumes and a Supplement, in English, French and German, during 1913–1938. The second, revised edition of this encyclopaedia too, published during 1954–2004, essentially reflected traditional European biases, notably its Sunni-centrism, though numerous Shiʿi texts had become available during the intervening decades.

It was under such unfavourable circumstances that Ivanow was commissioned in 1931 to investigate the history and teachings of the Ismailis on the basis of their literary heritage. Ivanow had, some two decades earlier, met groups of Ismailis in Persia, and had had the opportunity to handle a small collection of Ismaili manuscripts in the Asiatic Museum. In fact, he had made copies of some of these texts, which he edited and published in due course. This represented a significant milestone in Ivanow's chequered life. Henceforth, systematic recovery of the hidden literary treasures of the Ismailis became the prime concern of our Russian exile who was to spend the next three decades in Bombay, where members of both branches of the Ismaili community lived and preserved collections of manuscripts.

Asaf A. A. Fyzee

---

[26] See Asaf A. A. Fyzee, 'Materials for an Ismaili Bibliography: 1920–1934', *Journal of the Bombay Branch of the Royal Asiatic Society*, New Series, 11 (1935), pp. 59–65, and Daftary, *Ismaili Literature*, pp. 137, 138, 139, 140.

Ivanow's formal association with the Nizari community served him well in terms of facilitating access to Nizari Ismaili texts, all written in Persian and preserved in Central Asia, Afghanistan and Persia. However, his friendship with a number of Ismaili Bohra scholars put him in touch with the rich Arabic Ismaili literature of the Fatimid period and later Tayyibi Ismailis possessed by them. In this context, particular mention should be made of Asaf A. A. Fyzee (1899–1981), who studied law at the University of Cambridge and belonged to the most learned Sulaymani Tayyibi family of Ismaili Bohras in India. Possessing a valuable collection of Ismaili manuscripts, which he later donated to the Bombay University Library,[27] Fyzee made these available to Ivanow and other scholars. He also made modern scholars aware of the existence of an independent Ismaili school of jurisprudence through his numerous publications, including his critical edition of the legal code of the Fatimid state, *Daʿāʾim al-Islam*, written by al-Qadi al-Nuʿman (d. 974), the foremost jurist of the Fatimid period.[28]

Modern scholarship in Ismaili studies was thus initiated in the

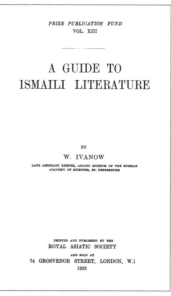

Title page of *A Guide to Ismaili Literature*

---

[27] M. Goriawala, *A Descriptive Catalogue of the Fyzee Collection of Ismaili Manuscripts* (Bombay, 1965), containing descriptions of some 200 manuscripts. Photocopies of the manuscripts contained in the Fyzee Collection have been acquired also by the library of The Institute of Ismaili Studies. See A. Gacek, 'Library Resources at The Institute of Ismaili Studies, London', *British Society for Middle Eastern Studies Bulletin*, 11 (1984), pp. 63–64.

[28] Al-Qadi Abu Hanifa al-Nuʿman b. Muhammad, *Daʿāʾim al-Islam*, ed. Asaf A. A. Fyzee (Cairo, 1951–1961), 2 vols; English trans., *The Pillars of Islam*, tr. A. A. A. Fyzee, completely revised by I. K. Poonawala (Delhi, 2002–2004), 2 vols. See also Ismail K. Poonawala, 'Al-Qadi al-Nuʿman and Ismaʿili Jurisprudence', in Daftary, ed., *Mediaeval Ismaʿili History and Thought*, pp. 117–143.

1930s in India. This breakthrough resulted mainly from the pioneering efforts of Ivanow and a few Ismaili Bohra scholars who had been educated in Europe and held important collections of Ismaili manuscripts. Benefitting fully from his Ismaili connections, Ivanow soon compiled the first detailed catalogue of Ismaili works, citing some 700 separate titles which attested to the hitherto unknown richness and diversity of Ismaili literature and intellectual traditions. The initiation of modern Ismaili studies may indeed be traced to the publication by the Royal Asiatic Society in 1933 of this very catalogue,[29] which, for the first time, provided an academic framework for further research in the field. Recognising the importance of continuing institutional support for Ismaili publications,

Title page of *Diwan of Khaki Khorasani*

in the same year Ivanow founded in Bombay the Islamic Research Association with the collaboration of Asaf Fyzee and a few other Ismaili friends. Sultan Muhammad Shah Aga Khan III acted as the patron of this institution. Four of Ivanow's own earliest editions of Persian Nizari Ismaili texts appeared in 1933, in lithograph form, in the institution's series of publications.[30]

Subsequently, Ivanow turned to aspects of early Ismailism, while editing several more Arabic and Persian texts, including the enigmatic *Umm al-kitab*, which has been preserved in an archaic form of Persian by the Nizaris of Badakhshan, but which does not contain any Ismaili doctrines.[31] His early studies culminated in the publication of *Ismaili Traditions Concerning the Rise of the Fatimids* (1942), which also contained extracts from a number of Arabic Ismaili texts, published

---

[29] W. Ivanow, *A Guide to Ismaili Literature* (London, 1933), based partially on the *Fahrasat al-kutub* of the Daʾudi Bohra author Ismaʿil b. Abd al-Rasul al-Majdu (d. ca. 1769), which has now been edited by Ali Naqi Munzavi (Tehran, 1966). See also Paul Kraus, 'La bibliographie Ismaëlienne de W. Ivanow', *Revue des Études Islamiques*, 6 (1932), pp. 483–490.

[30] Reference to items 58, 59 and 60 in Appendix 1, Works of Ivanow.

[31] Items 64, 67 and 68 in Appendix 1, Works of Ivanow.

for the first time together with their English translations. Ivanow had already published studies on the early Ismailis and their relationship to the dissident Qarmatis,[32] laying the preliminary foundations for the more accurate later works of S. M. Stern (1920–1969) and W. Madelung on the subject.[33] Meanwhile, Ivanow had made modern scholars aware of an important schism that had occurred in the Nizari Ismaili community in the early decades of the 14th century, dividing the line of the Nizari Imams and their followers into the Qasim-Shahi and Muhammad-Shahi (or Mu'mini) branches.[34]

In his research, Ivanow supplemented literary sources with archaeological and epigraphic evidence. In 1937, for instance, he discovered the tombs of several Nizari Imams in the villages of Anjudan and Kahak, in central Persia, enabling him to fill important gaps in the post-Alamut history of the Nizari Ismailis.[35] In fact, it was Ivanow himself who recognised the hitherto unknown Anjudan revival in the religious and literary activities of the post-Alamut Nizaris – a period stretching from the middle of the 15th century to the end of the 17th century. Subsequently, Ivanow published selected works by a number of Nizari authors who lived during the Anjudan period.[36] He also embarked on several archaeological surveys of Alamut and other Nizari fortresses of

Husayn F. al-Hamdani

---

[32] Items 86 and 91 in Appendix 1, Works of Ivanow.

[33] See, for instance, S. M. Stern, 'Isma'ilis and Qarmatians', in L'Élaboration de l'Islam. Colloque de Strasbourg 12–14 juin 1959 (Paris, 1961), pp. 99–108; reprinted in his Studies in Early Isma'ilism, pp. 289–298; and W. Madelung, 'Fatimiden und Bahrainqarmaten', Der Islam, 34 (1959), pp. 34–88; English trans. (slightly revised), 'The Fatimids and the Qarmatis of Bahrayn', in Daftary, ed., Mediaeval Isma'ili History and Thought, pp. 21–73. See also F. Daftary, 'Carmatians', EIR, vol. 4, pp. 823–832.

[34] Item 82 in Appendix 1, Works of Ivanow.

[35] Item 80 in Appendix 1, Works of Ivanow.

[36] Items 110, 116, 125, 141, 144 and 147 in Appendix 1, Works of Ivanow.

Persia, which culminated in his 1960 book on the subject.³⁷ By the time Ivanow's article 'Ismaʿiliya' was published in 1938 in the supplementary volume to the first edition of *The Encyclopaedia of Islam*, the Ismailis were already treated with much greater accuracy by contemporary scholars.

Meanwhile, two other Ismaili Bohra scholars, both educated in England, had provided their own impetus to furthering Ismaili studies. They were Husayn F. al-Hamdani (1901–1962) and Zahid Ali (1888–1958), who produced original studies as well as editions of texts on the basis of their families' collections of Arabic Ismaili manuscripts. Husayn al-Hamdani, from an eminent Daʾudi Tayyibi family of scholars with Yemeni origins, had received his doctorate in 1931 from the School of Oriental Studies in London, where he studied under Professor Hamilton A. R. Gibb (1895–1971). In

Zahid Ali

addition to a number of pioneering studies, he made his vast collection of manuscripts available to Ivanow and numerous other scholars such as Paul Kraus (1904–1944) and Louis Massignon. Indeed, he played an instrumental role in opening up the field of Ismaili studies to Western scholarship.³⁸ Zahid Ali, who hailed from another learned Daʾudi Tayyibi Bohra family, received his doctorate from the University of Oxford, where, in the late 1920s, he prepared a critical edition of the *Diwan* of poetry of the Ismaili poet Ibn Hani (d. 973) for his doctoral thesis under the supervision of Professor David S. Margoliouth (1858–1940). He was also the first author in modern times to have written, in Urdu, on the basis of a variety of Ismaili sources, a scholarly study of Fatimid history as well as a work on Ismaili doctrines.³⁹

---

[37] Items 44, 79 and 143 in Appendix 1, Works of Ivanow.

[38] See H. F. al-Hamdani, 'Some Unknown Ismaʿili Authors and their Works', *Journal of the Royal Asiatic Society* (1933), pp. 359–378.

[39] See Daftary, *Ismaili Literature*, p. 422.

Husayn al-Hamdani's collection of manuscripts was distributed among some of his descendants, and a major portion came into the possession of his son Professor Abbas Hamdani, who donated these manuscripts in 2006 to The Institute of Ismaili Studies in London.[40] The Zahid Ali collection, of some 226 Arabic Ismaili manuscripts, was also donated in 1997, by Professor Zahid Ali's sole surviving son Abid Ali, to the same institution,[41] where they have been made available to scholars worldwide. It may be noted here in passing that both Husayn al-Hamdani's father Fayd Allah al-Hamdani (1877–1969) and Zahid Ali, together with their families, were excommunicated by the traditionally oriented leadership of the Da'udi Tayyibi community for their scholarly activities.

Meanwhile, due to a variety of difficulties recounted in his *Memoirs*, Ivanow had effectively transformed the Islamic Research Association into the Ismaili Society of Bombay, a new institution that would openly and formally promote research on all aspects of Ismaili history, thought and literature.[42] Founded in 1946, again under the patronage of Sultan Muhammad Shah Aga Khan III, Ivanow himself acted as the Ismaili Society's honorary secretary and the general editor of its series of publications. It was also through Ivanow's efforts that the Ismaili Society came to possess an extensive library of Arabic and Persian Ismaili manuscripts. These manuscripts, eventually numbering some 600 titles, were transferred in the early 1980s to the library of The Institute of Ismaili Studies in London. The Ismaili Society with its collection of manuscript sources and series of publications played a central role in furthering Ismaili studies.

The bulk of Ivanow's own Ismaili monographs as well as editions and translations of Ismaili texts appeared in the Ismaili Society's various series of publications. In fact, the Society's publications were launched in 1946 with a book by Ivanow that aimed at deconstructing the centuries-old myth of Abd Allah b. Maymun al-Qaddah, the non-Alid personality introduced into anti-Ismaili polemics of medieval

---

[40] F. de Blois, *Arabic, Persian and Gujarati Manuscripts: The Hamdani Collection in the Library of The Institute of Ismaili Studies* (London, 2011).

[41] Delia Cortese, *Arabic Ismaili Manuscripts: The Zahid Ali Collection in the Library of The Institute of Ismaili Studies* (London, 2003).

[42] F. Daftary, 'Anjoman-e Esmaʿili', *EIR*, vol. 2, p. 84.

times as the founder of the Ismaili movement and the progenitor of the Fatimid caliphs.[43] It was also Ivanow who, for the first time, classified Ismaili history in terms of its main phases in a work published in 1952,[44] representing the first scholarly survey of Ismaili history. This small book was evidently written for the benefit of a broad, non-specialist readership.[45]

Ivanow recovered and published several significant texts written during the Anjudan revival in Nizari Ismaili history, also identifying their authors for the first time. These textual sources included the *Pandiyat-i jawanmardi*,[46] containing the sermons of Mustansir bi'llah (d. 1480), the 32nd Nizari Ismaili Imam whose grave in Anjudan had been discovered in the late 1930s by Ivanow himself. One of the earliest doctrinal treatises compiled during the Anjudan period, the *Pandiyat*, preserves unique evidence on Nizari–Sufi relations in the early post-Alamut period of Nizari history. Other authors of the period introduced by Ivanow to scholars of modern Ismaili studies were Abu Ishaq Quhistani (d. after 1498),[47] and Khayrkhwah-i Harati (d. after 1553),[48] who also composed

Title page of *The Alleged Founder of Ismailism*

---

[43] W. Ivanow, *The Alleged Founder of Ismailism*. Ismaili Society Series A, 1 (Bombay, 1946); with its 2nd revised edition as *Ibn al-Qaddah* (Bombay, 1957). See also F. Daftary, 'Abd Allah b. Maymun al-Qaddah', *EIS*, vol. 1, pp. 167–169.

[44] W. Ivanow, *Brief Survey of the Evolution of Ismailism* (Leiden, 1952).

[45] See *Correspondance Corbin-Ivanow*, pp. 78–80, 83–85 (containing some corrections to the book in question), 86–87, 104, 106–107, 109–111. A French translation of this work, undertaken by F. Max, a French diplomat, was never published.

[46] Item 125 in Appendix 1, Works of Ivanow.

[47] Item 141 in Appendix 1, Works of Ivanow.

[48] See items 8, 64, 110, 116, 144 and 147 in Appendix 1, Works of Ivanow. See also Daftary, *Ismaili Literature*, pp. 123–124.

poetry under the pen name (*takhallus*) of Gharibi. Through the writings of Shihab al-Din Shah al-Husayni (d. 1884),[49] the eldest son of Ali Shah Aga Khan II (d. 1885), the 47th Nizari Imam, Ivanow also called attention to a modern revival in Nizari literary activities in Persian. Ever since his early linguistic studies, Ivanow had also been interested in what he called 'popular forms of religion', forms that lacked theological complexities and formal organisation. In this context, he devoted some time to studying the so-called Ahl-i Haqq community and the connections of these obscure sectarians to the Nizari Ismailis of the Anjudan period.[50]

The Nizari Ismailis of the earlier Alamut period (1090–1256) had not produced any substantial religious literature. However, two major texts of the period, one erroneously known as the *Haft bab-i Baba Sayyidna*,[51] and the other one entitled *Rawdat al-taslim*,[52] have survived directly, and they were edited and published for the first time by Ivanow. At the time of Ivanow, the authorship of the *Rawda*, the major Nizari work of the Alamut period, was attributed to Nasir al-Din al-Tusi (d. 1274), the eminent Shi'i theologian and philosopher who spent some three decades in the Nizari fortress communities of Persia and voluntarily converted to Nizari Ismailism.[53] However, more recent scholarship has shown that the *Rawda*, completed in 1243, may have been compiled only under al-Tusi's supervision by another Nizari author and poet known as Salah al-Din Hasan-i Mahmud-i Katib (d. after 1243).[54] The same Hasan-i Mahmud-i Katib may also have

---

[49] Items 60, 108, 109, 132 and 151 in Appendix 1, Works of Ivanow. See also Daftary, *Ismaili Literature*, pp. 152–153.

[50] Item 126 in Appendix 1, Works of Ivanow. See also V. Minorsky, 'Ahl-i Hakk', *EI2*, vol. 1, pp. 260–263, and M. Jalali-Moqaddam and D. Safvat, 'Ahl-i Haqq', *EIS*, vol. 3, pp. 193–205.

[51] Item 59 in Appendix 1, Works of Ivanow.

[52] Items 45 and 120 in Appendix 1, Works of Ivanow.

[53] See al-Tusi's spiritual autobiography entitled *Sayr va suluk*, ed. and tr. by S. Jalal Badakhchani as *Contemplation and Action: The Spiritual Autobiography of a Muslim Scholar* (London, 1998).

[54] See H. Landolt's introduction to Nasir al-Din al-Tusi, *Rawda-yi taslim*, ed. and tr. S. J. Badakhchani as *Paradise of Submission: A Medieval Treatise on Ismaili Thought* (London, 2005), pp. 1–11. See also S. Jalal Badakhchani, 'Poems of the Resurrection: Hasan-i Mahmud-i Katib and his *Diwan-i Qa'imiyyat*', in Omar Ali-de-Unzaga, ed.,

Opening page of a manuscript of the *Pandiyat-i jawanmardi*, Ismaili Society of Bombay

been the author of the anonymous *Haft bab-i Baba Sayyidna*, written around 1200, and attributed wrongly to Baba Sayyidna, namely Hasan-i Sabbah (d. 1124) who lived several decades earlier.

Fortresses of the Intellect: Ismaili and Other Islamic Studies in Honour of Farhad Daftary (London, 2011), pp. 431–442.

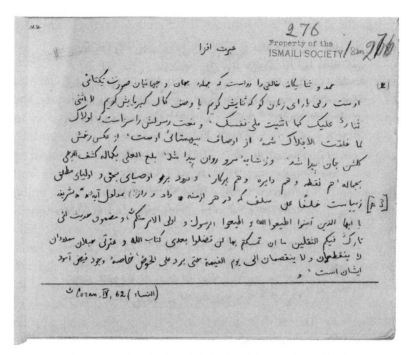

A page from Aga Khan I's *Ibrat Afza* copied in Ivanow's own handwriting

Another of Ivanow's contributions, which has generally remained unknown, was his production of an edition, for the first time, of the section on the Nizari Ismaili state of Alamut contained in the second volume of Rashid al-Din's *Jami al-tawarikh*, completed in 1310. As is now known, the Persian Nizaris maintained a historiographical tradition; they compiled chronicles in Persian recording the events of their state and community according to the reigns of the successive lords of Alamut, starting with Hasan-i Sabbah.[55] These chronicles, retained at the famous library in Alamut and other fortresses, have not survived, but a few later Persian historians of the Mongol Ilkhanid period had access to them. Using the Nizari chronicles, these historians, notably Juwayni (d. 1283), Rashid al-Din Fadl Allah (d. 1318) and Abu'l-Qasim Kashani (d. ca. 1337), wrote accounts of

---

[55] See F. Daftary, 'Persian Historiography of the Early Nizari Isma'ilis', *Iran, Journal of the British Institute of Persian Studies*, 30 (1992), pp. 91–97; reprinted in his *Ismailis in Medieval Muslim Societies*, pp. 107–123, and his *The Isma'ilis: Their History and Doctrines* (2nd ed., Cambridge, 2007), especially pp. 303–308.

the Ismailis as part of their histories. Their sections on the Nizari state in Persia provide our chief primary sources on the subject.

The account by Juwayni, the earliest of these histories, had been meticulously edited by the Persian scholar Muhammad Qazwini (1877–1949) for the Gibb Memorial Series.[56] Kashani's history, the most detailed account of the Persian Ismailis, came to light only in 1964 on the basis of a single known manuscript.[57] Meanwhile, various parts of Rashid al-Din's Universal History had appeared in print since the 19th century. However, the Ismaili section of his *Jami al-tawarikh* still remained unpublished when Ivanow decided, in the early 1950s, to prepare an edition of the portion on the Nizari Ismaili state in Persia. In the event, he did produce an edition, based chiefly on the manuscript copies held at the Bibliothèque nationale, Paris, and one obtained from Lahore.[58] But the Ismaili Society did not approve its publication due to the overtly anti-Ismaili stance of its author. The text of this history, as edited by Ivanow, was later published in Tehran by a Persian scholar, who himself was acknowledged as its editor.[59]

Meanwhile, Ivanow had maintained his systematic efforts to recover Ismaili manuscripts and promote research in the field. By 1963, when he published an expanded edition of his Ismaili catalogue,[60] he had identified a further few hundred Ismaili titles, while the field of Ismaili studies as a whole had witnessed incredible progress. Numerous Ismaili texts had now begun to be critically edited, preparing the ground for further scholarship. As noted, Ivanow generously shared

---

[56] Ata-Malik Juwayni, *Tarikh-i jahan-gusha*, ed. M. Qazwini (Leiden and London, 1912–1937), vol. 3, pp. 106–278; English trans., *The History of the World-Conqueror*, tr. John A. Boyle (Manchester, 1958), vol. 2, pp. 618–725.

[57] Abu'l-Qasim Abd Allah Kashani, *Zubdat al-tawarikh: bakhsh-i Fatimiyan va Nizariyan*, ed. M. T. Danishpazhuh (2nd ed., Tehran, 1987).

[58] See *Correspondance Corbin-Ivanow*, pp. 34, 48, 81, 105, 108, 111, 113, 115.

[59] Rashid al-Din Fadl Allah, *Fasli az Jami al-tawarikh: tarikh-i firqa-yi rafiqan va Isma'iliyan-i Alamut*, ed. M. Dabir Siyaqi (Tehran, 1958); for the subsequent editions of the full Ismaili history of Rashid al-Din, also containing the sections on the early Ismailis and the Fatimids, see *Jami al-tawarikh: qismat-i Isma'iliyan va Fatimiyan va Nizariyan va da'iyan va rafiqan*, ed. M. T. Danishpazhuh and M. Mudarrisi Zanjani (Tehran, 1959), and *Jami al-tawarikh: tarikh-i Isma'iliyan*, ed. M. Rawshan (Tehran, 2008). See also Charles Melville, 'Jame al-Tawarik', *EIR*, vol. 14, pp. 462–468.

[60] W. Ivanow, *Ismaili Literature: A Bibliographical Survey* (Tehran, 1963).

his knowledge as well as the manuscript resources of the Ismaili Society with other scholars. In particular, he established a close working relationship with the French Islamicist Henry Corbin (1903–1978), who commuted between Paris and Tehran, where he had founded in the immediate aftermath of World War II the Iranology Department of the Institut Franco-iranien. As attested in the regular correspondence exchanged between these two scholars, cited above, during 1947–1966, Ivanow readily prepared (handwritten!) copies of the Ismaili manuscripts at his disposal in Bombay and sent them to Corbin, who initiated his own Bibliothèque Iranienne Series of publications, in which several Ismaili works appeared simultaneously in Tehran and Paris.[61] Corbin represented a new generation of scholars interested in Ismaili studies. Another early member of this generation was Muhammad Kamil Husayn (1901–1961), the Egyptian scholar who edited several Ismaili texts of the Fatimid period in his own Silsilat Makhtutat al-Fatimiyyin Series, published in Cairo. Through Ivanow's efforts, he also co-edited the *daʿi* al-Kirmani's chief work, written in the tradition of 'philosophical theology', for the Ismaili Society of Bombay.[62]

Henry Corbin

Muhammad Kamil Husayn

---

[61] See Daniel de Smet, 'Henry Corbin et études Ismaéliennes', in M. A. Amir-Moezzi et al., ed., *Henry Corbin, philosophies et sagesses des religions du livre* (Turnhout, 2005), pp. 105–118, and D. Shayegan, 'Corbin, Henry', *EIR*, vol. 6, pp. 268–272. See also R. Boucharlat, 'France. xiii. Institut Français de Recherche en Iran', *EIR*, vol. 10, pp. 176–177.

[62] Hamid al-Din Ahmad al-Kirmani, *Rahat al-aql*, ed. M. Kamil Husayn and M. M. Hilmi (Leiden and Cairo, 1953). See also F. Daftary, 'Hamid-al-Din Kermani', *EIR*, vol. 11, pp. 639–641.

Although Ivanow concerned himself with various aspects of Ismaili history and thought,[63] his enduring contributions more particularly relate to the Nizari branch of Ismailism. He indefatigably recovered, published and studied a good number of the extant Persian Nizari sources and, as such, he may rightfully be considered as the founder of modern Nizari Ismaili studies. It was, in fact, Ivanow's foundational work on Nizari Ismailism that enabled Marshall Hodgson (1922–1968) to write the first comprehensive and scholarly study of the Nizari Ismailis of the Alamut period, which finally replaced von Hammer-Purgstall's fanciful book as the standard reference on the subject.[64]

Soon, others representing yet another generation of scholars, such as B. Lewis, S. M. Stern, A. Hamdani and W. Madelung, produced their own original studies on Ismaili history, including investigations of its obscure early pre-Fatimid phase, as well as the relations between the Fatimids and the dissident Qarmatis. Meanwhile, a number of Russian scholars, such as Liudmila V. Stroeva (1910–1993) and Andrei E. Bertel's (1926–1995), had maintained the earlier interest of their compatriots in Ismaili studies. However, the Russian scholars of the Soviet era generally investigated the Ismailis within narrow Marxist frameworks. At the same time, Rudolf Strothmann (1877–1960) of Hamburg University, who had a particular interest in Shi'i Islam and its

Rudolf Strothmann

---

[63] Asaf A. A. Fyzee, 'Wladimir Ivanow (1886–1970)', *Journal of the Asiatic Society of Bombay*, New Series, 45–46 (1970–1971), p. 93, and F. Daftary, 'Ivanow, Vladimir', *EIR*, vol. 14, p. 300.

[64] Marshall G. S. Hodgson, *The Order of Assassins: The Struggle of the Early Nizari Isma'ilis against the Islamic World* (The Hague, 1955; reprinted, New York, 1980; reprinted, Philadelphia, 2005), based partially on his doctoral thesis submitted to the University of Chicago in 1951; and his 'The Isma'ili State', in *The Cambridge History of Iran*: Volume 5, *The Saljuq and Mongol Periods*, ed. John A. Boyle (Cambridge, 1968), pp. 422–482.

Prince Karim Aga Khan IV

diverse manifestations, had published several Ismaili texts of the Tayyibi tradition, while Arif Tamir (1921–1998), from the small Muhammad-Shahi Nizari community in Syria, made a number of Ismaili texts of Syrian provenance available to scholars, albeit often in faulty editions. And Marius Canard (1888–1982), the French orientalist, published a corpus of original studies on the Fatimids drawing on Ismaili sources. Madelung summed up the current state of scholarship on Ismaili history in his seminal article 'Ismaʿiliyya', published in 1973 in the new edition of *The Encyclopaedia of Islam*.

Progress in Ismaili studies has proceeded at an astonishing rate during the recent decades through the efforts of yet another generation of scholars, including I. K. Poonawala, H. Halm, P. E. Walker, A. Nanji, A. Asani and D. de Smet. This progress in recovery and study of Ismaili texts is well reflected in Professor Ismail Poonawala's monumental catalogue, which identifies some 1,300 titles written by more than 200 authors.[65] Many Ismaili texts have now been published

---

[65] I. K. Poonawala, *Biobibliography of Ismaʿili Literature* (Malibu, CA, 1977). Professor Poonawala has identified many additional titles in the course of his ongoing efforts to produce a second edition of this standard work of reference.

in critical editions, while an increasing number of studies on all aspects of Ismailism have resulted from the efforts of at least four successive generations of scholars, as documented in this writer's bibliography of Ismaili literature.

Scholarship in Ismaili studies promises to continue at an ever greater pace as the Ismailis themselves are becoming increasingly interested in studying their literary heritage and history. In this context, a major contribution is being made by The Institute of Ismaili Studies, established in 1977 in London by Prince Karim Aga Khan IV, the 49th and present Imam of the Nizari Ismailis.[66] This institution, with its collection of more than 3,000 Ismaili manuscripts in Arabic, Persian and Indic languages, is already serving as a point of reference for Ismaili studies, while making its own contributions through various programmes of research and publications, including especially its Ismaili Texts and Translations Series. Numerous scholars worldwide participate in the Institute's academic programmes, and many more benefit from the accessibility of the Ismaili manuscripts now held at the Institute's Ismaili Special Collections Unit, representing the largest collection of its kind in the West. With these developments, the scholarly study of the Ismailis, which by the final decades of Ivanow's life had already greatly deconstructed and explained away the seminal anti-Ismaili tales of medieval times, promises to dissipate the remaining misrepresentations of the Ismailis rooted in either 'hostility' or the 'imaginative ignorance' of the earlier generations.

---

[66] See Paul E. Walker, 'Institute of Ismaili Studies', *EIR*, vol. 12, pp. 164–166.

The rock of Alamut, photographed by W. Ivanow

The rock of Alamut, photographed in 2014 by Dr Janis Esots

3

Autobiography

My Family and Childhood

My parents were of pure Russian stock, without any admixture of non-Russian blood, and had nothing to do with the East. My father,[1] grandfather,[2] great-grandfather and remoter ancestors were native Petersburgians. My father first graduated from the Faculty of Physics and Mathematics at St Petersburg University and then from the Faculty of Medicine at Moscow University. After that he served as a military doctor for the rest of his life.

My mother, Maria Philippovna Marchenko, was from Kharkov, now the capital of the industrial region of Ukraine. In the early 1880s, she moved to St Petersburg and entered the special university for ladies, which was founded by Professor Bestuzhev.[3] At that time women in Russia still could not enter 'male' universities. She did not graduate, because she married and devoted all her time to her family and children. She was a real intellectual and a very cultured woman, especially well read in Russian and French history. She preserved a keen interest in literary news until a very old age and kept reading the so-called 'thick journals'. She was also an exceptionally gifted teacher, who was able to teach even the most obtuse of children, showing

---

[1] Aleksei Andreevich Ivanow.

[2] Andrei Aleksandrovich Ivanow, a teacher in St Petersburg.

[3] Konstantin Nikolaevich Bestuzhev-Riumin (1829–1897), Professor of Russian history at St Petersburg University, was the founder of the largest higher education institution for women in Russia, known as Bestuzhevskie kursy (Bestuzhev Courses). See R. A. Kireeva, 'Bestuzhev-Riumin, K. N.', in A. A. Chernobaev, ed., *Istoriki Rosii: Biografii* [Russian Historians: Biographies] (Moscow, 2001), pp. 237–244, and Rochelle G. Ruthchild, *Equality and Revolution: Women's Rights in the Russian Empire, 1905–1917* (Pittsburgh, PA, 2010).

extraordinary patience and never losing her temper. She was always ready to help even the most challenging and talentless pupils.

I was born on 3 November 1886 in St Petersburg, in the headquarters of the Izmailovskii Regiment;[4] my mother's first child. She was not just a mother to me; for many years she remained my only friend, influencing my character and guiding my education. Everything that is good in me is owed to her. In 1894, we moved to Moscow, and then, for some time, to Yaroslavl on the Volga River,[5] and later on to the railway station town of Laptevo on the Moscow–Kursk line. I cannot remember now whether this place, some 120 km from Moscow and 40 km from Tula,[6] was in the Kashira or the Veniov district of Tula province. In 1899, we returned to Moscow and soon moved again to St Petersburg, where I enrolled in the second grade of a gymnasium, namely, a school where classical languages were taught.

I remember my time at the gymnasium as unending dark, cold days of intense boredom. I was always tired and occasionally even felt sick because of the tedium. The reason for this was that when I joined the school I was much better educated than the rest of my classmates. From the very beginning, I was the best in the class and in the fifth grade I even tried to skip a year by passing all the necessary examinations, but the school authorities did not allow me to do so. In the spring of 1907, I passed my final examinations and won the highest distinction – the gold medal.

Thus my time at school, which for me was nothing but an unpleasant duty, was finally over. I should say that the school did not really educate me; rather, with the help of my mother I taught myself. I read much, painted, regularly visited the numerous museums of St Petersburg as well as various factories and dockyards. During two holiday seasons, I worked as an unpaid apprentice on a locomotive at the construction site of the St Petersburg–Vitebsk railway. I even

---

[4] Founded in 1730, this was one of the oldest guards regiments in the Russian army. The regiment operated under the patronage of different Russian emperors and empresses until 1917 when it was disbanded.

[5] Yaroslavl is situated some 250 km to the north-east of Moscow, in the centre of the Yaroslavl oblast of Russia.

[6] Tula, an industrial city, is located 193 km to the south of Moscow, in the centre of the Tula oblast of Russia.

wanted to get a job in the repair shop of the Western railways in St Petersburg, but they did not take me since I was still under age.

At that time we were living in the town of Tsarskoe Selo,[7] now known as Pushkin, some 25 km from St Petersburg. It was the emperor's residence and full of palaces. I was an enthusiastic cyclist and walker, always keen to explore the entire neighbourhood for tens of kilometres at a time. I cycled to Revel, now Tallinn in Estonia, via Narva, and travelled up the Neva River to its source in Lake Ladoga, then took a steamer to Valaam and Sortavala, a town on the northern shores of the lake, and from there by rail to the town of Iensu via Antrea, where everything has a very Arctic look. From there I travelled by the Puikha-Vesi and Saima-Vesi lakes and the Saima canal to Vyborg and then returned to St Petersburg through the Gulf of Finland. I even began to learn the Finnish language, which I have completely forgotten now. I also spent a summer in Belorussia in Vitebsk province, then another summer in Kharkov and Chuguev[8] and then three months in the Crimea, in Balaklava[9] and Sebastopol.[10] I always travelled alone, hating any kind of group excursion that prevents people from seeing what they really want to see. Generally, I was not an outgoing person. I did not drink, smoke or play cards, though I was not a spoiled boy either. My mother trusted me and permitted me to go on these trips, while my father and paternal relatives disapproved.

University

Thus, the boring gymnasium days were over. To the great astonishment of my classmates and acquaintances, I decided to enter the Faculty of Oriental Languages at St Petersburg University, rather than taking up a career in engineering as everyone had

---

[7] Town to the south of St Petersburg, where the Catherine and Alexander Palaces are located. It is now part of the town of Pushkin in Russia.

[8] Chuguev (Chuhuiv), a city in the Kharkov oblast of Ukraine.

[9] Balaklava, a town in the Crimean Peninsula, which is now a district of the city of Sebastopol. It was the scene of numerous battles, including the famous Battle of Balaklava, during the Crimean War of 1854.

[10] Sebastopol (also Sevastopol), the port city on the Black Sea coast of the Crimean Peninsula.

expected. This was a sharp turn in my life. In the gymnasium my nickname was Ivanov-Parovoz (Ivanow-locomotive), since there were two boys called Ivanov in my class. Everyone knew about my love of machines and all kinds of engineering knowledge.

At that time, demand for people with higher technical education was rapidly growing in Russia and graduation from the fashionable Institutes of Mining, Communications and Electrical Engineering promised well-paid careers. Now, in my old age, when I try to explain my thinking at the time, I suppose two factors contributed to my decision. One was my genuine interest in, and fascination with, the study of the East, a subject I read about a great deal; and another was my general disillusionment with an engineering career, which by that time I saw as an embodiment of crude materialism. I realised that I would not be immediately allowed to design machines or build railways. First, I had to pass through a long period of office drudgery with all its mortifying monotony. What attracted me much more was an academic career in Oriental studies.[11] With the immense materials available from the East, it promised better chances of discovering new and interesting things.

---

[11] Oriental studies (*vostokovedenie*) emerged as a field of study in Russia at the beginning of the 18th century. The initial political and military interests of the Russians in the Orient gradually led to the establishment of an academic discipline for the systematic study of the cultures and languages of the East. Major contributions to the field were made by the establishment of chairs in the Persian and Arabic languages at the Universities of Moscow, Kharkov and Kazan in 1804, the Asiatic Museum of the Imperial Russian Academy of Sciences in St Petersburg in 1818, and the Faculty of Oriental Languages at St Petersburg University in 1855. In the Soviet era, Oriental studies expanded further with the newly centralised network of institutes and departments in various universities, the largest of which was the Institute of Oriental Studies in Moscow. At the same time, traditional studies on the history and philology of the Orient continued at Leningrad, later renamed St Petersburg again, at a branch of the Institute of Oriental Studies of the Academy of Sciences of the USSR (Institut Vostokovedeniia Akademii Nauk SSSR). See W. S. Vucinich, 'The Structure of Soviet Orientology: Fifty Years of Change and Accomplishment', in W. S. Vucinich, ed., *Russia and Asia* (Stanford, 1972), pp. 52–134; M. Kemper and S. Connermann, ed., *The Heritage of Soviet Oriental Studies* (London, 2011), especially essays in Part I, and D. Mikoulski, 'The Study of Islam in Russia and the Former Soviet Union', in A. Nanji, ed., *Mapping Islamic Studies: Genealogy, Continuity and Change* (New York, 1997), pp. 95–107.

So, returning from the Crimea in November 1907, I began to attend lectures at St Petersburg University. My first impression was not much different from that I had of the gymnasium. It was the same cramming, only this time not of simple Latin grammar, but of much more unpleasant Arabic verbs. About a hundred men took the course, all of them aspiring to become diplomats and eventually ambassadors to the East. After the Christmas holidays, there were only 25 of us left. In the subsequent term there were only 11,

Fedor Ippolitovich Shcherbatskoi

and merely three completed their course of studies by 1911. I myself found my studies increasingly interesting after the initial difficulties and stumbling blocks had been overcome. Of course, much depended on the teachers and they were of different moulds. The most important were those who possessed creative minds like Barthold (Bartol'd),[12]

---

[12] Vasilii Vladimirovich Barthold (Bartol'd) (1869–1930), prominent Russian orientalist and author of more than 650 works on the history of Islam, as well as the ethnography, geography, numismatics, epigraphy and philology of the peoples of Central Asia, the Caucasus and the Middle East. Barthold began his teaching career at St Petersburg University in 1896; and in 1906, he was appointed as professor there, a post he retained until the end of his life. Barthold published his doctoral thesis entitled 'Turkestan v epokhu mongol'skogo nashestviia' (St Petersburg, 1898–1900), which was subsequently revised and translated into English by Barthold himself, with the assistance of Sir Hamilton A. R. Gibb (1895–1971), under the title of *Turkestan Down to the Mongol Invasion*, and published in the E. J. W. Gibb Memorial Series (London, 1928), with subsequent revised editions. With his thorough knowledge of Arabic, Persian and Turkish, Barthold may also be regarded as the founder of this branch of Oriental studies in Russia. See B. V. Lunin, *Zhizn' i deiatel'nost' akademika V. V. Bartol'da* [Life and Works of the Academician V. V. Bartol'd] (Tashkent, 1981); 'Bartol'd, Vasilii Vladimirovich', in Sofia D. Miliband, ed., *Biobibliograficheskii slovar' otechestvennykh vostokovedov s 1917 g* [Biobibliographical Dictionary of Native Orientalists from 1917] (Moscow, 1995), vol. 1, pp. 128–131, and the following works by Yu. Bregel: 'The Bibliography of Barthold's Works and the Soviet Censorship', *Survey*, 24 (1979), pp. 91–107; 'Barthold and Modern Oriental Studies', *International*

Zaleman (Salemann),[13] Shcherbatskoi (Scherbatsky),[14] and Turaev.[15] They were already Members of the Imperial Russian Academy of Sciences,[16] or were soon to be elected as such. Students did not merely learn something under their guidance, but were able to study their subjects in depth with these teachers. Unfortunately, I did not meet one of them, Baron V. R. Rozen,[17] the famous Arabist who died early in 1908.

Another type amongst our teachers were the people who once had talent and ambition but had quickly exhausted their potential.

Journal of Middle East Studies, 12 (1980), pp. 385–403, and 'Barthold', *EIR*, vol. 3, pp. 830–832.

[13] See note 25 below.

[14] Fedor Ippolitovich Shcherbatskoi (1866–1942), Russian scholar of Sanskrit, Indian languages and Buddhist philosophy. Regarded as the founder of Indology and Buddhology in Russia, he became the director of the Institute for the Studies of Buddhist Culture in 1928, and the Indo-Tibetan Department at the Leningrad branch of the Institute of Oriental Studies in 1930. See Vera Tolz, *Russia's Own Orient: The Politics of Identity and Oriental Studies in the Late Imperial and Early Soviet Periods* (Oxford, 2011), pp. 101–110, and the introduction to his selected works by B. V. Semichov and A. N. Zelinskii, in F. I. Shcherbatskoi, *Izbrannye trudy po buddizmu* [Selected Works on Buddhism] (Moscow, 1988), pp. 15–41.

[15] Boris Aleksandrovich Turaev (1868–1920), Russian scholar of the Ancient East, Egyptology and Ethiopian studies. Turaev published more than 300 works, including his major studies entitled *Drevnii Egipet* [Ancient Egypt] (Petrograd, 1922), and *Istoriia drevnego vostoka* [History of the Ancient East] (Leningrad, 1935). See M. A. Korostovtsev, 'Istoriografii drevnogo vostoka' [Historiography of the Ancient East], in M. V. Nechkina et al., ed., *Ocherki istorii istoricheskoi nauki v SSSR* [Essays on the History of the Historical Sciences in the USSR] (Moscow, 1963), vol. 3, pp. 368–373, and the entry on him in Sofia D. Miliband, ed., *Biobibliograficheskii slovar*, vol. 2, pp. 508–510.

[16] The Imperial Academy of Sciences (Imperatorskaia Akademiia Nauk), the highest academic institution in Russia from 1803 to 1917, was based in St Petersburg. See Y. S. Osipov, *Akademiia nauk v istorii Rossiikogo gosudarstva* [The Academy of Sciences in the History of the Russian State] (Moscow, 1999).

[17] Victor Romanovich Rozen (1849–1908), a leading Arabist, was the director of the Asiatic Museum from 1881 to 1882. An aristocrat of German descent from Russia's Baltic regions, he institutionalised Oriental studies in Russia where in 1886 he founded the first scholarly periodical devoted to Oriental studies, *Zapiski Vostochnogo otdeleniia Russkogo Imperatorskogo arkheologicheskogo obshchestva* [Proceedings of the Oriental Department of the Imperial Russian Archaeological Society]. Rozen

Vasilii Vladimirovich Barthold

Karl Germanovich Zaleman

Victor Romanovich Rozen

Valentin Alekseevich Zhukovskii

Amongst such unpleasant types was V. A. Zhukovskii,[18] who was Professor of Persian, the subject I was most interested in. He resembled a provincial schoolteacher who somehow had been raised to the position of a headmaster. He liked to discipline the students and shouted at them in a very authoritarian manner. Another teacher, V. D. Smirnov,[19] was a very good specialist in Turkish, but he was too talkative and liked to digress from his subject in order to criticise Count L. Tolstoy,[20] and the Reds in general. Another type was represented by young scholars known as 'privat-docents',[21] but there was none among them working on the subjects of my interest.

I was very happy to be on good terms with the Professor of Islamic and Central Asian history, V. V. Barthold, whom I deeply respected for

---

served as dean of the Faculty of Oriental Studies at St Petersburg University from 1893 to 1902. A number of eminent Russian orientalists, such as Barthold, Oldenburg and Shcherbatskoi were trained by Baron Rozen. See I. Iu. Krachkovskii, ed., *Pamiati akademika V. R. Rozena: stat'i i materialy k sorokaletiiu so dnia ego smerti (1908–1948)* [In Memoriam Academician V. R. Rozen: Articles and Material on the Fortieth Anniversary of his Death (1908–1948)] (Moscow, 1947); Tolz, *Russia's Own Orient*, pp. 1–22, and D. Schimmelpenninck van der Oye, 'The Imperial Roots of Soviet Orientology', in Kemper and Conermann, ed., *The Heritage of Soviet Oriental Studies*, pp. 29–46.

[18] Valentin Alekseevich Zhukovskii (1858–1918), Russian scholar of the folklore, language and literature of Iran. In addition to his doctoral thesis on the Persian Sufi poet Awhad al-Din Muhammad Anwari (d. after 1160), Zhukovskii produced a number of studies on the Sufi orders and dervishes of Persia. See V. V. Bartol'd, 'Pamiati V. A. Zhukovskogo' [In Memoriam V. A. Zhukovskii], *ZVORAO*, 25 (1921), pp. 399–414; S. F. Ol'denburg, 'Valentin Alekseevich Zhukovskii (1858–1918)', *Izvestiia Rossiiskoi Akademii Nauk*, 2 (1919), pp. 2039–2068, and F. Abdullaeva's entry on 'Zhukovskii', in *EIR*, available online at http://www.iranicaonline.org/articles/zhukovskii-valentin-alekseevich.

[19] Vasilii Dmitrievich Smirnov (1846–1922), Russian Turkologist. His publications include *Ocherk istorii turetskoi literatury* [Essays on the History of Turkish Literature] (St Petersburg, 1891). See N. K. Dmitriiev, 'V. D. Smirnov: A Memoir', *Journal of the Royal Asiatic Society*, 2 (1928), pp. 408–410.

[20] Lev Nikolayevich Tolstoy (1828–1910), Russian aristocrat, philosopher and novelist. His well-known works include *Voina i Mir* (*War and Peace*), and *Anna Karenina*.

[21] Privat-docent (in French), or Privatdozent (in German) is an academic title conferred by some European universities, especially in Germany, on someone with certain formal qualifications, without holding tenure or professorship, enabling them to teach at those universities.

his academic achievements. Very soon, he was made a Member of the Imperial Russian Academy of Sciences. In return, he valued my academic efforts and expressed his appreciation in an unofficial way by frequently inviting me to his home for fish pie lunches. He was married to Professor Zhukovskii's sister, who was an expert cook and made excellent pies. Publicly often dry and even irritable, Barthold was quite a different person at home.

I worked with interest and intensely, and in 1910, as a reward, I received a scholarship for a three-month visit to Persia to improve my practical knowledge of the Persian language. As it turned out, I spent not three but five very useful months there. On my way to Persia, I passed through Bukhara and Samarkand, which proved valuable when I was sent on field research to Bukhara in 1915.

The Asiatic Museum

The Asiatic Museum of the Imperial Russian Academy of Sciences,[22] as it was officially styled, was founded in 1818, combining certain

---

[22] The Asiatic Museum (Aziatskii Muzei) was founded in 1818 in St Petersburg by Count Sergei Uvarov (1785–1855), president of the Russian Academy of Sciences. It became the main centre for the collection and study of Oriental manuscripts in Imperial Russia. From 1901 until 1925, the Asiatic Museum remained located in its old quarters near the main building of the Academy of Sciences in the Tamózhenniy pereulok. In 1925, the Museum was transferred to a new building above the Library of the Academy of Sciences. See I. Y. Krachkovsky, *Among Arabic Manuscripts: Memoirs of Libraries and Men*, tr. T. Minorksy (Leiden, 1953), pp. 62 ff., 72. In the Soviet era, in 1930 the Asiatic Museum was incorporated into the newly founded Institute of Oriental Studies; and then, in 1951, into the Department of Oriental Manuscripts at the Leningrad branch of the Institute of Oriental Studies of the Academy of Sciences of the USSR. From 1960 to 1970, it was part of the Institute of the Peoples of Asia of the Academy of Sciences. In 2007, this branch of the Institute of Oriental Studies was transformed into the independent Institute of Oriental Manuscripts of the Russian Academy of Sciences, in St Petersburg. The manuscripts of the Institute, including the Asiatic Museum's original collections, are now housed in the Novo-Mikhailovskii Palace, one of St Petersburg's celebrated buildings on the banks of the Neva. It had formerly belonged to Grand Duke Michael Nikolaevich (1832–1909), the son of Tsar Nicholas I (1796–1855), a scion of the Imperial Romanov family. See S. F. Ol'denburg, *Aziatskii Muzei Rossiiskoi Akademii Nauk 1818–1918* [The Asiatic Museum of the Russian Academy of Sciences 1818–1918] (Petrograd, 1919), and Yuri A. Petrosyan, 'Introduction', in Y. A. Petrosyan et al., *Pages of Perfection: Islamic Paintings and*

departments of the 'Kunstkamera' of Peter the Great (1682–1725).²³ It was set up by Ch. D. Fraehn, a Member of the Academy and an outstanding orientalist.²⁴ Nowadays, it is known as the Institute of the Peoples of Asia and Africa and serves as a centre for the popularisation of the knowledge of the East. When I was still a student, it was very little known to the general public, and few students of the Faculty of Oriental Languages were aware of its existence. In fact, the Asiatic Museum was rather like a library since, apart from a few stone relics, it possessed a first-class collection of Oriental manuscripts in many languages. It was nevertheless called a museum because it also had a most valuable numismatic collection, which could hardly interest the general public. In my time, the director of the Museum was a

Ch. D. Fraehn

Calligraphy from the Russian Academy of Sciences, St Petersburg (Lugano, 1995), pp. 27–31. See also note 75 below.

²³ Kunstkamera, located in St Petersburg, was the first museum to be founded in Russia (in 1714). Originally, it contained Oriental manuscripts and collections of other items of interest to Peter the Great. In 1878, the separate Museums of Anthropology and Ethnography, located in the Kunstkamera building in St Petersburg, were merged into one institution, and named Peter the Great Museum of Anthropology and Ethnography in 1903. See Ch. M. Taksami, *285 let Peterburgskoi Kunstkamere: Materialy itogovoi nauchnoi konferentsii MAE RAN posiashchennoi 285-letiiu Kunstkamery* [285 Years of the Petersburg Kunstkamera: Materials of the Closing Academic Conference of the Museum of Anthropology and Ethnography of the Russian Academy of Sciences, Dedicated to the 285th Anniversary of the Kunstkamera Collection of the MAE], vol. 48 (St Petersburg, 2000).

²⁴ Christian Martin (Danilovich) Fraehn (1782–1851), German scholar and numismatist. He was a graduate of Kazan University where he became Professor of Oriental literature. He served as the first director of the Asiatic Museum from 1818 until 1842 when he was succeeded by Bernhard Dorn (1805–1881); the latter retained the directorship until his death. See V. L. Ianin, 'Numizmatika', in Nechkina et al., ed., *Ocherki istorii istoricheskoi nauki v SSSR*, vol. 2, pp. 672–676, and Schimmelpenninck van der Oye, 'The Imperial Roots of Soviet Orientology', in Kemper and Conermann, ed., *Heritage of Soviet Oriental Studies*, pp. 32–35.

Institute of Oriental Manuscripts of the
Russian Academy of Sciences, St Petersburg

Member of the Academy, Karl G. Zaleman,[25] the famous specialist in Iranian studies and the Palaeo-Asiatic languages of Siberia. He was also the director of the Second Department (namely European literature) of the Library of the Academy, and taught at the University. He was a typical old-fashioned Baltic German scholar and a very good

---

[25] Karl Germanovich Zaleman (1849–1916), or Carl Hermann Salemann in German, a leading Iranologist. He was a Baltic German, born in Revel (now Tallinn) in Estonia. In 1890, he succeeded V. V. Radlov (1885–1890) as the director of the Asiatic Museum of the Imperial Russian Academy of Sciences in St Petersburg, and held that post until his death in 1916. Zaleman greatly expanded the Asiatic Museum's collections of manuscripts, also sending a number of expeditions to Central Asia for this purpose. His main fields of academic interest were the lexicography and grammar of the Iranian languages, such as Pahlavi, Soghdian and Persian. In particular, Zaleman made significant contributions to the study of the Eastern Iranian languages, especially Ossetic and Pamiri (Shughni and Yaghnobi). Zaleman also produced critical editions of several Persian, Chaghatai and Turkish texts based on the manuscripts held at the Asiatic Museum. See V. V. Bartol'd, 'Karl Germanovich Zaleman: 1849–1916', in his collected works entitled *Sochineniia* (Moscow, 1963–1977), vol. 9, pp. 599–618, and a detailed entry by D. Durkin-Meisterernst on 'Salemann, Carl Hermann', in *EIR*, available online at: http://www.iranicaonline.org/articles/salemann-carl-hermann.

man by nature. I attended his lectures on the Avestan language. He reportedly knew some sixty languages, though his Russian was less than perfect. He was a very good scholar.

Asiatic Museum, exterior

I discovered the Asiatic Museum, incidentally, through an Armenian monk from Echmiadzin.[26] He was working on a learned dissertation on historical issues and used the Armenian manuscripts in the collections of the Asiatic Museum. I wanted to consult a book, which was available only there,

Asiatic Museum, interior

and the learned monk volunteered to help me. After two years of university studies I knew nothing of the Museum. We entered the building and the feeling of quite a different world seized me. The world of the university was that of cramming, examinations, occasional political demonstrations, and all sorts of prosaic problems. But here, in the Asiatic Museum, I could breathe the air of science and scholarship. It offered a peaceful and restful refuge from the noise and excitement of the outside world in St Petersburg. I began to come and go there more and more frequently, and soon felt myself at home there. Later on, during World War I and the Revolution, I almost took up residence there, working in the evenings wrapped up in a soldier's overcoat and cap since it was very cold, by the light of the Christmas tree candles because of frequent power cuts. At lunchtime, the

---

[26] Echmiadzin, known in Armenian as Vagharshapat, is situated some 15 km to the west of Yerevan, the present capital of Armenia. This city was one of the historical capitals of Armenia. See S. Peter Cowe, 'Ejmiatsin', *EIR*, vol. 8, pp. 278–281.

Museum was a gathering place for university professors and lecturers, who came there to have a cup of tea with rolls and to discuss the latest news in a friendly and even brotherly atmosphere.

These gatherings were presided over by the learned Assistant to the Chief Keeper, a Baltic German, F. A. Rozenberg,[27] who was a scholar of rare cultural refinement and erudite knowledge. He did not hold a professorial position but from him one could learn much more than from official professors.

But let us return to my student years. As I mentioned above, after three years of studies I received a scholarship for a visit to Persia in the summer of 1910. On my return from Persia, I had to write my examination paper, attend lectures, and from time to time I visited my mother and brothers who lived in Tsarskoe Selo. It was also necessary to think about the approaching final examinations and contemplate my future in general. After their graduation, the students of the Oriental Faculty usually joined the Teaching Section of the Ministry of Foreign Affairs. This was a standard way of utilising their knowledge and eventually getting a diplomatic posting. But this path did not appeal to me. I wanted to get a position at the Asiatic Museum and pursue an academic career.

Fedor Aleksandrovich Rozenberg

The dream of hard-working and advanced students was to be 'retained by the department of preparation for professorial activities' [i.e. postgraduate studies]. But teaching did not interest me either. Besides, shortly before my graduation the Professor of Persian chose one of his students for this position. He was not particularly bright, which suited his mentor since it guaranteed that the student would

---

[27] Fedor Aleksandrovich Rozenberg (1867–1934), Russian scholar of Iran. He studied Firdawsi's famous epic-poem, *Shah-nama*, ancient Persian epigraphy, Persian literature and Soghdian documents. See S. F. Ol'denburg, 'Zapiska ob uchenykh trudakh F. A. Rozenberga' [Notes on the Academic Works of F. A. Rozenberg], *Izvestiia Rossiiskoi Akademii Nauk*, 6 (1923), pp. 369–371, and I. Iu. Krachkovskii, 'F. A. Rozenberg (1867–1937)', *Izvestiia Akademii Nauk SSSR*, 7 (1935), pp. 895–918.

never 'outshine' the teacher. Thus, there were no funds left for me.

I never had any particular admiration for the Arabic language or literature, yet I punctually attended the lectures and language classes taught by a Syrian Christian Arab called Anton Khashshab,[28] a native of Beirut. He taught at the University on a part-time basis and his main employment was with the Loan and Discount Bank of Persia [Uchetno-ssudnii Bank Persii].[29] This was simply one of the departments of the State Bank of Russia established for purely political purposes. Students rarely attended Khashshab's lectures, because he held his classes early in the morning, so very often I was the only student present. Thus, our friendship started and he began to invite me to visit him at his home. He was married to a Polish lady, who was an excellent housewife, and their home had a peaceful and tranquil atmosphere.

---

[28] Anton Feodulovich Khashshab (1874–1920), teacher of Arabic at the University of St Petersburg from 1904 until 1917. Author of a number of Arabic language books, after the Russian Revolution he migrated to Tehran, where he died in 1920. See M. Iu. Sorokina, *Rossiiskoe nauchnoe zarubezh'e: materialy dlia biobibliograficheskogo slovaria* [The Russian Academic Frontier: Material for a Bibliographic Dictionary] (Moscow, 2010), vol. 3, pp. 210–211.

[29] This bank was originally established in Tehran in 1890 as Ssudnoe obshestvo v Persii [Loan Society in Persia] by Y. S. Poliakov, a Russian resident in Persia with extensive commercial interests there. It was later reorganised as a bank under the name of Ssudniy Bank Persii [The Loan Bank of Persia]. In 1894, it was brought into the Russian system of state banks, and its loans were managed by the Imperial State Bank of Russia. By 1914, the bank had opened branches in the Persian cities of Tehran, Rasht, Meshhed, Tabriz, Kermanshah and other localities, with agencies in Isfahan, Qazwin, Sabzewar, Hamadan and Birjand amongst other places. The Bank was renamed Uchetno-ssudnii Bank Persii [The Loan and Discount Bank of Persia] in 1903. The operations of this bank, also known as Banque d'Escompte de Perse, were closely related to the political activities of Russia in Persia; and the management of the bank generally fell under the jurisdiction of the Russian diplomatic legation in Tehran. In 1921, the bank was turned over to Persia by the Soviet government. It may be added here that by 1907 the Russians and the British had already reached agreement on identifying their respective zones of influence in Persia. See A. I. Aksenov et al., ed., *Ekonomicheskaia istoriia Rossii s drevneishikh vremen do 1917 goda* [Economic History of Russia from Ancient Times to 1917] (Moscow, 2008), pp. 1019–1020, and Marvin L. Entner, *Russo-Persian Commercial Relations, 1828–1914* (Gainesville, FL, 1965), pp. 39–80.

Naturally enough, I discussed my future with him. It should be noted here that the most important thing in being selected for 'preparation for the professorial position' was a two-year trip to the East. But the stipend was not particularly lavish and thus did not allow much travelling. Khashshab, who was well aware of all these matters, offered a solution which I liked very much. He suggested that I join his bank. With my first-class degree the bank would enthusiastically take me on board and give me a position in some remote part of Persia still untouched by foreign influences, and where the way of life remained as it always had been. Usually the bank employees were less than enthusiastic about taking up such jobs. But there was not much work in these places, the pay was not bad, living was quite cheap and I would have much time for my academic pursuits. All this sounded very attractive.

After this conversation, I happened to meet Barthold, who again invited me to a fish pie lunch. Naturally, we discussed the forthcoming final examinations and my future. Barthold regretted that the appointment of the successor to Zhukovskii had already been made and kindly offered his plan for my consideration. Some time earlier, a learned Baltic German, Baron V. G. Tizenhausen,[30] had started working on the history of the Golden Horde.[31] He had published several works, which were acknowledged as valuable, and was elected a Corresponding Member of the Academy. He had died in 1902, leaving a substantial estate to finance the continuation of his work. Besides, for work of this kind it was possible to get funding from the Committee

---

[30] Vladimir Gustavovich Tizenhausen (1825–1902), Baltic German artistocrat and orientalist. A historian of the Golden Horde, he was also a numismatist. His major works include *O Samanidskikh monetakh* [The Coins of the Samanids] (St Petersburg, 1855). See B. A. Vvedenskii, ed., *Bol'shaia Sovestkaia Entsiklopediia* (Moscow, 1956), vol. 42, p. 422, and V. N. Ianin, 'Numizmatika', in Nechkina et al., ed., *Ocherki istorii*, vol. 2, p. 676.

[31] A dynasty of Mongol *khans*, descendants of Chingiz Khan, ruling over western Siberia, Khwarazm and southern Russia from around 1227 to 1502, when the Golden Horde was absorbed into the Crimean Tatar Horde. From 1341, the *khans* of the Golden Horde were all Muslims. See B. Spuler, *Die Goldene Horde. Die Mongolen in Russland 1223–1502* (2nd ed., Wiesbaden, 1965); German A. Fedorov-Davydov, *Obshchestvennyi stroi Zolotoi Ordy* [The Social Structure of the Golden Horde] (Moscow, 1973), and P. Jackson, 'The Dissolution of the Mongol Empire', *Central Asiatic Journal*, 22 (1978), pp. 186–243.

for the Study of Central and Eastern Asia. This was an international organisation with its headquarters in the building of the Russian Geographical Society. Provided I decided to accept this plan, I had to give up my specialisation in Persian and change to the languages of the Turkic group, because the bulk of the sources were in those languages.

Barthold's proposal did not suit me at all. For some reason I had never felt any attraction for these languages, and the history of the Golden Horde did not interest me in any way. I said this to Barthold and informed him of the plan suggested by Khashshab. He listened carefully to me, chewing his pie and asking no questions. Something – I cannot remember what – interrupted our conversation and Barthold never returned to it. 'Silence is the sign of consent' – so I interpreted it. But it would be better to make things absolutely clear. So before making the final decision, I went to see Zaleman. He burst into his usual exclamations: 'They are all fools there. There are so many Turkic scholars, but no good students of Persia. Changing your field of speciality is like changing your religion. Money may be found; go to Persia even under the flag of the bank, collect materials for your Master's thesis and work!'

Service in the Bank

So I did as Barthold had advised and joined the Loan and Discount Bank of Persia, and on 29 November 1911 left for Persia via Turkestan, stopping on the way in Tashkent, Samarkand and Bukhara. I was posted to Birjand [as assistant manager of that branch], at that time a small provincial town in the south-eastern corner of Persia [in the province of Khorasan], on the way to Sistan and India. Letters from Russia were sent there via England and India, taking about two months each way. My first year in Birjand – 1912 – was the happiest time in my adult life, and was never to be repeated. I was completely immersed in my studies and field research, read much in Persian and Arabic, collected specimens of the local variant of colloquial Persian, rural poetry and tales,[32] and explored an area of about 30 km in the

---

[32] The results of this early fieldwork were later published in several articles; see items 1, 2, 5, 6 and 37 in Appendix 1, Works of Ivanow. This was a turbulent period in the modern history of Persia, coinciding with the earlier years of the reign of Ahmad Shah (1909–1925), the last Qajar monarch of Persia.

surroundings, where I found dervishes, Ismailis and Baluchis. I lived my life to the full.

By the beginning of 1913, rumours began to circulate that the bank was about to be closed. Frankly speaking, from a commercial point of view this bank should have been closed much earlier and, better still, never have been opened at all. Some dignitaries who looked at the map and chose its particular location, having no idea of the real conditions on the spot, had established it to serve 'a higher purpose'. This branch not only made no profit at all, but its operations were limited to paying employees' salaries. So its closure was decreed. And I was relocated to the bank's branch in Kermanshah, close to the Turkish border in Mesopotamia [now the Iran–Iraq border]. I did not like being transferred from the south-east to the west of the country. The only consolation was the possibility of a desert trip by roads usually not used by foreigners. This journey turned out to be quite difficult. I had to travel by camel, which shed their winter coats in spring and become very weak during this change. We travelled mostly by night, as it was too hot in the daytime and there was no shade in which to seek refuge from the sun.

We reached Isfahan after having crossed the Central Desert [Dasht-i Kavir]. I spent a week there trying to find pack ponies and then moved to Hamadan. I had to stay there for two months in order to familiarise myself with banking operations. Later on, I left for Kermanshah via Senendaj or Senenduj, the centre of Persian Kurdistan. It was a picturesque but poor locality. As my Persian friends, who visited it not long ago, have told me, it still remains the same dull town.

After finding new pack ponies, I embarked on my journey to Kermanshah. The road went through mountainous country, which brought to mind ancient times, Assyrian and even earlier. Our convoy of one hundred horses moved at night. The moon rose late and it was very dark because of the dust raised by so many horses. Our servants were Kurds, all of them armed. From time to time shooting would start somewhere ahead and nobody knew who was shooting or why. At dawn we entered a village. From somewhere a small party of horsemen trotted towards us, headed by a young man without mustachios. He approached us with polite questions about who we were and where we were going. During this conversation an altercation arose between my man and his. Seizing the opportunity, I asked who this man was.

The answer was: 'This is not a man, it is a woman, Kokeli Khanum, daughter of the *khan*.' She then rode alongside me, offered me some pistachios and told me that she could shoot well, often came to Kermanshah and knew the Russian Consul there. Later on I discovered all this to be true.

Kermanshah, the last town before the Mesopotamian frontier, was at that time a dirty place, inhabited by a motley crowd of Kurds, Persians, Azeri Turks, Armenians, 'Baghdad Jews', as they were then called, and all sorts of riff-raff elements. It was an important commercial hub, through which a great amount of German goods were imported to be dispatched further on into the Persian heartland. There was much work in the bank. I had to be constantly on the alert because I had to deal with experienced and crafty crooks. The Kermanshah of today looks quite different with its electric lights and modernised buildings – all this came after World War I and the discovery of oil in Persia.

After the idyllic Birjand, Kermanshah appeared very unpleasant to me. The whole day was taken up with banking operations and it was often necessary to take work home. At the New Year, the central office sent me a surprise 'gift' – I was summoned to St Petersburg. Everything was done very negligently; it was not clear whether it was a transfer or only an invitation to a conference. As it transpired later, the intention was to introduce various changes, get rid of an Armenian agent, who had proved to be a crook and appoint somebody familiar with the local life as the bank's manager. But at the time, I knew nothing about all these decisions.

Journey to India

It became increasingly difficult to follow my original plan and use this banking appointment for my academic pursuits. Zaleman was then travelling abroad and I was unable to get from him any new information as to the possibility of my employment at the Asiatic Museum. If the bank retained me in St Petersburg I would be obliged to spend more time in the office. And there was no possibility of continuing my research in Kermanshah if I returned there. On the other hand, it was so tempting to use this unique chance, which could never come up again in my life, and travel to 'fabulous India', which

Autobiography

Bombay, 1921

was so close to Persia. After long deliberation, I finally decided that I had enough money to go to India, although in quite a modest style. I submitted my letter of resignation, and at the beginning of February 1914 rode on horseback to Baghdad.

In 1914, Baghdad was still under the Ottoman Turks and, although preserving its original style, was of very little interest. As I hear from reliable people, by now Baghdad has changed considerably. I decided not to stay there for long and only made a short tour of the ruins of Babylon excavated at that time by a German archaeological mission headed by Professor Koldewey.[33] I really wanted to see the famous Shi'i holy places, which was difficult to arrange, so I set out in a boat for Basra. The River Tigris (Dajla) has a very strong and rapid course; and, therefore, boats cannot be towed by a barge. Instead, the barges are on both sides of the boat. They sail only during daytime and at night they anchor by the shore. In Basra, there was a steamer sailing to India and so I bought a ticket and sailed the next morning. It took two weeks to reach Bombay, with stops at various ports for loading cargo.

---

[33] Robert Koldewey (1855–1925), German architect and archaeologist known mainly for his discoveries at Babylon; see his *The Excavations at Babylon* (London, 1914).

However, the steamer always anchored far from the shore, making it impossible to disembark and go onshore for a walk. In Bushir, for example, it took three hours to get onto the shore and the same time to return to the steamer. Now, there are motor launches, which greatly speed up the matter. The same thing happened in Bandar-i Abbasi. It took the steamer 12 days to arrive in Bombay. On board I was studying Hindustani intensely, with the help of the steamer's doctor, a Hindu. We arrived at Karachi at 10 o'clock at night. I quickly disembarked and went into the town. It proved to be a rather uninviting port town, with dusty streets and the walls of many houses seemingly dirty from dampness. There was nothing in it resembling Indian fairytales or simply India. The city looked like an artificial transplant from England. And it is still the same, as I witnessed in 1962 when I stayed there for eight months.

The sea-route from Karachi to Bombay is of absolutely no interest. It is much better to go by aeroplane, as one can nowadays. The shores of Kathiawar [in Gujarat] are monotonous; besides, the boat keeps far away from them. We arrived in Bombay early in the afternoon. Again I saw nothing fairytale or even distinctly Indian in it. I went to the local branch of the Royal Asiatic Society and discovered that they possessed only 30 quite uninteresting Persian manuscripts, fewer than I myself owned. After four days, I left by train for Calcutta. There was a Russian Consulate there. The Consul General Nabokov,[34] a brother of the politician Nabokov who was later shot in Berlin,[35] lived in Simla. His secretary, P. A. Rogalskii-Lazarevets, who was seriously interested in India, offered me a room at the Consulate. It enabled me to spend about four months in Calcutta, working on Persian manuscripts kept in the library of the Asiatic Society of Bengal, the oldest orientalist institution in the world founded in 1784.[36]

---

[34] Konstantin Dimitrievich Nabokov (1872–1927), Russian diplomat who served as Consul General in Calcutta during 1912–1915, and, subsequently, as Consul and head of mission in London. He published his memoirs under the title of *The Ordeal of a Diplomat* (London, 1921).

[35] Vladimir D. Nabokov (1870–1922), politician and co-founder of the Kadet party, was the father of the famous novelist and entomologist Vladimir V. Nabokov (1899–1977), the author of *Lolita* and many other works.

[36] See note 50 below.

It was, however, necessary to think about returning to St Petersburg. To take full advantage of my journey, I planned to visit the most famous Indian cities – Benares, then Lucknow, Agra, Delhi, Amritsar, Lahore, Multan and, on my way to the south, Ajmer, Hyderabad and Madras. Then in Colombo I intended to take the Russian steamer *Perm*, travelling between Vladivostok and Odessa. But the outbreak of war made all my plans superfluous. And I had to go through Persia. The troubles started when the police, who did not understand my passport, which was in Russian and French, demanded English documents. I wrote to Consul General Nabokov, and he was kind enough to send me the required documentation straight away. The German warship *Geben* sank the steamer *Perm* in Chinese waters. This news reached me in Ajmer, and I returned to Karachi and took a boat going up the Persian Gulf, to Bushir. It was August and it was terribly hot in Bushir, where I was kindly received by the head of the [Russian] Consulate, Ivan Ivanovich Loiko, who was later killed by brigands as he travelled through Turkish Kurdistan towards the Russian border. I therefore went to Shiraz where I remained for two months. Eventually, via Yazd and Tabas, Sabzewar and Quchan, I reached Ashkabad, from where I took the train to St Petersburg.

In St Petersburg, Zaleman received me in the most friendly way. He immediately gave me a Persian manuscript, which he planned to edit and publish. Unfortunately, I became ill with malaria which I had picked up somewhere in Multan. Nothing helped me and in April 1915 Zaleman suggested that the best cure for malaria would be a change of climate and offered me the opportunity to go to Bukhara to collect Persian and Arabic manuscripts for the [Asiatic] Museum. I hastened to Bukhara where my malaria was, indeed, cured by the head doctor of the local hospital, V. A. Dobrokhotov.[37] This was long before vitamins became fashionable but he used exactly the same method, and in addition to mixtures, he made me eat fruit and butter.

There was much work to be done in Bukhara. I succeeded in

---

[37] Vladimir Arkadievich Dobrokhotov, Russian physician active in the Emirate of Bukhara during the early decades of the 20th century.

acquiring 1,047 manuscripts,[38] some of them quite old and important. Moreover, I dispatched a collection of ancient ceramics to the Museum of Anthropology and Ethnography in St Petersburg, on the instructions of its director, and a Member of the Academy, V. V. Radlov.[39]

Vasilii Vasil'evich Radlov

Military Service

Newspapers were then publishing announcements on the mobilisation of reservists of various categories and my turn had also come, as it was now the turn of those who were short-sighted. I returned to St Petersburg in mid-December, and had to report to the mobilisation centre in January. I wanted to do my military service on the Caucasian front due to my knowledge of Oriental languages. I wrote a letter requesting as much, but I received a reply to the effect that only Cossack units served there and that I would, therefore, have to join the Cossacks, which would take much time. Finally, I was recruited for my knowledge of several Oriental languages and dispatched to the 'team of soldiers' attached to the

---

[38] See V. A. Ivanov, 'Spiski rukopisei Bukharskoi kollektsii' [List of the Manuscripts of the Bukharan Collection, with Foreword and Notes by Yurii E. Borshchevskii], *Pis'mennye pamiatniki Vostoka: Istoriko-filologicheskoe issledovaniia, Ezhegodnik 1970* (Moscow, 1974), pp. 407–436, and Kratchkovsky, *Among Arabic Manuscripts*, p. 68. See also Oleg F. Akimushkin et al., *Persidskie i Tadzhikskie rukopisi Instituta Narodov Azii AN SSSR* [Persian and Tajik Manuscripts in the Institute of the Peoples of Asia, the USSR Academy of Sciences], ed. N. D. Muklukho-Maklai (Moscow, 1964), 2 vols., and *Correspondance Corbin-Ivanow. Lettres échangées entre Henry Corbin et Vladimir Ivanow de 1947 à 1966*, ed. Sabine Schmidtke (Paris and Louvain, 1999), p. 190.

[39] Vasilii Vasil'evich Radlov (1837–1918), Turkologist and director of the Asiatic Museum (1885–1890), and then of the Museum of Anthropology and Ethnography (1894–1918). A prolific scholar, Radlov also headed numerous archaeological, ethnographic and linguistic expeditions to Central and East Asia. See Aleksandr N. Samoilovich, 'V. V. Radlov kak turkolog' [V. V. Radlov as a Turkologist], *Novyi Vostok*, 2 (1922), pp. 707–712.

general staff headquarters at its Foreign Department in St Petersburg. Soon, I was transferred to the 'special office', organised to deal with the representatives of the allied armies. In the 'special office', everything was 'secret and urgent'. Although there was so much secret correspondence there were only a few staff. Therefore, there was much work to do and we often missed breakfast. Sometimes even a cup of tea brought by a guard in the morning had to be sent back. At the same time, I continued my evening work at the Asiatic Museum, normally from 8 p.m. until midnight. I had no holidays, no leave, and this intense workload affected my health. My malaria reoccurred and, in January 1917, I had to spend three weeks in hospital. When I left the hospital, what was later called the February Revolution was already in full swing.[40]

To my great sorrow, K. G. Zaleman had died on 30 November [1916] of a cardiac arrest. Professor S. F. Oldenburg (Ol'denburg),[41] a Member of the Academy, replaced him as the director of the Asiatic Museum. He specialised in Indian studies and possessed a truly encyclopaedic knowledge. Apart from being the director of the Asiatic Museum, he held a plethora of other posts, including that of Permanent Secretary of the Academy and even Member of the State Council. He was a man of almost unbelievable

Sergei Federovich Oldenburg

---

[40] The Russian Revolution of February 1917 succeeded in uprooting the Romanov monarchy and installing a Provisional Government for running the affairs of the state. The Provisional Government itself was toppled by the Bolshevik Revolution of October 1917 led by V. Lenin, initiating the Soviet era in modern Russian history.

[41] Sergei Federovich Oldenburg (1863–1934), Russian Indologist. Succeeding K. G. Zaleman, he was director of the Asiatic Museum during 1916–1930. See V. M. Alekseev, 'Sergei Federovich Ol'denburg kak organizator i rukovoditel' nashikh orientalistov' [S. F. Oldenburg as Organiser and Leader of our Orientalists], *Zapiski Instituta Vostokovedeniia Akademii Nauk SSSR*, 4 (1934), pp. 31–57, and P. E. Skachkov and K. L. Chizhikova, *Bibliografiia trudov S. F. Ol'denburga* (Moscow, 1986), pp. 122–153.

energy and capacity for work. His working day started at 8 a.m. and continued until well after midnight. In spite of being such a busy person, he never made a visitor wait or refused a meeting, even after he became Minister of Education. I worked in the Museum at night and he often came to my office at about midnight and we had conversations then. Eventually, he made my affiliation to the Academy official and offered me the position of Assistant Keeper at the Museum. Although the Persian language and its literature were not his subject, I was often surprised by his knowledge of these subjects, which was rare even among those who claimed to be specialists. At that time, it was not safe to walk at night because of the so-called drunken shootings. Therefore, Oldenburg insisted that I should spend the nights in his office as the Permanent Secretary of the Academy. And I spent many nights there, sleeping on a couch. In January 1918, I received my demobilisation papers and my employment at the Academy was confirmed.

It was a difficult time, the northern winter days were short, and there was no electricity due to the scarcity of fuel. Quite coincidentally, I had bought several packets of Christmas tree candles. These tiny things burned for an hour and twenty minutes each. By their light, and clad in my overcoat and cap, I worked on my edition of the (Ismaili) manuscript of the *Ummu'l-kitab*,[42] brought from the Pamirs in 1916 by the late I. I. Zarubin.[43]

---

[42] W. Ivanow's edition of this text appeared much later in *Der Islam*, 23 (1936), pp. 1–132. Written in archaic Persian and containing the discourses of the early Shi'i Imam Muhammad al-Baqir (d. ca. 732) in response to questions posed by an anachronistic group of disciples, including Jabir al-Ju'fi and Muhammad b. al-Mufaddal, this work does not contain any Ismaili doctrines. However, it was adopted into Ismaili literature and eventually found its way into the private manuscript collections of the Nizari Ismailis of Central Asia. See W. Ivanow, 'Notes sur l'Ummu'l-kitab des Ismaëliens de l'Asie Centrale', *Revue des Études Islamiques*, 6 (1932), pp. 419–481; H. Halm, *Kosmologie und Heilslehre der frühen Isma'iliya: Eine Studie zur islamischen Gnosis* (Wiesbaden, 1978), pp. 142–168; his *Die islamische Gnosis: Die extreme Schia und die Alawiten* (Zurich and Munich, 1982), pp. 113–198, 218–230, containing a partial German translation of the work, and F. Daftary, 'Umm al-Kitab: 2. Among the Shi'a', *EI2*, vol. 10, pp. 854–855.

[43] Ivan Ivanovich Zarubin (1887–1964), Russian scholar of Eastern Iranian languages. Together with the French Iranologist Robert Gauthiot (1876–1916), Zarubin participated in research expeditions to the Pamirs, in Badakhshan, in 1914

So it continued like that until the spring of 1918, when the situation regarding food became very critical. Old men began to die, and the young ones, like myself, became so weak that they were unable to lift a weight of ten kilograms. The administration of the Academy then found it unavoidable to offer its employees application for a three-month leave to go to the interior of the country, where the scarcity of food was not so acute.

Persia Again

Of course, I applied for this kind of leave, but Oldenburg changed it into an academic mission for collecting Persian and Arabic manuscripts, if the currency still had any value, and if not, I was to go to Yaghnob, a mountain region to the south of Samarkand, to study a local dialect which was believed to be a remnant of the ancient Soghdian language. It should be noted that we in St Petersburg had heard absolutely nothing of either the great upheaval which had taken place in Turkestan in 1916, or about the sad events of 1917. Reporting news of this kind in the newspapers was strictly prohibited. When I arrived in Central Asia, through the Volga River and the Caspian Sea to Krasnovodsk, these events were still very fresh in the minds of the local population and their attitude was definitely hostile. The Basmachis were moving in gangs every-

---

and again in 1915. He collected extensive materials on the religious rituals of the Ismailis of the Pamir region. Zarubin's linguistic and ethnographic records are now held at the Institute of Oriental Manuscripts in St Petersburg. Zarubin also collected several Ismaili manuscripts in the Shughnan and Rushan districts of Badakhshan in 1916. These Persian manuscripts were later described by Ivanow in his article: 'Ismailitskie rukopisi Aziatskogo Muzeia. Sobranie I. Zarubina, 1916g', *Izvestiia Rossiiskoi Akademii Nauk*, 6 Series, 11 (1917), pp. 359–386; summarised in E. Denison Ross, 'W. Ivanow, Ismaili MSS in the Asiatic Museum, Petrograd 1917', *Journal of the Royal Asiatic Society* (1919), pp. 429–435. Zarubin is, indeed, considered to be the founder of the Pamirovedenie or Pamirology branch of Soviet Oriental studies. See V. I. Abaev, ed., *Iranskii Sbornik: k semidesiatiletiu Professor I. I. Zarubina* [Iranian Collection: On the 70th Birthday of Professor I. I. Zarubin] (Moscow, 1963); V. S. Rastorgueva, 'I. I. Zarubin (Nekrolog)', *Narody Azii i Afrika*, 4 (1964), pp. 273–275, and R. R. Rahimov, 'Ivan Ivanovich Zarubin (1887–1964)', *Sovestkaia Etnografiia*, 1 (1989), pp. 111–121.

where.[44] Russians could not stay in hotels or caravanserais; it was impossible to go to the bazaar without an accompanying Bukharan soldier. The doctor who had cured me of malaria, V. A. Dobrokhotov, offered me shelter in his hospital, putting me up in his study, but, of course, it was an emergency measure only, and the arrangement could not be expected to last for a long time. It was impossible to think about going to Yaghnob. And it was equally impossible to stay in Bukhara. I could return to St Petersburg, but that too was meaningless. The only reasonable solution was to try to go to Persia. The Bukhara Emirate was not yet incorporated into the Russian territories and enjoyed the status of a protectorate comparable to that of Hyderabad in British India. A resident, who was an official of the Ministry of Foreign Affairs, represented the Russian government there. He resided in Kagan, a railway station near the city.[45]

At the time, instead of a resident's office, there was the headquarters of the Soviet of the Workers and Soldiers Deputies. The doctor, who was on good terms with them, called their office and asked whether they could issue a pass to Persia for me. They answered that if I was indeed on a mission for the Academy of Sciences and could present official papers to that effect such a pass could be issued. Documents

---

[44] The Basmachi movement, lasting from 1917 to the mid-1930s, represented the popular armed struggle of the local inhabitants of Bukhara, the Fergana Valley in Turkmenistan and other Central Asian regions, against Russian, and later Soviet, rule. A Turkish word designating 'bandits', the Basmachis gradually organised a military movement led by their tribal chiefs and foreign military officers. The destruction of the rural economy and the traditional ways of life of the indigenous populations by the Soviet regime has been referred to as the main driving force of the Basmachi movement. See M. Broxup, 'The Basmachi', *Central Asian Survey*, 2 (1983), pp. 57–81; B. Penati, 'The Reconquest of East Bukhara: The Struggle against the Basmachi as a Prelude to Sovietization', *Central Asian Survey*, 26 (2007), pp. 521–538; John S. Schoeberlein-Engel, 'Basmachis', in *The Oxford Encyclopedia of the Islamic World*, ed. John L. Esposito (Oxford, 2009), vol. 1, pp. 317–318, and A. Mikaberidze, 'Basmachi Revolt (1918–1924)', in A. Mikaberidze, ed., *Conflict and Conquest in the Islamic World: A Historical Encyclopedia* (Santa Barbara, CA, 2011), pp. 197–198.

[45] Kagan, or Kogon in Uzbek, is a small town near Bukhara, in present-day Uzbekistan. Kagan acquired some prominence during the 19th century due to the establishment of a railway station there, on the Trans-Caspian line, built by the Russians.

were presented, and something like a diplomatic passport was issued to me. On 3 June 1918, I left for Meshhed.

In 1917, Persia was terribly affected by intense drought and famine, but in the spring of 1918 there was ample rainfall, and so the crops were in a good state. On my arrival in Meshhed, I discovered that the Russian colony of consular officials, bank employees and businessmen were all cut off from Russia and they were now surviving by selling their possessions. And the British were suspicious, while the Persians were still too medieval in their outlook. My old friends told me that a certain Armenian merchant of Nishapur wanted to learn English. So I went there, but the matter did not proceed beyond negotiations. At that time, an old friend, with whom I had worked in the bank and who was a widower with two young children, invited me to teach his children in exchange for food and lodging. He lived in Sabzewar and I moved there in August. His name was Asʿad Kassis. He was a Syrian from Beirut; now we should call him Lebanese. He belonged to the Greek Orthodox Church and had been married to a Russian lady. I spent six months in Sabzewar, which I enjoyed very much. In fact, it was second best after Birjand. I was able to do much work there and studied rural Khorasani and Khorasani Kurdish, as well as the local dervishes.[46]

However, the general situation was worsening. Kassis, being tired of waiting, decided to go to Baku to find out whether it was possible to travel to Moscow or St Petersburg. He arrived in Baku only to discover that the city was completely cut off from the rest of the world. He returned to Sabzewar utterly disappointed. There was nothing for him to do there, and while he still had some money left he decided to return to his native Syria. By that time I, too, had almost no money left and all my job applications had proved unsuccessful.

Dervish by Antoin Sevruguin (ca. 1837–1933)

---

[46] For the results of these studies, see items 13, 20, 28, 31 and 37 in Appendix 1, Works of Ivanow.

At the time of World War I, the Russian government had concluded an agreement with the British to patrol the Persian–Afghan border, through which German and Turkish agents were then penetrating into Afghanistan and the North-West Frontier areas to stir up trouble among the local Muslim populations of these provinces that are now part of Pakistan. The Russian government stationed along the Persian–Afghan frontier two Cossack cavalry regiments from Semirechye, a province in Turkestan bordering China. The Cossacks did their work very efficiently, but in 1916, during the troubles in Turkestan, they heard that native tribes had raided their villages. After the 1917 Revolution, they decided that the war was over for them, and they left their officers behind and rushed back home to punish the natives. The British Indian government was much alarmed by these developments and hastened to dispatch to the border area various units from the Quetta Division in Baluchistan. As was the usual practice in the British Indian Army, an enormous number of non-combatants, servants, clerks, and so forth, moved along with the troops. There were no roads in this desert region, and supplies could be found only in the north, in Khorasan. It demanded an enormous amount of transport capacity to carry things along the lines of communication. Such was the situation by the end of 1918 and the beginning of 1919.

A Russian letter in Ivanow's own handwriting on the subject of dervishes

And my own situation was constantly becoming more and more difficult. Kassis concluded that it was pointless to waste more time waiting for the conditions to return to normalcy either in Russia or in Persia, and decided to return to Syria with his family. My attempts to get a job proved fruitless. With Kassis's departure looming over my head, I found myself with the equivalent of three pounds sterling in my pocket and no hope of finding any employment. At that time the British military attaché at the Meshhed Consulate was a certain Lieutenant Colonel Reddle, who could speak and write in Russian, but not correctly. I sent one of my letters of application to him. He replied that the British Army did not employ interpreters, but, nevertheless, he forwarded my letter to [Brigadier] General Dickson, the Communications Commanding Officer of the Malmisa Force (it was known as the hush-hush brigade).[47]

Service in the British Indian Forces

According to his subordinates, General Dickson was a very good commander and a gentleman. And he was full of goodwill towards the Russians. After the war, he published an interesting book on southeastern Persia.[48] It was believed that he even knew Russian. It was said that he had lived as a child in Tehran where his father held a diplomatic post. At that time, he had a Russian nanny. I had been introduced to him during his visit to Meshhed but he spoke to me only in English. The reason behind my eventual employment at the Supplies and Transport Service was that its Indian staff were unspeakably corrupt. Of course, bribery and stealing are endemic when clerks deal directly with contractors, but the Indians in the Force displayed these qualities in truly 'tropical' proportions. The British Army spent considerable sums not only in order to purchase food and forage but also to hire means of transport – more than 5,000 camels and over 1,000 pack-ponies and mules. The British officers who could not speak any Persian totally depended on the Indian *baboos*,[49] who took full advantage of the situation. Thus, I was appointed to the Transport Office where reliance on an expert in the local language was the greatest. We had to deal with Persians, Kurds, Turks, Afghans and Baluchis, who often were rather rough people of the desert, and local contractors and Indian clerks cheated them left and right. They were

---

[47] William Edmund Dickson (1871–1957), who was born in Persia, was at the time, in fact, the Inspector-General of the East Persian Line of Communications, earlier known as East Persian Cordon.

[48] W. E. R. Dickson, *East Persia: A Backwater of the Great War* (London, 1924). General Dickson states (p. 91) that he could speak Persian fluently; he had spent his childhood in Tehran (p. 256).

[49] In British India, especially in Bengal, the Hindi term *baboo* referred to an Indian clerk. It also denoted a sense of slight disparagement in reference to someone superficially cultivated and educated in English bureaucratic norms.

absolutely furious when I introduced some order, but it satisfied my superiors.

The pay was not very generous, but the army provided everything: lodging, meals, clothes and even a servant, so I could start saving money for a rainy day. This was very useful since it was obvious that it was not a permanent job and it could come to an end at any time. But at that stage I could even afford to order books from Europe.

There are allegations in the press that the British Indian government planned to annex Turkestan. I was in the British service for almost two years from March 1919 until 13 November 1920, and over that period I acquired the impression that the British were afraid of worse developments rather than preparing for an aggression. I may mention that the Force kept in the stables 300 pack-ponies and mules which had been hired at inflated rates in order that they could be ready for duty within two hours to form a 'moveable column'. To maintain them was one of the most important responsibilities of the Transport Office. From time to time, alarming news on the movement of Russian forces were telegraphed from one of the Persian border telegraph points: 'The Bolshis are coming!' The moveable column would be despatched at once. This happened many times during the two years of my service, and it was always a false alarm – there was no invasion. But it is amusing that every time this 'false' alarm was taken quite seriously.

I asked for some explanation from the former head of the Semirechye Brigade of the General Staff, Colonel Sergei Efimovich Gushchin, a Cossack from the Don region of Russia. He was a balanced, calm and respected person. He reassured me by saying that from a military point of view the British would never dream of going to Turkestan due to 'geographic conditions'. Their military forces were far removed from the Russians. The British bases in India were more than three thousand miles away across deserts and roadless mountains. They themselves knew very well their position.

Let me tell you about one particular case. One evening there was an alarm and we sent out the mobile column. Our unit got ready to head south through some deserted areas, where there was straw to feed our camels and horses. A huge pile of kit was placed on the ground. The commandant of the camp, Major White, came to check all this. He was a young man, as energetic as a devil, efficient and clever, according to his friends. In order to see closely how we could ascend a mountain from where the whole camp could be viewed, he asked me: 'How many soldiers do you think we still have now, after the departure of the mobile column yesterday?' I told him the Persians confirmed that there were 20,000 troops in the camp. 'OK, I will tell you,' he said, 'we have now only 15 armed men. If the Bolshis only knew this.' 'Why do you think, sir, that they are interested to know this?' I asked him. 'Why!' he said. 'They are going to take over the world.' Such were the sentiments of the time. Of course, it all depended on the personality of the speaker and his state of mind. Gradually I acclimatised to this environment. The people around me could be divided into three categories. There were a few young and low-ranking officers. They were not devoid of the 'military spirit' that infected our pre-revolutionary army in Russia. Then there were the doctors, like the type of ordinary army doctors everywhere, with whom I had the most contact. There were also former insurance agents and clerks from established firms, who had been mobilised and were now dressed in officer's uniforms. They were not interesting or pleasant types. They were very bored, and often drowned their boredom in booze. Some of them were even drunk from the early morning. The same was true of a small number of ordinary British soldiers.

In September 1920, we were ordered to evacuate to India. According to our instructions, we had to move in four columns, each one marching in accordance with an elaborate timetable towards Duzdap, which is now called Zahidan. At that time, Duzdap was just a camp by the railway lines. I had to remain on duty until the disbandment of the Force on 13 November 1920, and accompany the fourth column, which was the largest, taking 1,500 camels. We were carrying 44 camel-loads of silver as well as ammunition for machine guns and two cannons of the Second Kashmir Mountain Battery travelling with us, and many other items as well. Because of bad desert roads, our convoy stretched 15 km long, men and animals kept injuring their feet and there was much work to do. Eventually, we reached Burmuk, a small village close to Duzdap where we had to get on the train. It took us more than two days to reach Quetta, a small shabby town, which later on was made even more desolate by an earthquake.

Calcutta Again

I received a permit to go to Calcutta, where I hoped to get a job at the Asiatic Society of Bengal.[50] The Force was disbanded on 13 November 1920 and on the same day I took the Delhi train. It was my second visit to Calcutta since 1914. I had with me references from the military authorities and letters of recommendation addressed to the friends of my British friends. The most effective one proved to be the letter addressed to Colonel George Ranking,[51] a retired military doctor. He was a specialist in Persian and had published the thickest Grammar of the Persian language,[52] which contained interesting information, but was too bulky to use. At the time, he was lecturing at Calcutta University. He received me with great empathy and a friendly attitude. He introduced me to Sir Ashutosh Mukherjee,[53] Chief Justice and President of the Asiatic Society of

Sir Ashutosh Mukherjee

---

[50] The Asiatic Society of Bengal was established in 1784 in Calcutta, through the efforts of the British orientalist Sir William Jones (1746-1794), as a research institution. In time, the Society became a leading research centre in the fields of geology, archaeology, history and law, as well as an institution for the study of its extensive collections of manuscripts in Sanskrit, Bengali, Arabic, Persian and other Asian languages. See S. K. Mitra, *The Asiatic Society* (Calcutta, 1974); R. Chakrabarty, *The Asiatic Society 1784-2008* (Calcutta, 2008); Arthur J. Arberry, *Oriental Essays: Portraits of Seven Scholars* (London, 1960), pp. 48-86, and N. H. Ansari and S. H. Qasemi, 'Bengal. ii. Royal Asiatic Society of Bengal', *EIR*, vol. 4, pp. 141-143.

[51] George S. A. Ranking (1852-1934), British surgeon and scholar of Persian. From 1875 he was in the Indian Medical Service, also serving as a Professor of Arabic and Persian in India. From 1894 to 1905, Ranking was an examiner in Oriental languages in India, before becoming a lecturer in Persian at Oxford University (1909-1920). See C. Hayavadano Rao, *Indian Biographical Dictionary* (Madras, 1915), p. 352.

[52] G. S. A. Ranking, *A Grammar of the Persian Language* (Oxford, 1911).

[53] Ashutosh Mukherjee (1864-1924), Bengali educator and founder of a number of higher education institutions. He also served as a High Court Judge and Vice-Chancellor of Calcutta University. See A. Basu, *The Growth of Education and Political Development in India, 1898-1920* (New Delhi, 1974), pp. 30-44, and D. P. Sen Gupta,

Calcutta, 1922

Bengal, who was an exceptionally intelligent and talented man of enormous influence and connections in Calcutta – he could do anything. The Asiatic Society was often called the Society of admirers of Sir Ashutosh. He received me very warmly and told me that the Society owned many rare and valuable Oriental manuscripts, but they could not be used because there was no descriptive catalogue. Thus, he offered me the opportunity to prepare this catalogue. His words were strong enough to override the Council's objections, which was often portrayed as a 22-headed hydra, with each head trying to devour another. I had now something to do and, although I received a pittance salary, I liked the work. I stayed with the Society until 1930 and, before my work was interrupted, published four volumes of a descriptive catalogue of the Persian manuscripts (1,922 pages) and the larger part of a catalogue of the Arabic manuscripts.[54]

Indians, both Muslims and Hindus, resented my appointment and they all united against me. Their argument was that I could not know the Persian language because I did not even speak fluent Urdu. My meagre salary loomed like a fortune in their eyes. All of them were

---

'Sir Ashutosh Mookerjee – Educationist, Leader and Institution-Builder', *Current Science*, 78 (2000), pp. 1566–1573.

[54] See items 18, 22, 27, 36 and 85 in Appendix 1, Works of Ivanow.

convinced that I had been hired because I was a European, 'a white'. One of the elected secretaries, Ma'mun Suhrawardy, a brother or nephew of Huseyn Shaheed Suhrawardy,[55] later a Prime Minister of Pakistan, launched an attack against me. It was quite usual in India that members of such 'notable' families were hopeless degenerates, but they traditionally retained some influence and thus were able to do much harm. This Ma'mun Suhrawardy knew no shame, and he did not blush when he declared at the Council meeting that he knew me very well, that I was a private soldier who had deserted from the Russian Army, fled to Persia and there, while loitering in the bazaars, had picked up some colloquial Persian. He also knew that my real purpose was to have access to the valuable books in the library and steal them. His scurrilous remarks about me were not believed by the scholars at the Council meeting. One of them, A. Harley,[56] the successor to Sir E. Denison Ross[57] in the position of

Sir E. Denison Ross

---

[55] Huseyn Shaheed Suhrawardy (1892–1963), Bengali politician and statesman. He served as the Prime Minister of Bengal in British India (1946–1947), and later as the Prime Minister of Pakistan (1956–1957). See Mohammad Talukdar, *Memoirs of Huseyn Shaheed Suhrawardy, with a Brief Account of his Life and Work* (Oxford, 2009).

[56] Alexander H. Harley (1882–1951), scholar of Hebrew and Arabic languages. He taught Semitic languages at the University of Edinburgh before going to India in 1911 to become the Principal of the Calcutta Madrasah. He stayed in that post until 1926, and later became the Principal of Islamia College in Calcutta. See C. Whitehead, *Colonial Education: The British Indian and Colonial Education Service 1858–1983* (London, 2003), pp. 34–35.

[57] Edward Denison Ross (1871–1940), British orientalist specialising in Persian literature. During 1891–1893, he studied Oriental languages at the Collège de France and the École des Langues Orientales Vivantes, in Paris, with a number of eminent scholars, including Charles Schefer (1820–1898). Later, Ross continued his studies in Strasbourg and St Petersburg. He spent the period 1901–1914 in India, serving as the Principal of the Calcutta Madrasah, founded in 1781 with an Arabic Department and an Anglo-Persian Department. He also served as the philological secretary in the

Principal of the Calcutta Madrasah, said that apparently Suhrawardy had mixed up Mr Ivanow with someone else, 'because Ivanow's paper, published by the Asiatic Society, demonstrates the sound orientalist education of the author'.[58] Ma'mun burst into indignation and stopped attending the Council's meetings. And the following year he was not re-elected. Not long before this incident, I was informed that he, then officially a 'joint philological secretary', had expressed his disapproval that I had started my work without having seen him first. Since he rarely came to the Society, I went to see him at his private address. During our conversation, he said that the proposed catalogue had to be published under his name, but in the preface he would express his gratitude to me for my help. When I asked him why, he rather seriously replied that he would 'guide' me. I was outraged by his audacity and told him that having been trained academically at the Asiatic Museum of the Russian Academy of Sciences, I had no need for any supervision. He was furious and could only say: 'We shall see!' Next morning, when I went to the Society to work, I found some of the reference books on my desk missing. I found out that the 'secretary' had taken them, although according to the rules of the library, the members could not borrow them.

Such parasitic plagiarism was, and still is, practised in India, where 'authorities', who may be even illiterate in the language of a book, pose as its author, while their subordinates do all the work. Indian *iskolars* (as they pronounce the English 'scholar') constantly perpetuated this atmosphere of meanest intrigues and mutual hostility. The only exception was Professor Haraprasad Shastri,[59] an eminent Sanskritologist

---

Asiatic Society of Bengal. In 1916, Ross became the first director of the School of Oriental (and, from 1938, African) Studies (SOAS) in London, a position he held until his retirement in 1937. He was also one of the founding editors of the *Bulletin of the School of Oriental (and African) Studies*. See E. Denison Ross's own *Both Ends of the Candle: The Autobiography of Sir E. Denison Ross* (London, 1943), and R. L. Turner, 'Obituary: Sir Edward Denison Ross', *Bulletin of the School of Oriental and African Studies*, 10 (1940), pp. 832–836.

[58] Reference to item 8 in Appendix 1, Works of Ivanow.

[59] Haraprasad Shastri (1853–1931), also known as Haraprasad Bhattacharya, was an Indian Sanskritologist and historian of Bengali literature. He taught Sanskrit at the Sanskrit College and the Presidency College in Calcutta. He also served as Professor of Bengali and Sanskrit at Dhaka University. Shastri was also the librarian and cataloguer of Sanskrit and Bengali manuscripts in the Bengal Library (1886–1894), and then at

who had worked on a monumental descriptive catalogue of Sanskrit manuscripts in the Asiatic Society's Library. He was able to understand the nature of my work and its difficulties and requirements. He was a poor man, belonging to a comparatively low caste, but possessed a rare quality in India, namely honesty, and, therefore, he was respected. The people who supported me in my fight were English biologists, chemists, geologists and other scientists, some of whom required translations from Russian academic journals. I was, so to speak, working with one hand and parrying intrigues with the other, and despite this succeeded in carrying on for nine years. In addition, I also managed to collect manuscripts in various Indian cities, such as Lucknow and Hyderabad, in the Deccan and, in 1928, even in Persia.

It was difficult to live under such circumstances while waiting for further developments. The natives' hatred of the British was apparently on the rise. Because of that I decided to go on an acquisition mission to Persia to see if it was possible to find a job there. Unfortunately, it was equally chaotic over there. But in Bombay, on my way to Persia, I established contacts with the Ismailis of the Aga Khan's branch.[60] Later on, these contacts led me to the study of the history and literature of the Ismaili movement.

Life in India was difficult for me especially on my miserable salary. All Indians were united in their xenophobic feelings, while at the same time Hindus and Muslims hated each other. And there was also animosity between various branches of Muslims. The British plainly tried to placate the different parties, but the Muslims appeared more pliable than the Hindus, and they were more in favour with the government. In the Asiatic Society, the Hindus were irritated that the

---

the Royal Asiatic Society of Bengal, where he also served as president during 1919–1920. He produced several works on Sanskrit manuscripts, including *A Descriptive Catalogue of Sanskrit Manuscripts in the Government Collection under the Care of the Asiatic Society of Bengal* (Calcutta, 1917).

[60] The author is here referring to the Nizari Ismailis who are known as Khojas in South Asia. During 1885–1957, the Nizari Ismailis were led by their 48th Imam, Sultan Muhammad (Mahomed) Shah, Aga Khan III. The honorific title of Aga Khan (Agha Khan), meaning 'chief lord', was bestowed by Fath Ali Shah (1797–1834), the second Qajar monarch of Persia, on Sultan Muhammad Shah's grandfather, Hasan Ali Shah (1804–1881). See F. Daftary, *A Short History of the Ismailis* (Edinburgh, 1998), pp. 195–199, and 'Aga Khan (Aqa Khan)', in *EIS*, vol. 3, pp. 153–159.

Society's modest budget was spent on the catalogue of Muslim manuscripts, and worthless Muslim *iskolars* were equally indignant that they could not pocket the money. So the Society decided to appease them all. My catalogue of the Arabic manuscripts, of which approximately 200 pages had been printed, was discontinued on the pretext that the Society had no more funds left for cataloguing. This was a lie; after I had left the money was found, so it was only an excuse. The work was entrusted to the most notorious *iskolar*, a certain Hidayat Husain, of whom the joke was that 'honesty was not his strong point'.[61] He was employed once by Sir E. Denison Ross to buy old books.[62] He did not get anything valuable but, as was widely rumoured, had pocketed about 10,000 rupees. The collection I purchased for the Society cost 6 rupees per book and that included the costs of travelling, hotels, etc.; while his cost was 18 rupees per book.

And now I would like to travel back in time for a while. In 1915, in the Bukhara bazaar I had met by chance Sir Aurel Stein.[63] He was returning from Central Asia, and was on his way

Sir Aurel Stein

---

[61] This work was published much later as *Catalogue of the Arabic Manuscripts in the Collection of the Royal Asiatic Society of Bengal*, Volume I, prepared by Wladimir Ivanow, and revised and edited by M. Hidayat Husain. Bibliotheca Indica, 250 (Calcutta, 1939). Muhammad Hidayat Husain was a scholar of Arabic sources in the Royal Asiatic Society of Bengal.

[62] As the philological secretary to the Royal Asiatic Society of Bengal, E. Denison Ross was made responsible for collecting and purchasing Arabic, Persian and Turkish manuscripts for the Society during 1903-1907; and Hidayat Husain assisted Ross in this endeavour, also producing the *List of Arabic and Persian Mss. Acquired on Behalf of the Government of India by the Asiatic Society of Bengal, 1903–1907* (Calcutta, 1908), describing 1,106 manuscripts.

[63] Marc Aurel Stein (1862–1943), Hungarian archaeologist, explorer and Sanskritologist. Between 1900 and 1916, he participated in four expeditions along the Silk Road in Chinese Turkestan (now the Sinkiang or Xinjiang province of China) and Central Asia. He also travelled extensively through Persia and Iraq. See A. Walker, *Aurel Stein: Pioneer of the Silk Road* (London, 1995); R. Whitfield, *The Art of Central*

to Sistan. On account of the scope of his journeys, S. F. Oldenburg described him as the last of the great travellers. I was very glad to make his acquaintance. He wrote down my address and thus our correspondence started, ending only with his death in Kabul. When I came to Calcutta, he wrote about me to the then Minister of Education in Hyderabad of the Deccan, Sir Akbar Hydari,[64] who was a Sulaymani Ismaili Bohra,[65] and an exceptionally intelligent and highly educated person. He immediately offered me the commission of cataloguing the Persian and Arabic manuscripts of the Asafiyya Library in Hyderabad.[66] Later, I discovered there were no unique books there, but, in general, that library possessed some interesting material. I received an official notification from the Ministry of Education in Hyderabad offering me the job, and discussing remuneration and similar matters. Usually when one gets a letter

Sir Akbar Hydari

Asia: The Stein Collection in the British Museum (Tokyo, 1982), and C. Edmund Bosworth, Eastward Ho! Diplomats, Travellers and Interpreters of the Middle East and Beyond 1600–1940 (London, 2012), pp. 245–254.

[64] Sir Mahomed Akbar Nazarally Hydari (1869–1942), Muslim politician and reformer in India, belonging to the Sulaymani branch of Ismaili Shi'ism. He organised the archaeological department of the Hyderabad State University and also played a key role, in 1918, in the foundation of the Osmania University in Hyderabad. Hydari was for many years a leading figure in the government of the Nizam of Hyderabad.

[65] The Tayyibi Ismailis represent the smaller of the two main Ismaili communities, after the Nizaris. The Tayyibis, who are known as Bohras in South Asia, have split into Da'udi, Sulaymani and Alawi groups. The Sulaymanis are concentrated in Yemen, with a very small community of Sulaymani Bohras mainly in Gujarat and Bombay. See F. Daftary, 'al-Tayyibiyya', EI2, vol. 10, pp. 403–404, and I. Poonawala, 'Sulaymanis', EI2, vol. 9, p. 829.

[66] The Asafiyya Library, now known as the State Central Library, was founded in 1891. It was named after the Asaf Jahi dynasty, also known as the Nizams of Hyderabad (1720–1948), who ruled over parts of the Deccan in southern India. In 1955, the Asafiyya Library became the State Central Library for the Hyderabad state of India.

like this from a minister of a recognised state, even under protectorate, one can start packing one's suitcases. But it was not so in my case. I had to wait for no less than 17 years. I visited Hyderabad, wrote letters and invariably received the answer that the matter was under consideration and would be decided 'next week'. Eventually Sir Akbar Hydari died and I settled in Bombay.

However, the explanation was simple. His Exalted Highness the Nizam of Hyderabad,[67] reportedly the richest person in the world, knew Persian well and even wrote poetry in that language. Besides, he was a paranoiac, affected by the mania of avidity for good manuscripts. So he 'borrowed' the most valuable manuscripts from various state libraries and even from private collections – 'just to have a look'. My appointment depended entirely on his goodwill and its postponement until the 'next week' was quite a reasonable action on his part. If a local man, a *mulki*,[68] was employed he would keep silent about the Nizam's misappropriations. But a foreigner, not initiated into all these secrets, could make an issue out of the missing books and that would be bad publicity. This is why I had to waste 17 years waiting for nothing.

The Nizam of Hyderabad

In Calcutta, I met the Russian engineer P. I. Mashmeer-Patrik, who became my friend and played an important role in my life. He was from St Petersburg and had graduated from the Faculty of Mathematics at the University of St Petersburg, and later from

---

[67] The Nizams of Hyderabad ruled over this part of India from 1720 to 1948. The particular Nizam referred to here was Osman Ali Khan (1886–1967), who succeeded his father Mir Mahbub Ali Khan in 1911. He ruled as the last Nizam until 1948, when Hyderabad was annexed to India. The Osmania University established in 1918 was named after him. For more on this Nizam's life and rule over Hyderabad, see V. K. Bawa, *The Last Nizam: The Life and Times of Mir Osman Ali Khan* (New Delhi, 1992), and C. Edmund Bosworth, *The New Islamic Dynasties: A Chronological and Genealogical Manual* (New York, 1996), p. 339.

[68] A native or inhabitant of the former state of Hyderabad in India.

The Institute of Railways. By the time we met, he was already an old man. Before the Revolution he held the important position of chief engineer of the Turksib (i.e. Turkestan–Siberia) railway. He was also a talented linguist, passionately devoted to the study of classical and modern Greek. And he also knew many modern languages. The Revolution deprived him of his position and forced him to emigrate to India via Persia. He found a job in India, but his position was not comparable to that he had held in Russia – he was put in charge of building a section of a new railway. It branched off from the main Calcutta–Madras line at the station of Visakhapatnam, and went through the small principality of Bobbili,[69] to Raipur.[70] His office was in the station-town of Rayagada,[71] close to the confluence of the Nagawali and Rayagada rivers. In the jungles of eastern India with their monkeys, mosquitoes, snakes, black panthers and elephants, it was surreal to find a room where the poetry of Sappho or the descriptions of Mycenaean antiques and books about the 6th-century church of Saint Irene in Thessalonica were kept. These were extremely exotic for the Gond people of the remote Rayagada.[72] He invited me to stay with him for a while and enjoy the 'real' India. As mentioned above, my work in Calcutta had ended and I was awaiting the outcome of the decision for my study of the history and literature of the Ismailis in Bombay. Therefore, I gratefully accepted my friend's invitation and stayed with him from June until December when I left for Bombay.

Mashmeer fell ill in Rayagada and had to leave India for treatment. He later settled in Baghdad and worked on the new railway there. I met him in Iraq in 1937. However, as old age came upon him, he retired and went to live in the south of France. He bought a house in the town of Puy l'Évêque, where he died. He was a very good and interesting person. As we were both away from home, we got along very well with each other.

---

[69] Bobbili is a town in the Vizagapatam district of the Indian state of Andhra Pradesh. The town (and kingdom) of Bobbili was founded in the 17th century.

[70] Administrative centre of the Raipur district, and, from 2000, the capital of the state of Chhattisgarh in India.

[71] Centre of the Rayagada district in the Indian state of Odisha. Rayagada was earlier part of the Jeypore administrative area.

[72] See note 52 in Chapter 4.

Naturalisation as a British Subject

As mentioned above, the Asiatic Society of Bengal sent me to Persia to collect manuscripts. Therefore I had to take a necessary step, which I had continually postponed, namely, my naturalisation as a British subject. As noted, everything was changing in the Asiatic Society of Bengal and the end of my employment there was increasingly imminent. It was still before the oil boom which brought a fortune to Persia and things were still not promising, so I returned to India.

However, this trip raised the question of my passport. I had a sort of certificate issued by the Russian Imperial Consulate in Meshhed, Persia, but obviously it was not a regular passport. By that time the regime in Russia had changed and this consulate no longer existed. When in 1928 the Society sent me for three months to Persia to acquire manuscripts, I had to get my documents in order. The Persian Consul refused to recognise my certificate. The police did not bother me, but they too refused to recognise my certificate, saying that I could leave the country with it, but it was unlikely that I would be allowed to return on it. I succeeded in getting an interview with an officer in charge of the Department of Foreigners. He patiently and politely listened to me and said: 'We cannot issue any passport to you, and your Meshhed certificate has lost its validity with the change of regime in your country.' He told me: 'You have to apply to the Soviet Embassy in London and it will certainly take much time. But why do you not apply for naturalisation? You have lived for more than five years in India uninterruptedly, your papers are in order, and you may acquire British citizenship easily. This will save you any trouble.' I answered that I was determined to return to my country and that I was afraid of public disapproval. He advised me to consider it as a *force majeure* when no other options were left. I thanked him for his advice and said I would think about it. I spent the night pacing up and down my room and it became clear to me that there was no other alternative. Next morning I submitted my application. In less than two months, I received the certificate of naturalisation and my British passport. Now I was saved from police interrogation and could travel. I must add, however, that my naturalisation did not change anything in my status as a foreigner. Like other nationals of the British Commonwealth, in the eyes of the law I remained a British subject, not a citizen of the UK. But, nevertheless, it was a considerable step towards some peace of mind.

I can recall that after World War I and the Russian Revolution, the British considered themselves offended by the behaviour of the new regime. Even in 1921, the mere possession of Soviet currency was a criminal offence punishable by imprisonment. When at the beginning of 1922 I read in a newspaper that the ban on sending letters to Russia had been lifted, I at once wrote a letter to my mother and went to post it as registered mail at the central post office in Dalhousie Square in Calcutta. When the Indian clerk saw the address on the envelope, he turned green (Indians do not get pale when emotional, but turn greenish) and rushed out shouting, 'Russia, Russia'. Eventually, he returned and with his hands still trembling issued a receipt. Gradually things became more normal, I corresponded regularly with my mother and later on could even send her money through 'Torgsin', the Soviet organisation for trade with foreign countries. So, I went to Persia via Bombay and Bushir, bought a box of manuscripts in Shiraz and returned by train to Calcutta via Tehran, Meshhed and Duzdap.

Bombay

It is well known that 'defensive silence' (*taqiyya*) on their religious matters is one of the main duties of the Ismailis.[73] They have to pretend to be members of the orthodox Sunni community, knowing nothing about Ismailism. In India only their clothes and general appearance could distinguish them, but their way of dressing is conditioned by their caste, not religion. In Persia, Syria, Turkestan and other countries they do not differ from non-Ismailis. One may know a person for years without being aware that he is an Ismaili. The only way to draw an Ismaili into a conversation on religious subjects is to give him a hint that the questioning party already possesses some

---

[73] *Taqiyya* is an Arabic term denoting precautionary dissimulation of one's true beliefs, especially in times of danger. *Taqiyya* has been used especially by the Twelver (Ithnaʿashari) and Ismaili Shiʿis. The practice of *taqiyya* has conveniently protected these Shiʿi Muslims from persecution, frequently serving to safeguard their survival under hostile circumstances. See E. Kohlberg, 'Some Imami-Shiʿi Views on *taqiyya*', *Journal of the American Oriental Society*, 95 (1975), pp. 395–402; reprinted in his *Belief and Law in Imami Shiʿism* (Aldershot, 1991), article III.

reliable knowledge. The first time I met Ismailis while knowing who they were was at the beginning of 1912 in the village of Sedeh, on the road from Qa'in to Birjand, in eastern Persia.[74] They themselves denied they were Ismailis and told me nothing interesting. I also met Ismailis in other places such as Birjand, Nishapur and various villages, but with very little success in terms of finding access to their literature.

My entire knowledge of Ismailism was based on the study of Syrian manuscripts in Arabic bought at the beginning of the 19th century from a Levantine dealer, Rousseau,[75] for the Asiatic Museum. I could lay my hands on real Ismaili books only in 1916 in the Asiatic Museum, when I. I. Zarubin brought a collection of Ismaili

---

[74] This region of south-eastern Khorasan was known as Quhistan in Arabic (Kuhistan in Persian) in medieval times, when it was an important territory of the Nizari Ismaili state in Persia (1090–1256). At the time of Ivanow's visit, the Nizari Ismailis of Sedeh, and a few surrounding villages, were led by a certain Murad Mirza (d. 1936), who operated in an independent manner. In fact, he broke away from the Nizari Ismailis of Khorasan while developing his own doctrinal position. The majority of Murad Mirza's followers, known as Murad Mirza'is, eventually embraced Twelver Shi'ism. See Daftary, *The Isma'ilis: Their History and Doctrines* (2nd ed., Cambridge, 2007), pp. 490–493.

[75] Jean Baptiste Louis Jacques Rousseau (1780–1831), better known as Joseph Rousseau and hailing from the famous French Rousseau family, was the French Consul in Aleppo, Tripoli and Baghdad, then in Ottoman domains, from 1809 to 1816. He was also interested in Oriental studies, collected Oriental manuscripts and maintained close academic relations with A. I. Silvestre de Sacy (1758–1838), the most distinguished orientalist of his time. Rousseau was, in fact, the first person to draw the attention of European orientalists to the existence of the contemporary Ismailis as well as to their local traditions and literature in Syria. In 1819 and 1825, through the intervention of A. Silvestre de Sacy, Rousseau sold some 700 Arabic manuscripts to the then newly founded Asiatic Museum in St Petersburg. Rousseau also acquired a few Ismaili texts, which were later sent to Paris. See J. B. L. J. Rousseau, 'Mémoire sur les Ismaélis et les Nosaïris de Syrie, adressé à M. Silvestre de Sacy', *Annales des Voyages*, 14 (1811), pp. 271–303; his 'Extraits d'un Livre qui contient la doctrine des Ismaélis', *Annales des Voyages*, 18 (1812), pp. 222–249; Henri Dehérain, *Silvestre de Sacy 1758–1838. Ses contemporains et ses disciples* (Paris, 1938), Part I, pp. 65–92, and Part II, pp. 25–35; Kratchovsky, *Among Arabic Manuscripts*, pp. 75–76; Oleg F. Akimushkin, 'K istorii formirovaniia fonda musul'manskikh rukopisei Instituta Vostokovedeniia AN SSSR' [On the History of the Formation of the Collection of Islamic Manuscripts of the Institute of Oriental Studies of the USSR], *Ezhegodnik Pamiatniki pis'mennosti Vostoka* (Moscow, 1978–1979), p. 9, and O. F. Akimushkin et al., 'The Triumph of the Qalam', in Petrosyan et al., *Pages of Perfection*, especially pp. 68–75.

manuscripts from the villages of the Upper Oxus.[76] I published a short note on them in Russian,[77] and later edited some of these works in the original Persian together with English translations and commentaries. I sent some of my articles to the 'Ismaili' weekly, then published in Bombay in Gujarati with only a few pages reserved for articles in English. This generated an invitation from the editors to send them more material. When I was passing through Bombay in 1928, I called at their office, they telephoned the head of the local community and I was received with pomp and taken to some important people, all with much fuss.

In my letters to Sir Aurel Stein I had mentioned my complications with the Asiatic Society of Bengal and with his usual goodwill he wrote to his friend Sir Arthur Cowley,[78] the Librarian of the Bodleian in Oxford, recommending me for cataloguing their still uncatalogued manuscripts, acquired after the publication of the catalogue by H. Ethé in 1889.[79] I received from him a very kind letter, to which I replied with complete agreement. But this offer, too, came to nothing, because Cowley was then old and sick. He had to undergo an operation and died soon afterwards in 1931. I wrote to his successor and received a reply that the building extensions of the Bodleian Library had proved

---

[76] Upper Oxus (Arabic, *ma wara al-nahr*), is a designation used by European and Russian travellers during the 19th century in reference to the territories of Qarategin, Hissar, Darwaz, Shughnan, Rushan and Wakhan in Central Asia, where the Amu Darya (also known as the Oxus) has its tributaries. The largest tributaries of the Amu Darya are the Panj and Wakhsh rivers in the south-western parts of present-day Tajikistan. The territories from this point to the north-east of Tajikistan, up to the Pamir mountains on the border of the present Gorno-Badakhshan Autonomous Province of Tajikistan and the Badakhshan province of Afghanistan, were thus referred to as the Upper Oxus. Muslims designated the region north of the Amu Darya (Arabic, Jayhun) as Ma Wara al-Nahr, 'the land beyond the river', or Transoxania. See R. Mitchell, 'The Regions of the Upper Oxus', *Proceedings of the Royal Geographical Society*, 6 (1884), pp. 489–512, and B. Spuler, 'Amu Darya', *EI2*, vol. 1, pp. 454–457.

[77] Reference to item 4 in Appendix 1, Works of Ivanow.

[78] Arthur E. Cowley (1861–1931), British librarian and scholar of Semitic studies. He served as the head of the Bodleian Library at Oxford University from 1919 until 1931. See T. W. Allen, 'Arthur Ernest Cowley, 1861–1931', *Proceedings of the British Academy*, 19 (1933), pp. 351–359.

[79] Hermann Ethé (1844–1917), *Catalogue of the Persian, Turkish, Hindustani and Pushtu Manuscripts in the Bodleian Library*, vol. I (Oxford, 1889).

more costly than initially expected, hence no money was left for cataloguing, which had to be postponed. I must confess that life in the English climate, after so many years in the subtropics, did not particularly appeal to me.

However, it was still necessary to get a job and I decided to try the Khojas, who had received me so well. The answer soon came that His Highness the Aga Khan was travelling,[80] and as nothing could be decided without his consent, I had better wait until he returned. I was at that time staying in Rayagada, editing and translating the manuscript of the *Tasawwurat* kindly lent to me by the Khojas.[81] In December, I was informed that His Highness the Aga Khan had consented to my engagement in regular research on the history, literature and philosophy of Ismailism. I was certainly very glad and at the end of December I left via Hyderabad for Bombay, where I started my work on 1 January 1931.

---

[80] Sir Sultan Muhammad (Mahomed) Shah, Aga Khan III (1877–1957), the 48th Imam of the Nizari Ismailis, known in India as the Khojas. From early on, Aga Khan III concerned himself with the affairs and the welfare of his followers, especially those in South Asia and East Africa. In time, these concerns evolved in the form of specific modernisation policies. He worked vigorously for reorganising the Nizari Ismailis into a modern Muslim community, with high standards of education and social well-being, also paying particular attention to the emancipation of women. On this Imam, see his *The Memoirs of Aga Khan: World Enough and Time* (London, 1954), and his *Aga Khan III: Selected Speeches and Writings of Sir Sultan Muhammad Shah*, ed. K. K. Aziz (London, 1997–1998), 2 vols. See also Naoroji M. Dumasia, *The Aga Khan and His Ancestors: A Biographical and Historical Sketch* (Bombay, 1939; reprinted, New Delhi, 2008); F. Daftary and Z. Hirji, *The Ismailis: An Illustrated History* (London, 2008), pp. 198–231, and Daftary, *The Ismaʿilis*, pp. 480–496.

[81] Reference to item 120 in Appendix 1, Works of Ivanow. Mr Ali Mahomed Mecklai, the future first President of the Ismaili Society, had arranged for the loan in 1930 to Ivanow of a manuscript of the *Tasawwurat*, also known as *Rawdat al-taslim*, belonging to a Khoja cultural institution in Bombay. Ivanow's edition and English translation of this work appeared two decades later, in 1950. Meanwhile, Ivanow had published a note in 1931 (item 45 in Appendix 1) on this text, representing one of his earliest Ismaili publications after settling in Bombay. See also *Correspondance Corbin-Ivanow*, pp. 20, 34, 36, 43, 45, 53–54. For a more recent, and better, edition and translation of this text, see Nasir al-Din Tusi, *Paradise of Submission: A Medieval Treatise on Ismaili Thought*, ed. and tr. S. Jalal Badakhchani. Ismaili Texts and Translations Series, 5 (London, 2005).

Sir Sultan Muhammad (Mahomed) Shah, Aga Khan III

First of all, I started looking for Ismaili works. The Khojas had some religious books in Gujarati and other languages which I did not know. They had no such works in Arabic and possessed only two Persian manuscripts, one the above-mentioned *Tasawwurat* and another one of no particular importance. Fortunately, I received money for the purchase of Arabic Ismaili manuscripts from the Bohras, and Persian books from the Badakhshani and Persian [Nizari Ismaili] pilgrims, who came to Bombay for the ceremony of the *didar* of their Imam.

This was no easy task, but our collection of Ismaili works began to grow. My 'breakthrough' in the entanglement of traditional Ismaili secrecy and direct access to their genuine literature undoubtedly constituted an important step in the development of Islamic studies and the study of Ismailism. And this was hailed as such by eminent scholars such as the late L. Massignon,[82] R. Strothmann,[83] and others.

Surprisingly enough, it also provoked outbursts of excitement from certain circles in England and America, which bravely rushed to the defence of 'orthodox' Islam, condemning the 'subversive and heretical' Ismailism. Genuine Ismaili works that I edited and translated were shamelessly proclaimed as the 'apologetic propaganda of the Aga Khan', and it was claimed that for its forgery I was paid 'fabulous sums'. Lie upon lie was invented and began to circulate. I think it would be useful if I plainly state the facts here. The initiative for my engagement in the study of the history, literature and

---

[82] Louis Massignon (1883–1962), French orientalist and the foremost pioneer of modern Shi'i studies and Islamic mysticism in France. He led a selective group of French scholars, including especially Henry Corbin (1903–1978), who investigated Shi'ism with particular reference to its spiritual, esoteric and mystic dimensions, as manifested especially in its Twelver and Ismaili traditions. Amongst various academic positions at the École Pratique des Hautes Études at the Sorbonne, and elsewhere in Paris, Massignon was also the first director of the Institut d'Études Iraniennes, founded in 1947; see *Correspondance Corbin-Ivanow*, pp. 144–146, 154. A prolific scholar, Massignon devoted a lifelong interest to the celebrated mystic al-Husayn b. Mansur al-Hallaj (d. 922); see his *La passion d'al-Hosayn Ibn Mansour al-Hallaj, martyr mystique de l'Islam* (Paris, 1922; 2nd ed., Paris, 1975), 4 vols.; English trans., *The Passion of al-Hallaj: Mystic and Martyr of Islam*, tr. H. Mason (Princeton, 1982), 4 vols. See Y. Moubarac, 'Bibliographie de Louis Massignon', in *Mélanges Louis Massignon* (Damascus, 1956–1957), vol. 1, pp. 3–56. See also Carmela Baffioni, ed., *Atti del Convegno sul centenario della nascita di Louis Massignon* (Naples, 1985); Éve Pierunek and Y. Richard, ed., *Louis Massignon et l'Iran* (Paris, 2000), and J. Fr. Six, ed., *Louis Massignon* (Paris, 1970).

[83] Rudolf Strothmann (1877–1960), German orientalist and a leading pioneer of modern Shi'i studies in Germany. Professor Strothmann of Hamburg University was interested in the diverse manifestations of Shi'i Islam. He was one of the earliest European scholars to make pioneering contributions to Zaydi and Ismaili studies on the basis of original sources, in addition to pursuing his interest in Twelver Shi'ism. He also studied the religious doctrines of the Nusayri Shi'is, designated more commonly as the Alawis (or Alawites) since the 1920s. Strothmann trained a number of German scholars in Shi'i traditions, such as Wilferd Madelung who has made seminal contributions to the study of all the major Shi'i communities. See R. Paret, 'Rudolf Strothmann (4.9.1877–15.5.1960)', *Zeitschrift der Deutschen Morgenländischen Gesellschaft*, 111 (1961), pp. 13–15, and F. Daftary, *Ismaili Literature: A Bibliography of Sources and Studies* (London, 2004), pp. 111, 118, 119, 122, 160, 163, 165, 401.

philosophy of Ismailism came from the progressive circles of the Khoja community, not from the Aga Khan himself, though his consent was required. During my only conversation with the late Sir Sultan Muhammad Shah, the Aga Khan, concerning the programme of my research he emphasised that I should concentrate on the *history* of his ancestors. He recalled the well-known fact that his grandfather, Hasan Ali Shah [1804–1881], the original Aga Khan, was attacked in Sind by Baluchi brigands.[84] He himself escaped almost by miracle. His property, including precious books belonging to the family, was pillaged. Many attempts to recover them, in spite of promises of generous rewards, had failed – the books were most probably destroyed. The books I was mainly concerned with, the early Ismaili literature, were preserved in the Bohra community,[85] which had

---

[84] Hasan Ali Shah's predecessors as Nizari Ismaili Imams had all lived in Persia for some seven centuries. Hasan Ali Shah himself succeeded to the Nizari Imamate in 1817, upon the death of his father Shah Khalil Allah. He was later appointed to the governorship of the province of Kerman. However, his early dismissal in the reign of the third Qajar monarch, Muhammad Shah (1834–1848), led to a series of military confrontations between the Nizari Imam and the Qajar establishment of Persia, obliging the Imam to leave his ancestral home in 1841. After spending some time in Afghanistan, coinciding with the final years of the First Afghan War (1838–1842), Hasan Ali Shah proceeded to Sind, where he rendered some effective assistance to the British, who were then annexing the region to British India. After the conquest of Sind in 1843 by General Sir Charles Napier (1782–1853), the Nizari Imam lent further support to the British in their operations in neighbouring Baluchistan. It was perhaps as a reprisal for his assistance to the British that the first Aga Khan himself became the target of Baluchi raids and his books and other possessions were plundered. The Nizari Imam eventually settled permanently in 1848 in Bombay. Hasan Ali Shah, Aga Khan I, recounts the events of this period in his autobiography, written in Persian and entitled *Ibrat-afza* (lithographed, Bombay, 1862); see also William F. P. Napier, *The Conquest of Scinde* (London, 1845), pp. 369, 372, 404–405; his *The History of General Sir Charles Napier's Conquest of Scinde* (2nd ed., London, 1857), pp. 224, 226, 245; Priscilla Napier, *I Have Sind: Charles Napier in India, 1841–1844* (Salisbury, Wiltshire, 1990), pp. 155–156, 177, 238–240, 242, 258–260; Daftary and Hirji, *The Ismailis: An Illustrated History*, pp. 182–195, and Daftary, *The Isma'ilis*, pp. 463–476.

[85] The books, all in Arabic, related to the Fatimid and later periods of Ismaili history. They had been originally transferred mainly from Fatimid Egypt to Yemen, which in due course became the stronghold of Tayyibi Ismailism. These texts were preserved and copied generation after generation, and subsequently transferred to Gujarat and other parts of India where Tayyibi (Bohra) communities had evolved through the efforts of the Tayyibi leaders in Yemen.

Hasan Ali Shah, Aga Khan I

nothing to do with the Aga Khan. These works were lost centuries ago in his community.⁸⁶ Besides, they were quite out of tune with the

---

⁸⁶ The Nizari Ismailis of Persia, Afghanistan and Central Asia elaborated their own doctrines and literature, using the Persian language in preference to Arabic. As a result, they did not generally preserve the Ismaili literature produced earlier in Arabic. At the same time, the Nizari Khojas of India had elaborated their own indigenous Ismaili tradition, designated as Satpanth, or 'true path'. The eclectic Muslim–Hindu teachings of the Satpanth tradition are reflected in the *ginan*s, the devotional literature of the Nizari Khojas. Composed in a number of Indian languages and dialects of Sind, Punjab and Gujarat, these hymn-like poems, which were transmitted only orally until the 16th century, have been recorded mainly in the Khojki script developed in Sind by the Nizari Khoja community. See F. Daftary, 'Ismaili History and Literary Traditions', in H. Landolt et al., ed., *An Anthology of Ismaili Literature: A Shiʿi Vision of Islam* (London, 2008), pp. 1–29, and Ali S. Asani, 'From Satpanthi to Ismaili Muslim: The Articulation of Ismaili Khoja Identity in South Asia', in F. Daftary, ed., *A Modern History of the Ismailis: Continuity and Change in a Muslim Community* (London, 2011), pp. 95–128.

beliefs of the Khojas, so they would be quite useless as propaganda material. They had only historical and antiquarian interest for the community as well as for any serious student of the evolution of Islamic history.

As for the allegedly circulating accusation about 'fabulous sums paid to me by the fabulously rich Aga Khan', the facts are as follows. The main reason for my taking up this employment was not the money but the unique possibility to study Ismailism from within, relying on genuine [Ismaili] literature. I therefore was willing to join on probation for 12 months on a salary of 300 rupees per month. At that time, in the beginning of 1931, this was the equivalent of just over £22 [approximately £1,000 in today's terms], which was quite sufficient for a single man to live on. It had been agreed that on the termination of the probationary period my pay might be increased. But this did not actually happen, and I received the same salary for 14 years. Instead of being increased, it kept decreasing due to the fall in the [purchasing] power of the rupee. It was more and more difficult to make ends meet, and I had to find some extra work. Finally in 1944, the depreciation of the rupee and the increasing cost of living became unbearable and after much insistence, my pay was raised by 100 of these devalued rupees a month. I could survive only because I was lodged in the government's publishing house. After the end of World War II, and with great difficulties, I secured a salary of 1,000 rupees per month, and in 1957 1,200 rupees; it is still the same now. But the rupee is constantly being devalued; on 6 June of last year it lost 35 per cent of its value. By calculating all these devaluations, it comes to this: I started my fabulously paid work in 1931 on £22 of that time and after 37 years of continuous work I am now paid the equivalent of £9 of that time.

It is not so easy to answer the question of what the purpose was of this campaign of lies and speculations about fabulous sums paid to me for the alleged propaganda. I think it can be explained only by the monstrosity of our times. Various revelations in the press help to solve this puzzle. In America, there is a not particularly respectable institution called the Central Intelligence Agency (CIA), or simply an agency of espionage. Its agents' activities are not only confined to spying, they are also empowered to 'take measures for the containment of Communism'. It is difficult to comprehend by what insane process of reasoning such an arch-conservative and purely religious movement as Ismailism had come to be associated with theories of Communism. But it caused a flurry at the CIA – subsidised 'academic' publications and talks on the 'Order of Assassins' or the 'Cult of Murder', and so on. Really, it is worth remembering the axiom that the more shameless, stupid and absurd a lie, the quicker and easier it spreads and becomes generally accepted as unassailable truth.

But let us return to my work in Bombay. The first thing that I had to do was to find the coveted Ismaili literature. I have already mentioned what the situation was with Ismaili works. However, I succeeded in finding a number of persons who possessed them, among both the Khoja and Bohra Ismailis. The most valuable contact was an old man, a retired servant of the late Aga Khan, Musa Khan Khorasani by name.[87] Although himself devoid of much learning, he was an enthusiastic collector of Ismaili books in Persian. What was even more important, he wanted other people to study them. This was in sharp contrast to other collectors' attitudes, who usually zealously guarded their books from the world. Without any hesitation, he made his collection accessible to me and allowed me to copy and photograph his books. This Musa Khan wrote a legendary history of Ismailism. Some time ago his book was negligently edited by A. A. Semenov (Semyonov) in Russia,[88] who

Aleksandr Aleksandrovich Semenov

---

[87] Musa Khan b. Muhammad Khorasani (d. 1937) was a bibliophile and collector of Ismaili manuscripts, whose Persian ancestors had accompanied Hasan Ali Shah, Aga Khan I, from Persia to India in the early 1840s. The family had remained in the service of the Ismaili Imams. Musa Khan had established his own private library of Persian Ismaili manuscripts in Bombay and also copied some of these texts.

[88] Aleksandr Aleksandrovich Semenov (1873–1958), orientalist and a Russian pioneer in the study of the religious traditions of Central Asian Ismailis. In 1898, Semenov participated in the expedition sent to Badakhshan under the leadership of Count Aleksey A. Bobrinskoy (1861–1938), for collecting ethnographic information

erroneously attributed it to Fidaʾi Khorasani of Dizbad, near Nishapur.[89]

A young and wealthy Khoja businessman, Ismail Mohammed Jafer, offered to meet the printing costs of the edited versions of Musa Khan's manuscripts. However, the matter appeared to be rather complicated because of the hostility of some reactionary circles. It was decided that the best way forward would be to offer them for publication to a recognised academic institution, such as the Bombay Branch of the Royal Asiatic Society, which was founded at the beginning of the 19th century. It published a journal, memoirs and a

---

on the Pamir regions of Central Asia. This was also a pioneering effort on the part of Russian scholars and officials to study the Ismailis of Badakhshan; see A. A. Bobrinskoy, 'Sekta Ismailiya v Russkikh i Bukharskikh predelakh Sredney Azii' [The Ismaili Sect in Russian and Bukharan Central Asia], *Etnograficheskoe Obozrenie*, 2 (1902), pp. 1–20, and Bianca Marabini Zoeggeler et al., *Il Conte Bobrinskoj. Il lungo cammino dal Pamir alle Dolomiti* (Bozen, Italy, 2012). Semenov had an academic career at the then newly founded State University of Central Asia in Tashkent from 1920 to the 1940s. Subsequently, he served as the director of the Institute of History, Archaeology and Ethnography of the Academy of Sciences of Tajikistan in Dushanbe during 1951–1958. Semenov collected a number of manuscripts from Shughnan and other districts of Badakhshan, which were given to the Asiatic Museum; see his 'Opisanie ismailitskikh rukopisei, sobrannykh A. A. Semyonovym' [A Description of Ismaili Manuscripts, A. A. Semenov's Collection], *Izvestiia Rossiiskoi Akademii Nauk/Bulletin de l'Académie des Sciences de Russie*, 6 Series, 12 (1918), pp. 2171–2202. Semenov also published a number of Ismaili studies as well as editions of several Persian Ismaili texts. Based in Tashkent, Semenov was not spared the purges of Stalin's era; he spent 1931–1934 in prison. See Daftary, *Ismaili Literature*, pp. 112, 137, 139, 381–382. For a detailed study of Semenov's life and work, see B. A. Litvinskii and N. M. Akramov, *Aleksandr Aleksandrovich Semenov (Nauchno-biograficheskii Ocherk)* (Moscow, 1971).

[89] The work in question is Fidaʾi Khurasani's *Kitab-i hidayat al-muʾminin al-talibin*, ed. A. A. Semenov (Moscow, 1959). According to Ivanow's own earlier account (*Ismaili Literature*, Tehran, 1963, pp. 153–154), Musa Khan Khorasani had evidently added, in Bombay around 1910, only the final sections on the Aga Khans to this history; and the copy of the text edited by Semenov was actually the one revised and expanded by Musa Khan. Muhammad b. Zayn al-Abidin, better known as Fidaʾi Khorasani, was a Persian Nizari Ismaili author, poet and missionary (*daʿi*). Born around 1850 in the village of Dizbad, in northern Khorasan, Fidaʾi was made responsible by Imam Sultan Muhammad Shah, Aga Khan III, for overseeing the religious affairs of the Persian Nizari community. Fidaʾi died in 1923 and was buried in his native Dizbad. He composed several doctrinal works, which remain in

separate series of academic works. To some extent, it duplicated the work of the Asiatic Society of Bengal in Calcutta, but only on a much smaller scale. We decided to offer initially the four books [containing five Persian Nizari Ismaili texts] prepared by me for publication in their special series at the expense of our 'anonymous donor' mentioned above.[90]

My friend Asaf A. A. Fyzee,[91] a young advocate educated at the University of Cambridge, was the secretary of the Bombay Branch of the Royal Asiatic Society. We requested that he discuss our proposal at the meeting of their Council. It was submitted, put to vote and

---

manuscript form, as well as the *Kitab-i hidayat al-mu'minin*, permeated with errors, which has been preserved by the Nizari Ismailis of Badakhshan in present-day Tajikistan and Afghanistan; see Andrei E. Bertel's and M. Bakoev, *Alfavitnyi katalog rukopisei obnaruzhennykh v Gorno-Badakhshanskoi Avtonomnoi Oblasti ekspeditsiei 1959-1963 gg. / Alphabetic Catalogue of Manuscripts found by 1959-1963 Expedition in Gorno-Badakhshan Autonomous Region*, ed. B. G. Gafurov and A. M. Mirzoev (Moscow, 1967), p. 102, and F. Daftary, 'Feda'i Korasani', *EIR*, vol. 9, p. 470.

[90] Reference to items 58, 59, 60 and 64 in Appendix 1, Works of Ivanow.

[91] Asaf Ali Asghar Fyzee (1899-1981), Indian educator and one of the leading pioneers of modern Ismaili studies. Born into the prominent Tyabji-Fyzee family of Sulaymani Ismaili Bohras, Fyzee studied at St John's College, Cambridge. In 1925, he was called to the bar from the Middle Temple and became a barrister-at-law. Fyzee embarked on his legal career in 1926, as an advocate in the High Court of Bombay, a post he held until 1938. Meanwhile, he had started teaching law at the Government Law College, Bombay, where he eventually became the Principal and Perry Professor of Jurisprudence during 1938-1947. After the partition of India, he was designated as his country's first ambassador to Egypt during 1949-1951. Subsequently, he served (1957-1960) as the Vice-Chancellor of the University of Jammu and Kashmir at Srinagar. Fyzee made valuable contributions to modern scholarship in Ismaili studies, especially in the area of Ismaili jurisprudence, drawing on his own family collection of manuscripts, which he donated in 1957 to the Library of the University of Bombay. Fyzee, in fact, introduced to modern scholars the Ismaili school of jurisprudence (*madhhab*), as reflected mainly in the works of al-Qadi al-Nu'man (d. 974), the foremost jurist of the Fatimid period in Ismaili history. Meanwhile, Fyzee had started his lifelong academic collaboration with Ivanow, initially as the Executive Secretary of the Islamic Research Association. See F. Daftary, 'Professor Asaf A. A. Fyzee (1899-1981)', *Arabica*, 31 (1984), pp. 327-330; his 'The Bibliography of Asaf A. A. Fyzee', *Indo-Iranica*, 37 (1984), pp. 49-63, and Farhan A. Nizami, 'Fyzee, Asaf Ali Asghar', in *The Oxford Encyclopedia of the Islamic World*, vol. 2, pp. 281-282. See also M. Goriawala, *A Descriptive Catalogue of the Fyzee Collection of Ismaili Manuscripts* (Bombay, 1965); A. A. A. Fyzee, 'A Collection of Fatimid Manuscripts', in N. N.

rejected. One of the members of the Council, a retired Hindu official, had assured his colleagues that the proposal should be turned down because if they published the books, the Aga Khan might send his 'assassins' to murder them all. This evoked protests and a learned Parsi said that although such a thing was certainly quite improbable,[92] he advised that the proposal and the grant of money for it should be rejected because publication of such books might provoke street riots. All this now seems ridiculous, but it demonstrates what even the most educated people were then capable of believing.

My friends who attended the meeting informed me of the decision and we discussed what was to be done next. It was clear that repeating the same thing with some other learned institution would be a waste of time. I suggested founding an entirely new organisation under a neutral name, with no mention of Ismailism, that could publish our books under its auspices. So, after some discussion, the 'Islamic Research Association' was born.[93] Unfortunately, misunderstanding gradually cropped up again. From my point of view, the most important matter was the publication of genuine Ismaili works, but to some members of the organising group this appeared to be of secondary importance. They were more concerned with public images and all the theatricals of meetings, gatherings and speeches. And I remained the only worker [i.e. working scholar]. It was mentioned that the publication of further Ismaili works would turn the [Association's] series into the 'Ivanow's Ismaili Series'. The argument went like this: 'It was necessary to publish some non-Ismaili works, by another author, especially in Urdu – otherwise God only knows what people would think.' I felt repelled by this behaviour and, from early on, started to distance myself from the newly born body.

Gidwani, ed., *Comparative Librarianship: Essays in Honour of Professor D. N. Marshall* (Delhi, 1973), pp. 209–220, and *Correspondance Corbin-Ivanow*, p. 161.

[92] See note 57 in Chapter 4.

[93] The Association was formally founded in February 1933 with headquarters in Bombay. Its six 'founding members' were: A. M. Mecklai, Dr U. M. Daudpota, Saif F. B. Tyabji, Dr M. B. Rehman, W. Ivanow and Asaf A. A. Fyzee. Mr Mecklai served as President of the Association, and others, with him, constituted the Executive Committee. Asaf Fyzee served as the Association's Secretary. Aga Khan III was the Association's patron. By 1938, the membership of the Association stood at 83.

Having published five works, I prepared a new book for publication dealing with one of the most cardinal and difficult questions in the study of Ismaili history, namely the real role of Abd Allah ibn Maymun al-Qaddah.[94] The enemies of the Ismailis had portrayed him as the founder of Ismailism and the progenitor of the Fatimid caliphs, an arch-heretic, and so forth. When the book was ready I gave it for review to two members of the 'organising group', as was stipulated by the home-made 'constitution', and at a subsequent meeting I offered to send the manuscript for printing. But one of the group members, a non-worker himself, suggested giving the book to professors so-and-so for their approval. In fact, none of the suggested scholars had anything to do with the study of Ismailism, and it would have been a plain formality and waste of time, pure procrastination so dear to the bureaucratic mentality of the Indians. I became furious and told them that either the manuscript should be posted the next day or I would leave their Association.[95] They tried to change my mind, but I was fed up with all this and left. This Association still exists, but in a state of hibernation. In the last 14 years they have not published anything, although they still have some funds.[96]

Anyway, it had become clear that the publication of our Ismaili works would not cause any untoward events. Hence, I suggested to the President of the Association, Mr Ali Mahomed Mecklai, to start a new and independent organisation for the continuation of Ismaili

---

[94] Abd Allah b. Maymun al-Qaddah was a companion of the early Shi'i Imam Ja'far al-Sadiq (d. 765) and reporter of numerous *hadiths* from him. This respected non-Alid personality, who was a Shi'i traditionist from the Hijaz and died sometime during the second half of the 8th century, is introduced into anti-Ismaili polemics starting with Ibn Rizam, who flourished in Baghdad in the first half of the 10th century and wrote a major work around 951 in refutation of the Ismailis, more commonly known as the Batinis. His polemical work laid the foundation of a 'black legend' and set the tone for later refutations of the Ismailis. As a result, Ismailism was depicted as an arch-heresy designed to destroy Islam from within, and the Alid genealogy of the early Ismaili Imams and the Fatimid Imam-caliphs was also refuted. See F. Daftary, 'Abd Allah b. Maymun al-Qaddah', *EIS*, vol. 1, pp. 167–169, and his *The Isma'ilis*, pp. 100–107.

[95] This book by W. Ivanow, entitled *The Alleged Founder of Ismailism*, published in 1946, in fact, was to launch the Ismaili Society's new series of publications.

[96] A list of the publications of the Islamic Research Association, from 1933 to 1952, totalling 13 in number, as compiled by the editor, is given in Appendix 2.

publications, this time without masking its real purpose and calling it the 'Ismaili Society'.[97] Its membership was based on a number of principles, and would be open only to active researchers of Ismailism and not to the general public. Only those who had at least one published study of Ismailism could be eligible for membership. The proposal was approved and on 6 February 1946 the Society was born. Invitations to join were circulated among those eligible and 25 scholars were originally elected as members.

During the last 22 years, only a few new members have joined, while 22 have either died or resigned for various reasons. The remaining few keep irregular contact and do not do any academic work for the Society. Syrians and Egyptians have been the most industrious members, as for them Ismailism is part of their own history and heritage. But this is not the case in Persia and India. Since Arab and Persian Ismailis suffer from the want of literature on Ismailism, they willingly buy the most worthless booklets from commercial publishers. It is interesting that they pay no attention to the confessional origin of these works and buy materials produced by all branches and groups. During the last 22 years, the [Ismaili] Society has published 28 works in three series, with one more prepared for publication. The list of these publications is attached to this book.[98]

We also experimented with publishing a non-periodical collection of articles, designated as the 'Collectanea'.[99] But it was discontinued because of the shortage of contributors. And still the most important task remains the preparation of critical editions of genuine Ismaili texts. The difficulties are almost insurmountable. Ever since the

---

[97] See F. Daftary, 'Anjoman-e Esmaʿili', *EIR*, vol. 2, p. 84.

[98] This editor compiled the list afresh, as he could not find Ivanow's compilation referred to here; see Appendix 3. The additional title mentioned by Ivanow here, and never published, was an English translation by Ivanow himself of Khayrkhwah-i Harati's *Tasnifat*. By the early 1960s, in the aftermath of Ivanow's settlement in Tehran, the Ismaili Society and its library were effectively absorbed into the Nizari Ismaili community's Ismailia Association (later renamed Ismaili Tariqah and Religious Education Board, or ITREB) for Pakistan. The Ismaili manuscripts collected by Ivanow for the Ismaili Society of Bombay were transferred, in the early 1980s, to the library of The Institute of Ismaili Studies in London.

[99] Reference to item 113 in Appendix 1, Works of Ivanow. See also *Correspondance Corbin-Ivanow*, pp. 20, 31, 36–37, 50, 88, 100.

beginning of this work, I have done everything possible to invite and encourage additional contributors from amongst educated Persians and Arabs. But I have failed completely. The supposedly idealistic East proved to be far more materialistic than the materialistic West. No one wanted to work for the advancement of knowledge, and even for future monetary gain, but everyone demanded cash, and too much cash, which is not so easy to obtain.

But let us return to my biography. In July 1948, I attended the 21st Congress of Orientalists in Paris, representing the Ismaili Society.[100] Frankly speaking, it was of little interest and badly organised. It only proved that such grandiose gatherings have outlived their usefulness. International topical symposia would be more useful.[101]

In April 1954, I was invited by the Persian government to attend the celebrations of the 900th anniversary of the birth of Avicenna [Ibn Sina], in Tehran and Hamadan. It was a more specialised occasion, much better organised and, therefore, more useful.[102] I also took the opportunity to make some arrangements for my planned work in Alamut[103]

---

[100] See *Actes du XXIe Congrès International des Orientalistes*, Paris 23–31 juillet 1948 (Paris, 1949), p. 295, containing a reference to Ivanow's presentation on Nasir-i Khusraw's *Shish fasl*, in the session of 29 July on 'History of ideas and literature in Islam'. Other panellists of this session were Georges J. Haggar, Abbas H. al-Hamdani, M. Kamil Hussein and Henri Pérès. See also *Correspondance Corbin-Ivanow*, pp. 26–29, 49–50.

[101] For Ivanow's further negative comments on this Congress, see *Correspondance Corbin-Ivanow*, pp. 26–28.

[102] For Ivanow's presentation on Ibn Sina, the celebrated philosopher-physician who was born near Bukhara in 980 and died in Hamadan in 1037, at this international conference, see item 130 in Appendix 1, Works of Ivanow. See also *Correspondance Corbin-Ivanow*, pp. 52, 106–107.

[103] Alamut, name of a fortress located 35 km north-east of Qazwin, in an area of northern Iran known in medieval times as Daylaman. The fortress was originally constructed, in 860, on the summit of a high rock in the central Alburz mountains. In 1090, the Ismaili leader Hasan-i Sabbah (d. 1124) seized Alamut and used it as the seat of what was to become the Nizari Ismaili state of Persia. In 1256, Alamut was surrendered to the Mongols who demolished it. Ivanow published a couple of short studies on Alamut, in 1931 and 1938 (items 44 and 79 in Appendix 1), before producing his book on the subject (item 143 in Appendix 1). For the most recent study of the Ismaili fortresses, see P. Willey, *Eagle's Nest: Ismaili Castles in Iran and Syria* (London, 2005), and S. Sajjadi and E. Majidi (revised by F. Daftary), 'Alamut', *EIS*,

and Lamasar,[104] where I spent two seasons in 1957 and 1958.[105] This was made possible through a generous grant of £350 contributed by the Khojas of East Africa. I do not know what they expected of me, but the book giving careful descriptions and measurements of the relics [of these Ismaili fortresses], which was published in 1960 did not please the sponsors,[106] who complained that I wrote only about stones. Well, what should I have written about? In any case, my book will scare away all sorts of spurious 'expeditions' with their 'startling' discoveries, which are based on ignorance and misunderstanding.

---

vol. 3, pp. 449–461. Peter Willey (1922–2009) devoted some four decades of his life to studying the Ismaili fortresses, also identifying the sites of several of them.

[104] Lamasar, also known as Lanbasar, was a major fortress of the Nizari Ismailis in north-western Persia; it is situated some 43 km north-east of the city of Qazwin. The Nizaris fortified Lamasar into a major stronghold, also equipping it with ample water resources and cisterns, which are still in existence. Lamasar guarded the western approaches to Alamut, and it considerably enhanced the defensive capability of the Nizaris of northern Persia. Lamasar finally surrendered to the Mongols in 1257. In modern times, the site of Lamasar was first identified in 1931 by the British traveller Freya Stark (1893–1993); see her *The Valleys of the Assassins and other Persian Travels* (London, 1934), pp. 234–251. See also P. Willey, *The Castles of the Assassins* (London, 1963), pp. 269–279.

[105] See *Correspondance Corbin-Ivanow*, pp. 153–154, 155–156, 167–168.

[106] Reference to item 143 in Appendix 1, Works of Ivanow.

4

Impressions and Experiences

Persia

I was awakened at dawn in my cabin by a strange monotonous singing. The boat, its engine silent, was moving slowly. I could make out the words: 'Tweeeeelve', 'noooot touched'. It was clear that we were entering the port of Enzeli.[1] Later on, I heard this singing on many occasions, the languages were different but the tune was always the same, either in the Persian Gulf, or the Caspian, or in India. In the shallow waters of the Caspian and the Persian Gulf this measurement is a necessary routine.

It was June of 1910, my first journey to Persia. At the time, there were no complex customs formalities, passports were not checked, personal belongings were not examined and the landing did not take much time. By the customs, I saw the unforgettable Hamun marsh overgrown with weeds and full of white pelicans and pink flamingoes. I have never been there again, but I have heard that everything has changed. Because of the shallowing of the Caspian Sea, the Hamun is full of salt and mud now and the birds are gone.

In order to get to the local capital, Rasht, it was necessary to go by a wooden boat called a *kerdjim* through the Hamun marsh and a canal to the village of Pir-bazar. I do not know whether the canal is still in use, but now buses and taxis can reach the customs house by road. And Enzeli itself does not exist any more; now it is called Pahlavi. I have heard that today there are modern buildings in Rasht. At that time it was still very old-fashioned and full of houses with tiled roofs. All these

---

[1] Anzali (Enzeli), town in the northern Iranian province of Gilan, located 40 km from Rasht, the province's capital. It is Iran's main commercial port on the Caspian Sea. Anzali was renamed Bandar-i Pahlavi (after the ruling dynasty) from 1925 to 1979 when it again became Anzali. See M. Bazin, 'Anzali', *EIR*, vol. 1, pp. 143–145.

frequent rains, sticky mud, shabby shops, dampness and heat did not evoke much enthusiasm in me. It was not the Persia I had dreamt of. Only when the sky cleared could I see the forested mountains and high peaks covered with snow. Rasht proved to be of little interest and I left for Tehran. The journey took four days, by a *delijan*, a coach for eight passengers, drawn by four animals. Now it is a four-hour journey by car or bus.

The road climbs through a thick forest until it reaches the village of Menjil, where it crosses the Safid-rud River and then it goes along the south-facing foothills until it reaches Tehran. There is nothing to see by the road and the foothills block the view of the mountains. Nowadays, it is possible to see with binoculars a railway to Tabriz winding up at a considerable distance. The only town on the way [to Tehran] is the ancient Qazwin, which still preserves relics of the Safawid times and its old bazaars.[2]

Doroshke, Tehran, 1909

The modern Tehran of 1968 bears little resemblance to Tehran of 1910. The traffic has increased and the roads have improved. The way of life of its two million inhabitants [increased to 12 million by 2013] has changed considerably, and the city does not look the same now that its once numerous gardens have disappeared. In my time, only a few streets were cobbled, the main streets were still dusty and pedestrians walked in the middle of the road. It was full of dust and very hot and it was difficult to catch a *doroshke* (from the Russian *drozhka*); in general, it was of very little interest. At that time, there were greener gardens around the large houses of the well-to-do people, and there were no multi-storey buildings. There are also shops everywhere. Of course, there are many improvements now, but at that time it was incomparably cheap and

---

[2] The Safawids ruled over Persia and adjacent lands from 1501 to 1722. Qazwin served as the capital of the Safawids before they moved to Isfahan in 1597. See M. Haneda and R. Matthee, 'Isfahan. vii. Safavid Period', *EIR*, vol. 13, pp. 650–657.

Qahwa-khana, Isfahan, ca. 1910

easy to live in Tehran. In earlier times, there was not a single university there, nor any libraries, museums and newspapers in foreign languages.

After spending five days there I left for Isfahan. Those who could afford it could hired a *kalaske* (also from the Russian word *koliaska*), drawn by four ponies. But I was travelling on limited funds and, therefore, had to go by mail *ghari* (an Indian word).[3] It was a strongly built cart carrying mailbags and passengers, who had to squat. If you are not accustomed to it you will last only for a few minutes. These vehicles were usually overcrowded since Persians like travelling. Sometimes the cart had a sort of light roof, to protect passengers from the sun. The ponies were changed at stations. The road was just as it used to be at the time of [the Achaemenian] King Darius and Alexander the Great with bumpings and joltings that were unbearable. It was very hot during the daytime, hence we travelled mainly at night. I sat by the driver with my legs hanging down and on two occasions, being drowsy and terribly tired, nearly slipped under the wheels. When

---

[3] *Ghari* is a Hindi term referring to a 'vehicle' pulled by horses or other animals.

it was very hot the cart would stop at a roadside *chay-khana* [tea house]. Usually they are called *qahwa-khana*s [coffee houses], but I never saw coffee served in them. Because of heat and glare, it was impossible to sleep in the daytime. It was not only hellishly hot inside the *qahwa-khana*s, but the air there was always poisoned by opium (*teryak*), which almost every passenger smoked. It was quite a nauseating experience. Besides, there were flies and dust and no place to lie down. Then the night came and with it more shaking and a struggle not to fall asleep. On one occasion, we could not have a good night's rest because of a bandit raid, which was then quite a common thing. The *chapar*, a postal officer accompanying the mail, asked me to write a note in Russian confirming that we had been delayed by brigands.

On the fifth day, we reached the suburban gardens of Isfahan. As I found out later, the city resembles Damascus, but bigger. Persians have an annoying form of courtesy. When a tired traveller asks them how close he is to the final destination, he invariably receives the answer: 'Oh, we are almost there.' But it was still a long way to go and we reached Maydan-i Shah, the central square of Isfahan, only by sunset. I decided to visit the Russian Consul right away and ask for his advice. I asked for the way to the Consulate, which was nearby but the crafty Isfahanis forced me to hire a *kalaske* with four ponies. I had not yet properly taken my seat when they said, 'Here it is'. The Consul, P. G. Bogoiavlenskii,[4] who was mysteriously killed at the end of the same year, received me most hospitably and put me up in the vacant flat of his secretary who was then on leave.

There were two consulates in Isfahan at the time, the Russian and the British. The Russian Consul was a married man and, therefore, invited members of the Persian and foreign high society to weekly tea parties with the inevitable tennis. The British Consul, Mr Graham,[5] was a bachelor and he invited his guests to late dinners by moonlight. But his calendar was not very reliable and the dinner was scheduled for

---

[4] Bogoiavlenskii served as the Russian Consul in Isfahan from 1908; he was murdered there in 1911.

[5] Thomas George Graham (1861–1922) served as the British Consul in Shiraz (1903–1908) and then in Isfahan (1908–1917). See Hyacinth L. Rabino, *Great Britain and Iran: Diplomatic and Consular Officers* (London, 1946), p. 26.

Khaju Bridge, Isfahan, ca. 1911

an evening when the moon rose very late and the guests could hardly see what they were served. The Consul usually got up very early in the morning so occasionally he dozed off during dinner, right in the middle of conversation and often in most peculiar positions. He had a complicated life: for 14 years he was an actor and then did many other things. Isfahan was a beautiful and very interesting place. In my young years, I was a tireless walker and I went exploring every corner of the city and its suburbs. The ring of the hills surrounding the city and its famous buildings are more beautiful than those of Samarkand. Unfortunately, the main square, Maydan-i Shah, was barbarously *qashang*-ised [beautified] by some busybody municipal officials whose concept of beauty was that of a *chay-khana*. It is a relief that now the authorities try to stop this vandalism. However, various municipalities still do much harm to antiquities and old buildings. The picturesque bazaars of Isfahan were whitewashed and now they look dirty and have lost their style.

I was most interested in the Isfahani dervishes, who had first attracted my attention even before I went to university. Professor V. Zhukovskii, who many regarded as an expert on this subject, complained about his disappointment in the Sufism that he studied in Persia in the 1880s. And he deplored its degeneration. I did not expect much of the dervishes and my approach to this extremist Shi'i sect was purely ethnographical. I was not interested in their mystical or ascetic achievements, which were always exaggerated. Contrary to some abstract theories, real Persians considered dervishes as members of a certain profession, one of the classical 33 *sinfs* [professional guilds], which also included some surprising occupations like those of soldier, thief and beggar. They were closely associated with gypsies (*ustakar, qirishmal, kauli*, etc.).[6] However, they must be distinguished from the upper-class Sufi-minded amateur philosophers as well as from superstitious people worshipping saints like idols. There is a rich hagiographical Sufi literature on saints but their presentation is so idealised that it is impossible to trace in them any historical reality.

Once I was taken to their 'nest' in the Takht-i Fulad cemetery near the Khaju Bridge, on one or the other side of the Zayandeh-rud. Dervishes sprinkled the ground with water to cool the air, made the inevitable tea and we sat down to discuss pious subjects. I was particularly eager to hear their life-stories, even doctored versions of them. I met many dervishes in Birjand, Shiraz, Kerman, Meshhed and Sabzewar. It is difficult to regard their influence on the local population as completely negative. In the past, there were large and strong dervish organisations, but in my time there remained only one, the Gunabadi Brotherhood [an offshoot of the Ni'mat Allahi Sufi order] in Bidukht, an organisation to which all the servants as well as higher officials belonged. And I always regretted that I had no knowledge of shorthand to write down this material. I have been planning to write a comprehensive book on this subject, but unfortunately something more urgent always came up. It seems that it is already too late to start it now. By now, due to the advance of culture and economic difficulties, parasitical dervishes, who in the recent past used to sing religious poems in every bazaar, have completely disappeared in Persia. But there are still many people who remember these 'people of religion', in white or coloured turbans,

---

[6] Persian terms describing gypsies (*kaulis*) as clever people (*ustakar*), enticing dancers (*qirishmal*), etc. See J. P. Digard, 'Gypsy. i. Gypsies of Persia', *EIR*, vol. 11, pp. 412–415.

wandering the streets and living off all sorts of *waqfs* [religious endowments] and religious institutions. The Iranian government wisely made provisions to reduce their number.

Like many incipient orientalists, I was very interested in Sufism in my student years. I must confess that its amorphous nature and lack of precise organisational structure confused me greatly and I ended up none the wiser. However, [in Persia] I attempted to find Sufi dervishes. The two-month stay in Isfahan in the summer of 1910 was enormously useful for me in getting to know the dervishes. They were poor and simple Sufis who did not have anything in common with philosophical Sufism. Indeed, this popular form of Sufism had an ideology in terms of messianic beliefs. As I delved deeper into Sufism, it was not difficult to identify it essentially as a crude form of Ismailism.

I have mentioned the widespread existence of brigandage on the [Persian] roads. Sometimes the robbers operated openly in their villages, even during daytime. I am recounting my own observations here. In July 1918, I was living in a building that was earlier used as a cotton factory. It belonged to an Armenian company in Nishapur and was located at the northern gates of the city, beyond the walls of the governor's house. One day as I was going to 'my factory', I saw a gathering of the people with their belongings. It appeared that these people came from a village situated some 3 km away from the city. This village had just been robbed by brigands. I complained to the governor, a certain Moʻayer al-Dawla. However, he sent someone informing the people that we could not do anything for them as he had only five servants. The peasants stayed there for a while longer and then returned to their village.

In the years when there were Cossacks of the Semirechye Regiment in some of these localities, the brigands stayed on the mountain road to Nishapur, where the village of Zushk was famous for its robbers. The Russian army command dispatched a cavalry unit to that village at the request of the Persian government, but the brigands displayed fierce resistance and several people were killed in the shoot-out. On the departure of the Russian army, the brigands returned home and, once again, the road became dangerous for travellers. The government also used certain old methods of putting the robbers to work in various places. The recruited robbers had the right to collect taxes from visitors [as protection money], protecting them against other brigands. One could often meet these 'defensive robbers', known as *karasuran*. Sometimes the government adopted stricter measures to catch and execute the brigands. In 1918, on the road to Nishapur, about 3 km from Sabzewar, one could see the results of such measures in the form of clay structures in which bodies of robbers had been walled up alive.

I have already discussed the dangers of widespread brigandage at the beginning of the [20th] century. There are many bandit stories, but I think that mine might be of particular interest. In April 1913, I crossed the Central Desert [Dasht-i Kavir], travelling from Birjand to Hamadan via Isfahan with a small camel caravan. We went through Tabas, which is a notoriously hot place and therefore had to travel by night. After a long journey, in the darkness, we reached the small hamlet of Mihrijan. We were ushered to the *rabat*, a public caravanserai, allegedly built during the reign of the Safawid monarch Shah Abbas I [r. 1587–1629]. Actually people say that all the old buildings in Persia were built by him. Someone brought a kerosene lamp and showed me to my place where I quickly went to sleep. When I woke up I thought I was going mad. I was lying near the wall in a large room looking like a Gothic hall pierced with columns of bright light coming down from the ceiling. It was full of men of a peasant appearance silently staring at me. My servant explained that they were *duzd-begir* – the government force charged with catching the brigands – and that they had been sent to chase a gang of local bandits. The men were unarmed and of quite a peaceful appearance. A man came forward and told me that their commander wanted me to sell him some *araq*, or raisin spirit. I answered that I did not drink it and, therefore, had nothing with me. They immediately accused me of lying since they saw some bottles in my luggage, but they were for water. My servant showed them the bottles and the crowd disappeared.

My camelmen came to say that they could not get any straw for their animals and the only way to procure it was to ask the commander of the *duzd-begir* force for some. The 'brigand-catchers' took everything by force without paying a penny. I was taken to the commander, a young bearded man, and I asked him to sell us some straw. He began to criticise the locals, saying that they hid everything and would not sell anything to his people.

It was true, the village was empty. Not a single human being or animal was visible. Everything was so well hidden that even the men of the force were unable to find anything. I returned to my men and gave them the news. A local peasant, apparently the village's headman, stood by. He quietly winked at me and I followed him. We went to a maze of vacated huts. He stopped, looked around and then whispered to me: 'We have straw, but we cannot sell it to you openly. These catchers of brigands are worse than any brigands; bandits rob people once and then go away, but these soldiers sit here watching us and if they see anything they take it by force and then beat us up. Tell everybody that you feel tired after your journey and want to rest a day or two, and when it gets dark, we shall bring the straw.' We did so and I stretched out on the bed. Soon a few men came in, obviously to nose around. They conveyed a request from their officer to take a picture of the entire force with the commander at the head. I did not mind doing it, but although I had a camera, there was no film left. Therefore, I told them that due to the heat, the 'oil' for photographs had dried out, but that I would return and take their pictures. It satisfied them and they went away. My men and I pretended that we were going to stay put until the following day. At the same time, we kept an eye on the soldiers hanging around. When they finally went away, two huge sacks appeared as if from nowhere. Everything was ready for departure. For those who have no experience of camel riding, I have to explain that camels walk almost without any noise, each of them tied to the pack-saddle of the animal in front. When the rope unties, the last camel stops and with him stops the rest of the 'chain' while the front animals continue to move. Therefore, they wear large bells on their necks. The camel is a large animal and a chain of 350 animals stretches for a mile. Each camelman looks after 8 to 12 animals. They memorise the sound of the bells of their camels and when they stop jingling the drivers know where the chain is broken.

So, we began to move with caution. As this story testifies, the Persian government of that time tried to suppress robbery. But there were insufficient means to do it. With the discovery of oil and the establishment of a regular army and police force, things changed completely and armed robbery became as rare as it is in Europe. But sometimes attempts to improve the situation can result in farce. This is what happened in the case which I describe below.

It is known that Birjand lies 50–60 km from the Persian–Afghan border. There, I went to a village called Tabas, not to be confused with the town of Tabas in [the same province of] Khorasan. I had travelled to the locality to see the border and peculiar windmills of the local villages with their 'wings' attached to vertical axes. These mills can only be found in Sistan. I heard that at the beginning of 1912 a strict order had come from Tehran to raise a suitable military force recruited from the local farmers. But the villages refused to provide young and able men, and decided to get rid of the elderly who were unable to work and 'ate their bread for nothing'. One of the [Qajar] *shah-zada*s, or princes, was appointed commander of this force. He was one of these innumerable parasitic princes who surrounded important officials and wealthy people. I have absolutely no idea whether the said *shah-zada* had any military qualification. Most probably he had none and was simply given a sinecure as a young man 'from a good family'. He lived close to the house where I stayed and almost every morning I could see the same picture on my way to the bank. A number of veritable Methuselahs sat along the wall of the prince's house waiting for the 'commander'. They were all very old men, probably over 80, many lame or with their backs bent. And these were the recruits of the intended army. The commander was always so obliging as to send out a *qalyan* (water pipe) for them, so that they could have a smoke while waiting. Sooner or later the commander himself would come out. A pony would be brought and he would be helped to mount to ride a short distance of only 100 metres. After that he would dismount, sit on a small carpet under a parasol, smoke his *qalyan* and start training his army. An hour at a time was quite sufficient. After that the commander would be helped back on his horse and retire to his quarters, again under an umbrella. I do not know how all this ended, but everything disappeared. It seems that the prince left Birjand and the old men returned to their villages.

This is a good example of a traditional, patriarchal society. It may look rather repulsive, as it was in the case of the attempt to 'catch the brigands', but sometimes it appears attractive and even touching. I shall never forget a gypsy wedding which I saw in Birjand. Gypsies from the whole district came to town for the celebration which was on a small harvested field near my home. The gypsy women looked really exciting in their traditional long colourful dresses. To a degree, they

Tup-khane Square, Tehran, early 1930s

reminded me of the pictures of the famous Russian painter Maliavin,[7] and I regretted that choreographers could not see them dancing. Perhaps nowadays only a few gypsies still remain in Persia. In 1937, I tried to collect samples of the dialect of the gypsies of Kerman, but I could not find anyone who could speak it well. Fifty years ago they were still considered members of one of the traditional bazaar trades and even had their own place in the bazaar. But later they were unable to compete with industrially manufactured goods. Some of them were really talented people who made the most beautiful objects with their primitive tools. Women made sieves of different styles. And gypsies could be found everywhere, but in 1957 when I was passing through Birjand I saw only one young gypsy at the site of their camp. They had these camp sites in many cities. I tried my best to study their dialect, or rather jargon, and published a few articles on it.[8] Later on, when I tried to check a few things, I was unable to find a single gypsy who could

---

[7] Filipp Andreevich Maliavin (1869–1940), Russian painter and draughtsman. In the 1890s, he studied under the eminent Russian realist painter Ilya Repin (1844–1930). In the Soviet era, Maliavin painted portraits of the Soviet leaders.

[8] Reference to items 1, 6, 10 and 30 in Appendix 1, Works of Ivanow.

speak the dialect; even the old people had completely forgotten their idiom.

All this is part of the sweeping process of modernisation which started after the two world wars and accelerated even more with the development of the oil industry. Large cities such as Tehran, Shiraz and Meshhed, and to a degree even small towns, have undergone extensive changes. Villages, too, were not left untouched. They were heavily influenced by the agrarian reforms introduced by the government and the campaign for total literacy. I can still vividly remember my first visit to Tehran, in June 1910, some 57 years ago. At that time, it looked quite different, and not only because there was no overwhelming traffic, asphalted streets, pavements or high buildings. The general style of the city, its 'atmosphere', was quite different. People were more polite and the city was less crowded.

Tup-khane Gate, Tehran, ca. 1910

The old Tehran extended only to a fraction of the space occupied by the modern capital city, everything was very close and the *doroshke*s were very cheap. There were many green trees. And everywhere one saw interesting locally produced things. Now imported products and their domestic imitations are everywhere and the prices have risen many times. Many places of interest, especially near the bazaar, are gone. There was no garden on the dusty main [Tup-khane] square where one could walk from the Ala al-Dawla Gate, which was demolished a long time ago, to Nasiriyya, which is now Nasir-i Khusraw Avenue.[9] Nasiriyya was the main venue for booksellers, who have now almost completely disappeared, and it was also full of shops selling paper. The appearance of bus and truck bays also changed Nasiriyya. It became noisy and filthy, full of crowds of pilgrims, some of them going east to Meshhed, some west to Mesopotamia. It was like

---

[9] Named after the renowned Persian poet and traveller, and Ismaili *daʿi*, who died not long after 1070.

Shams al-Imare, Tehran, ca. 1911

some kind of a moveable ethnological exhibition, with 'exhibits' from all parts of Asia, even from as far as Turkestan and India.

The name of Tup-khane, 'the cannon depot', was quite appropriate to the square, since there was a shed for brass guns on the very spot where now stands the huge building of the Tehran municipality. A big cannon was placed at the entrance to Nasiriyya, near the present international telephone exchange. It was believed that this gun possessed magic powers to cure women's diseases, and especially venereal ones. Actually it spread diseases rather than curing them and eventually it was removed in the interests of public health.

By Persian standards, Tehran is a young city. It was built on the site of ancient Rhagae or Rey, which nowadays is reduced to a miserable village surrounded by cemeteries and wastelands. A *dakhma*, or 'tower of silence', stands nearby. Zoroastrians used it for the exposure of dead bodies. There are still some Zoroastrians in Iran, mainly in Yazd and Kerman as well as neighbouring villages. There are only a few really old buildings in Tehran. The city has a small number of Qajar mosques and new buildings built by the present dynasty.[10] The only prominent thing is the Shams al-Imare, or the 'Sun of all Buildings', constructed at the time of the Qajars [1789–1925]. In the past, it served as a palace. However, it has not been repaired for a long time and still remains in deplorable condition. According to newspapers, the government now wants to restore it to its former glory.[11]

At present, the few remaining old buildings are often demolished to free up space for new ugly houses, which are nothing but brick boxes of various sizes. In the 1920s, the talented Russian architect Markov introduced a clever method of reducing the boring monotony of these 'boxes' by decorating them with majolica and coloured tiles. It looked nice and 'nationalistic'.[12] But this fashion did not last for long and the 'boxes' remained as they are now.

The whole endeavour to revive the former glory of Achaemenian and Sasanian art failed, and some of the buildings designed as replicas of the ancient palaces look like caricatures.[13] In general,

---

[10] Here Ivanow refers to the Pahlavi dynasty, which succeeded the Qajars in 1925 and was itself uprooted in 1979 by the Islamic Revolution.

[11] In subsequent decades this building was renovated and housed part of the royal library of the Golestan Palace.

[12] Nikolai Lvovich Markov (1882–1957), Russian architect and long-term resident of Iran. After a few years serving in the Cossack Brigade (contemporaneously with Reza Khan, the future founder of the Pahlavi dynasty, 1925–1979), established by the Russians in Persia, Markov set up his architectural practice in Tehran. In the 1920s and 1930s, Markov's eclectic buildings (mixing Persian and Western designs and motifs) appeared in Tehran in a variety of contexts. They included ministries, the old municipality building (Shahrdari) and the Alborz College, attended by this editor, as well as private villas; see Victor Daniel et al., *Nikolai Markov: Architecture of Changing Times in Iran* (Tehran, 2004).

[13] One such building, borrowing motifs from Persepolis, the Achaemenian royal capital, served as the central headquarters of the national police force (Shahrbani-yi kull-i kishvar), under the Pahlavis. Among the major architects of the period, mention may be made of Gabriel Guevrekian (1900–1970), who designed a number of public buildings, including the Officers' Club (Bashgah-i Afsaran) and the Ministry of Foreign Affairs, in Tehran during the 1930s, when he served as chief architect of the Tehran municipality. An Armenian avant-garde architect, Guevrekian studied in Vienna and Paris and was associated with the European circle of avant-garde architects, such as Henri Sauvage and Le Corbusier. Amongst other major architects of the period with works in Tehran, mention may be made of Nikolai Markov (1882–1957), André Godard (1881–1965) and Vartan Avanessian (1896–1982). See Mina

The shrine of Imam Reza, Meshhed, ca. 1911

architecture is not the strongest attraction of Tehran. However, the city can afford itself this sort of negligence since the majestic beauty of the Elburz range and the Demawend peak dominate its skyline. The latter is an extinct volcano, about 18,500 feet high, much higher and more picturesque than the Fuji-yama in Japan (about 12,000 feet). Despite its bad climate with strong winds and intense summer heatwaves, Tehran is still a comfortable place to live in and pursue cultural interests. Hopefully, it will continue as such in the future.

Of all the Persian cities under reconstruction which I have seen, Meshhed has benefited the most. Now it is a clean and friendly city full of vegetation. I lived in Meshhed for several years and my memories of it go back to as far as 1910, when it was full of ruins, collapsing mud walls and even fields under crops right in the middle of the city cut across by winding streets. Surprisingly, the city was most ugly in the

---

Marefat, 'Guevrekian, Gabriel', *EIR*, vol. 11, pp. 382–383; her 'Building to Power: Architecture of Tehran 1921–1924' (Ph.D. thesis, Massachusetts Institute of Technology, Cambridge, 1988), and her 'The Protagonists who Shaped Modern Tehran', in Ch. Adle and B. Hourcade, ed., *Téhéran, capitale bicentenaire* (Paris and Tehran, 1992), pp. 95–125.

The shrine of Imam Ali b. Abi Talib, Najaf, ca. 1948

vicinity of the holy enclave, the *haramat*.[14] The place was full of dirty and smelly caravanserais, miserable shops and heaps of rubbish. But now the city has changed completely – the streets are clean, paved, straightened and widened. The sacred structures now stand at the centre of the *falakiye*, that is, a circular street from where all the roads radiate. But even after the reconstruction of the city, because of some strange reasoning, all dirty businesses continued to be located near the sacred site. And now it is full of lorry garages, buses, repair shops, piles of old tyres and similar things.

The *falakiye* itself and its pavings have a sad history. Originally, a large cemetery occupied all the space around the *haramat* buildings. And pious people were prepared to pay good money in order to be buried near the tomb of Imam Reza and the various famous religious scholars. I found out how these graves were made available for prospective buyers. In Najaf, where similar *haramat* are the centre of pilgrimage, graves in the surrounding cemeteries are rented out for burial. They are looked after and kept in order as long as the rent is paid. When payments stop, the tombstone is removed and the place is

---

[14] The area is dominated by the shrine of Imam Reza (d. 818), the eighth in the line of the Imams recognised by the Twelver Shiʻis.

rented out to a new 'customer'. But Najaf is situated in the desert while in Meshhed, with its limited space, the renting of graves must be difficult. When the *falakiye* was paved, the practically minded authorities pulled out all the tombstones and used them for the pavement. I remember that I was able to read the names, dates and religious verses on these headstones while walking on the pavements. Later on, the stones were covered with cement. I have seen so much barbaric destruction of historical monuments that I am almost sure that the headstones were removed indiscriminately with absolute disregard to their historical value. Usually municipalities do not care about these trifles. And many important relics were broken or simply thrown away during these fits of modernisation.

I was always interested in the so-called 'archaeology of the way of life', and, therefore, I often visited Persian villages and stayed there for quite a time. Peasant mentality, popular religious ideas, folklore and vernacular languages have fascinated me. I have already published some of the collected materials,[15] but there is still a lot awaiting publication. Summing up my impressions of Persian rural life, I would praise Persian peasants, especially those living in remote areas, for their honesty and strong sense of responsibility and duty, which was spontaneous and deeply religious but in no way connected with the apprehension of punishment or gain. It was a manifestation of a genuine and powerful culture, which was not taught but naturally acquired from the surrounding milieu. Unfortunately, many of these things are disappearing. This attitude contrasted very much with the mentality of the bazaar men and, regrettably, even the so-called educated people. During all my travels, peasants never stole anything from me. I often stayed in their houses, trusting them completely, and they trusted me. They followed the unwritten rules of their culture, which found its expression in hospitality. Often the inhabitants of the house where I was staying went to sleep at their relatives' houses in order not to disturb me during my rest. Here is just one of the numerous examples illustrating my experience.

On my way from Birjand to Hamadan via Isfahan, I passed through the small ancient town of Golpayegan, which the learned Arabicised as

---

[15] Reference to items 2, 20, 23, 24 and 26, amongst others, in Appendix 1, Works of Ivanow.

Jurbadaqan. Our day march was long and we were all tired when our caravan entered the town about 10 p.m. The streets were empty. Following the usual practice my muleteers (*charwadars*) began to shout '*Ya Hasan*' at some houses, but there was no reply. We moved on down the street and soon heard sounds of music coming from a rich house. My servants decided that there had to be a wedding and knocked on the door. Three young men came out and my men told them that the Consul (that was a standard title for all European travellers) was looking for a place to spend the night. They warmly invited us in. I did not feel it was right to intrude into their house and interrupt their family celebration, but the hosts insisted. They brought me in, put [me] on a seat of honour and introduced me to the groom, but unfortunately not to the bride, whose dress I was so anxious to see. They fed my men and horses and the next morning I departed with their best wishes and determined refusal to accept any money. They explained to me that an unexpected arrival of a respected guest is regarded as a very good omen for a newly wed couple.

Superstitions apart, such a thing could not happen in India or Bukhara; but I can remember many similar situations in Persia, when I slept in the houses of schoolteachers and peasants and even on a table in a customs house. I also did this in a Druze house in Suwayda. The hosts always refused money and provided shelter simply because of their hospitality. And I always left their houses feeling uneasy for causing inconvenience.

I could write volumes about my good memories of rural Persia. Of course Persia changes and becomes more urbanised, as Westerners call it. But urban life brings mischief, swindle and fraud. And these things easily influence the masses. However, let us hope that what is good in the Persian village life will be preserved.

Bukhara

I have already mentioned that in April 1915 the director of the Asiatic Museum and Member of the Academy, K. Zaleman, gave me the opportunity to travel to Bukhara to collect Persian and Arabic manuscripts. I went there and succeeded in buying 1,047 volumes, the largest single collection ever acquired by the Museum. Earlier I had been to Bukhara twice, first in 1910 when returning from Persia and the second time in 1911 on my way back to that country. Nothing had changed in Bukhara during my third and fourth visits in 1915 and 1918. The only difference was a general feeling of tension caused by the Basmachi movement and exacerbated by the holy month of Ramazan, which always interrupts the normal course of life.[16] The city of Bukhara (the whole principality or emirate is also often called simply Bukhara) seems to be the only important city which has never changed in the course of its long history. Therefore, Bukhara is still built according to the medieval plan, with the crossing of two main roads as the central point of the city. This centre, known as the Chahar-su (four sides), forms a small circular square covered by a large cupola with shops along the walls. At that time they were selling books there. But the booksellers did not display all their stock and kept the bulk of their books in their homes.

For a foreigner, who is not supposed to be able to read in the language, buying books requires a special approach. When I came to the Chahar-su for the first time, the booksellers did not even want to talk to me. My unfailing method was to buy, almost without any bargaining, the first manuscript offered to me. The rumour spread quickly under the cupola and next time the newcomer would be taken seriously and offered more books. Then the normal trading would start. Since I spoke Persian fluently and could read Arabic, I was considered a Nogay, that is, a Volga Tatar. There were not many of them in Bukhara. They usually worked as teachers or carried out subversive pan-Islamic propaganda or promoted some other 'ideology'. They were rarely interested in books in general, still less in manuscripts.

I rented a room in a modern caravanserai near the Chahar-su. I think this guesthouse was called the 'Caravanserai of the Bazaar of the Comb-makers' (*shana-sazan*), and it was patronised by Russian petty merchants. My room was 'Russian', that is, with a wooden floor and a large window, facing the Mir Arab Mosque with a stork's nest on its dome and a high tower from which, in olden times, criminals were thrown down. Since I did not know how long I would stay in Bukhara, I did not want to spend too much money on furniture and I managed with just an unpainted table and a wooden bench, which served a variety of purposes. I did not have chairs and my rare visitors also sat

---

[16] See note 44 in Chapter 3.

on the bench. In the corner, on old newspapers, lay my books and also 'antiques', especially ceramics, which V. V. Radlov had commissioned me to buy for the Museum of Anthropology and Ethnography. It was in this room that I entertained Sir Aurel Stein. My place was close to the fruit market by the Lab-i Hauz Mosque, on the bank of a dirty square pond. There was plenty of excellent fresh fruit and some shops sold fried mutton and there were also many *chay-khana*s.

Unlike Persia, India and other Muslim countries, Bukhara traded in manuscripts which were quite rare elsewhere. These manuscripts were mainly Arabic grammars, manuals of logic, *fiqh*, glossaries and various types of commentaries. These books came mainly from the libraries of deceased learned people whose less-learned heirs sold them to the bazaar merchants. Books were loaded on donkeys in *khurjin*s, carried in baskets or tied up in bundles.

Buying manuscripts requires familiarity with calligraphy as well as a sort of encyclopaedic knowledge, or 'being well read', as many of the books are defective with missing pages either at the beginning or the end, or both. Thus, the buyer must be able to identify books without their 'title page'. When the price was negligible it was often more convenient to buy the book right away and identify it later, at home. From time to time, I was able to buy interesting books this way. Occasionally, books were sold wholesale in packs, but usually they were worthless. Before sunset my pious booksellers closed their shops and went for prayer, and I started my homework of identifying, registering and packing the books. Ever since the time of Peter the Great, according to the law, all parcels addressed to the Academy of Sciences or affiliated institutions, and weighing not more than a *pood* (40 lb), were sent free of charge. So I had to ensure that my parcels were not overweight, since otherwise I had to unpack and repack them.

Not far from the market of Chahar-su, on the road, there was a domed caravanserai whose name I cannot remember. There was a shop where an old Jewish man, Mullah Daud, was selling 'rare and old' things. He was considered

Bazaar in Bukhara, ca. 1898

a scholar because there were only a few learned people among the members of the fairly large and old Jewish community there. He was an organised and respected person. From him I always bought large collections of Central Asian polychrome ceramics which are not found in any European or American museum. I also bought some other things for the Museum of Anthropology and Ethnography of the [Russian] Academy of Sciences, the director of which was the Academician V. V. Radlov. Mullah Daud himself did not understand much about his artefacts, and his specific 'treasure' was a small copper box in which he kept the texts of Buddhist prayers written on thick white Tibetan papers. These papers could be purchased in any form in the markets of Kalimpong and Darjeeling for two or three rupees per sheet. I explained this to him but he was adamant that it was not in a Tibetan script but in Achamaenid cuneiform. He was terribly offended when Sir Aurel Stein, on his trip to Sijistan [Sistan] through Bukhara, entered the shop, pushed the 'treasure' aside and did not want to see it. In any case, when he saw that I worked with books, he sometimes used to ask 'scholarly questions', especially one which he asked many times. Is it true that in Central Asia there is a huge sandy desert, in which there is a city populated only by the Jews? The sand swirls around the city continuously for six days and stops on the seventh day, the 'Shabbat'. I told him many times that this was a legend, but he assured me that 'this was written in the sacred books, and they did not lie'.

I was greatly impressed by the celebrations for the two major Muslim holidays, the end of the [fasting] month of Ramazan and the Qurban Bayram [or Id al-adha, the feast of sacrifice]. On these days communal prayers are recited in an open-air Id-gah, or square designated for the celebration. This was located outside the city walls and the people gathered near Chahar-su from where the procession moved to the Id-gah. The participants were dressed in festival costumes, beautiful silk and brocade garments. The most interesting items of these dresses were the yellow turbans made from thin silk, which can be seen in Mughal miniatures. I have not seen them in regular use either in Bukhara or in India. I dearly wished I could get these costumes for the Ethnographic Museum. Of course, there was much silk and brocade on sale in a special row in the market, which was carefully protected, but these items were not 'authentic'. By contrast, there was another scenario, which was so awful that I can never forget it.

Close to my place, there was an old-fashioned caravanserai where Russian doctors stayed. Apart from the doctor I have already mentioned, there also lived two elderly lady doctors: Dr Garanovskaia, and an assistant in charge of the women's ward and the head of the maternity ward, which was independent from the central hospital. They were bored with their life in Bukhara and often invited me for lunches and dinners. One evening, I was returning home from one such dinner. The streets were empty and silent. Suddenly I heard a strange high-pitched sound. The sound was repeated and it was now possible to hear the melody. I turned to the main road and saw a singing procession of blind men led by a boy, walking with their hands on the belt of the person in front. They looked terrible with black or white holes in place of their eyes. The locals explained to me that they had not lost their sight because of disease but had been blinded in punishment for their offences. They were kept in jail, and by singing these nocturnal serenades they collected alms for their own survival. This method of making obnoxious or undesirable people harmless was widely practised in the Middle Ages. It was very popular in Persia in Safawid times. But the record belongs to the 'civilised' Byzantines when Emperor Basil Bolgar-machos (976–1025) blinded no fewer than 13,000 captured Bulgarians. The history of Byzantium is full of terrible stories of the blinding of heirs to the imperial throne, various relatives of the rulers and sometimes even children, whose eyelids were pulled up and pieces of white hot metal were pressed against the eyes. The party of only about a dozen blind men, seen by myself, would appear a trifle in comparison with such figures.

Being in contact with literate and sometimes even learned men, I decided to use this opportunity and enlighten myself with the 'light from the East' by studying with local scholars. I even attempted to settle in one of the famous local *madrasa*s, although life in such an institution did not promise much comfort and peace of mind.

I knew that under the Astrakhanid and later Mangit dynasties,[17] religious buildings had fallen into decay because of economic crises.

---

[17] The Ashtarkhanids or Toqay Temürids (also known as Janids) ruled over Transoxania and northern Afghanistan from 1599 until 1747, when the Mangits established their own rule over those regions. The Mangits (1747–1920) hailed from

A law was adopted that said a person contributing money to the repair of the *madrasa* cell he occupied could later sublet it to anyone. To become an occupant of such a cell was so temptingly exotic that I took up the matter quite seriously. But all the *madrasas* were closed for the summer holidays and nothing came of this idea. All the students had gone to their villages where they worked as *pish-namazes*, or leaders of communal prayers. For their services they received free meals and 50 roubles per season.

Coincidentally I bought a copy of the famous work by al-Ghazali, *Tahafut al-falasifa* (The Refutation of the Philosophers).[18] Al-Ghazali died in 1111, and this copy was transcribed only 50 years after his death. The manuscript was one of the jewels of the whole Bukhara Collection of the Asiatic Museum. To read it together with a Bukharan 'scholar' would be an interesting undertaking. So I made enquiries about a suitable person and was directed to a certain 'celebrity'. To my disappointment and irritation, he was an Indian. He was a well-fed man of just over 40, with the face of a policeman rather than a philosopher, studying in Bukhara. I introduced myself as a person interested in the study of Muslim philosophy, who would like to read the book of al-Ghazali under his guidance, the manuscript copy of which I had just acquired. I am almost sure that the 'professor' had never heard of this book, and I doubt very much whether even the name of al-Ghazali was at all familiar to him. He contemptuously looked at the manuscript and asked me whether I had read the *Sugra* and *Kubra*, two elementary booklets on logic intended for beginners. I replied that I had looked through them. 'Then recite!', he ordered me. In the scholastic world to 'read' means to study by heart and literally memorise texts. I answered that we never memorise books and that the

---

the Özbeg tribe of the same name, and they eventually evolved into the Khans of Bukhara. See B. Spuler, 'Djanids', *EI2*, vol. 2, p. 446; Y. Bregel, 'Mangits', *EI2*, vol. 6, pp. 418–419; Robert D. McChesney, 'Central Asia. vi. In the 10th–12th/16th–18th Centuries', *EIR*, vol. 5, pp. 176–193, and Y. Bregel, 'Central Asia. vii. In the 12th–13th/18th–19th Centuries', *EIR*, vol. 5, pp. 193–205.

[18] See Abu Hamid Muhammad b. Muhammad al-Ghazali, *Tahafut al-falasifa*, ed. M. Bouges (Beirut, 1927); ed. and tr. M. E. Marmura as *The Incoherence of the Philosophers* (Provo, UT, 1997). In this work of refutation, completed in 1095, al-Ghazali enumerated twenty maxims of the philosophers that he found objectionable or inconsistent with their own views.

understanding of their contents is quite sufficient. Besides, I had studied logic at St Petersburg University and passed my examination with distinction. He looked down at me and said, 'Then how can you talk about reading (i.e. memorising) such a thick book?' He was right, to memorise al-Ghazali's *Tahafut* would represent almost a superhuman achievement. So I lost the chance to enlighten myself with the light from the East. I made yet another attempt, with another teacher, a Bukharan, but he obstinately insisted on speaking the Chaghatai language, which I did not understand well. I have heard that things have greatly changed since my time in Bukhara, so my reminiscences may appear as referring to a bygone world.

Much has been written about the medieval methods of learning in the *madrasa*s of Bukhara and elsewhere in Turkestan. It took much time for the students to learn a few texts by heart. The same methods were still practised in the Muslim East. My overall impression of Bukhara, where I spent nearly a year, was one of helplessness. At the time of my stay, there were only a few educated individuals among the local inhabitants. In their general mentality the Bukharans were not only lower than the Persians but also of Arabs; they were closer to Indian Muslims. This may have been related to similarities in their educational systems. The Indians, thanks to the absence of an Indian lingua franca, study English from early childhood. In the Bukharan *madrasa*s, all the texts that were to be learnt by heart were in foreign languages, including especially the difficult Arabic language. Therefore, students could not learn to think clearly in their own language.

My personal recollections of Bukhara came to an end on 2 June 1918. On that morning I took my seat in a taxi going to Kagan [a town near Bukhara], in order to take an afternoon train to Kaahka, the first station on the way to Persia. The train was late and we arrived at Kaahka at 3 a.m. It was strangely dark. I shouted into the darkness, '*Hammal!*', a Persian word for porter, and a genuine Persian voice replied, '*Bale!*', or 'yes' in Persian. I was already close to Persia. I went to the station restaurant, but it was full. It was impossible to rest there and I sat on the bench outside the door. I fell asleep and was awakened by a Turkoman policeman who said, 'It is not decent to sleep in the street'. It was a yellow Turkestan dawn and I could hear caravan bells. I talked to the *charwadar* (muleteer), who said that the caravan was going to Persia without any loads and that animals were available. At 9 o'clock we started to climb up the long road to the old mud fortress where we spent a night before moving on. I was once again in Persia.

At the customs on the Russian side, I handed my papers to the head of the caravan; he submitted it to the officer in charge, who did not ask me any questions. It was the same in the Persian customs one kilometre along the road. It was apparently one of the outposts from where, later on, alarming messages were telegraphed to Meshhed about a Russian invasion. As I mentioned above, the year 1918 brought good rains to Persia and people were relieved after the drought and famine of 1917. Food was available, although the Russian currency did not cost much. The normal rate of exchange was 10 roubles for £1. Now a glass of tea with sugar cost 15 roubles. I paid 250 roubles for a pony ride to Meshhed, while the usual price was 4 or 5 roubles. Thus the prospects were not encouraging.

After a three-day journey, I was in Meshhed where I met some old friends who were very depressed. For three months there were no visitors from Russia. I was the first person who had come all the way from St Petersburg, and I had to tell them everything about the changes that had taken place.

Iraq

I have already mentioned that in Kermanshah, to where I was transferred from Birjand, I had resigned from my position at the Banque d'Escompe de Perse [Loan and Discount Bank of Persia] in order to travel to India. At the end of January 1914, I left for Baghdad which at that time was still under Turkish control. The Russian Consul there, E. K. Popov, kindly introduced me to Professor Koldewey who carried out very interesting excavations at Babylon near Hilla. But it was impossible to visit Najaf[19] and Karbala,[20] the Shi'i holy sites which

---

[19] The shrine of Ali b. Abi Talib (d. 661), the first Shi'i Imam, is situated in Najaf. It is the most important pilgrimage site for all Shi'i Muslims; see Y. Gholami, 'Ali b. Abi Talib. 12. Shrine', *EIS*, vol. 3, pp. 577–583.

[20] The shrine of Imam al-Husayn b. Ali (d. 680), who was murdered by the Umayyads, is situated in Karbala. Karbala, too, is a major pilgrimage site for the Shi'i Muslims, especially during the first ten days of the Muslim month of Muharram; Imam al-Husayn and his small band of relatives and companions were massacred on

I wanted to see. Baghdad itself was of no particular interest to me. Therefore, I took a boat to Basra. The slow four-day journey down the Tigris was very interesting. The Russian Consul there, N. Golenishchev-Kutuzov, was so kind as to send a Consular *kawas*, who could speak Persian, to meet me and I was put up in a hotel which was a typical Indian boarding house. There was nothing interesting to see in Basra. It was the beginning of March, it rained frequently and the mud was exasperating. A boat leaving for Bombay was ready. It was an old cargo ship infested with ants, which were a great nuisance and impossible to get rid of. It was a slow mail vessel sailing to Bombay on a two-week voyage. Yet I wanted to travel by this boat in order to see the marvels of the Persian Gulf. There were also fast mail boats, which made the journey in five days.

Few places have undergone such thorough changes as these. I can still remember a barren sandbank, which is now the town of Abadan with its forest of chimneys.[21] Over the past 55 years, I have travelled along this route from India several times, and I have seen everything changing. In 1914, at the mouth of Shatt al-Arab – the joint outlet of the Tigris and the Euphrates – I could see that the muddy river water did not mix with the green sea water for quite a while. When I passed there in 1959, it was gone, since the many boats going up and down have mixed the water.

I did not waste time while travelling and practised my Hindustani with an Indian doctor who was a fellow passenger. Regrettably, it was impossible to go ashore when the boat was loading because of attempts on the lives of foreigners. I could only go ashore in Bahrain and Chahbar [Chabahar]. Bahrain has changed immensely since the jetties were built; now its old 'underwater gardens' for pearl shells are gone. Like Abadan at that time, Kuwait was just a sandbank. Now it

---

the 10th of Muharram, in the Islamic year 61, corresponding to 10 October 680. See S. Husain M. Jafri, *Origins and Early Development of Shiʿa Islam* (London, 1979), pp. 174–221; W. Madelung, 'Hosayn b. Ali', *EIR*, vol. 12, pp. 493–498, and F. Mehrvash, 'Ashura', *EIS*, vol. 3, pp. 883–892.

[21] Abadan is an island and a city in the south-western Iranian province of Khuzistan, known for its oil fields. After the discovery of oil in the region and the construction of a major oil refinery at Abadan in 1912, the town developed and expanded rapidly into a major industrial and commercial centre on the Persian Gulf. See X. de Planhol, 'Abadan. ii. Modern Abadan', *EIR*, vol. 1, pp. 53–57.

is an enormous port and city. Thus after Bahrain the next real port of call was Masqat,[22] a narrow bay with its basalt rocks covered with the names of the ships that had called there. From there the boat went directly to Bandar-i Abbasi,[23] but it anchored several kilometres away from the shore. And I could see only the line of distant buildings. Now a large port has been constructed there. The further journey east towards Karachi is of no interest and I have already described Karachi above.

I visited Iraq for the second time in 1948 and certain traces of development were then already visible. The Baghdad of 1914 was a thing of the past. My friends who live in Baghdad say that it has much progressed since that time, in terms of both architecture and culture.

In Bandar-i Abbasi where I arrived in the winter of 1937 from Kerman, in order to take a boat to Bombay, I took the most interesting trip to the islands. At that time, the Iranian government tried to organise their National (Milli) Bank with the help of experts, the German *kultur-tragers*, who very soon were locked up in jail by the authorities for their unbelievable swindling, embezzlement and other crimes. The regulations that they had introduced in financial transactions appeared insane because of the confiscatory exchange rate. Knowing that, I approached the local agent of the British India Steam Navigation Company and offered to pay for my ticket in Bombay. The offer was gladly accepted and a telegram was sent to India. While waiting for the reply I visited Larak, Qeshm and Hormuz which 500 years ago was visited by my fellow countryman, Afanasii Nikitin.[24]

---

[22] Masqat (Muscat) is now the capital of Oman.

[23] Bandar-i Abbas (or Abbasi) is a port city in the southern Iranian province of Hormozgan, on the Persian Gulf, some 16 km north-west of the island of Hormuz. See X. de Planhol, 'Bandar-e Abbas(i)', *EIR*, vol. 3, pp. 685–687.

[24] Afanasii Nikitin (d. 1475), medieval Russian merchant and traveller, who travelled through Persia and India during 1468–1475. He wrote a detailed account of his travels entitled *Khozhdenie za tri moria* [A Journey Beyond Three Seas] (Moscow, 1948), referring to the Caspian Sea, Black Sea and Arabian Sea. See G. Lenhoff and J. Martin, 'The Commercial and Cultural Context of Afanasij Nikitin's Journey Beyond Three Seas', *Jahrbücher für Geschichte Osteuropas*, 37 (1989), pp. 321–344, and Mary Jane Maxwell, 'Afanasii Nikitin: An Orthodox Russian's Spiritual Voyage in the Dar al-Islam, 1468–1475', *Journal of World History*, 17 (2006), pp. 243–266.

Larak, a small island which is visible from Bandar-i Abbasi, was the most interesting place. It is of volcanic origin, with even the cone of an extinct volcano, traces of immense streams of lava and fantastic scenery. Apart from an old Portuguese fortress, a small village and a few palm trees, however, there was not much else to see. There were no animals except a few goats, not even dogs, cats or rats, and no vegetation except dry thorn weeds. The water there is salty, hence tea is horrible. The locals buy fresh water from visiting motor boats. The islanders are all Sunnis. They speak a peculiar dialect and the women wear black masks. They speak Kumzari, a specific southern dialect of the Persian language, which I recorded. It had two forms: one was spoken by the inhabitants of the village on the island and it had a greater mixture of Persian, and the other one was spoken by the Bedouin Shiʿi tribe living on the Arab side in the rocky coves of Musandam. They often crossed over to Larak in order to graze their cattle in the thorny grass fields. This dialect of Kumzari was full of Arabic words and expressions. Living in this manner, it was obvious that the inhabitants of Larak and other islands were engaged in smuggling, and the government took disciplinary measures against them from time to time. In addition, it seemed to me that the volcanic soil of Larak gave off some noxious substance. Until my visit to this island I had felt quite normal, but once there I began to feel dizzy and my memory became fuzzy. These islands consist of a solidified lava stream and there are what I believe to be the remnants of conical volcanoes in their western parts. The inhabitants also complained about the low birth rate there.

On the relatively larger neighbouring island of Qeshm, some time ago there existed a bazaar. During my visit there in 1937, there were only two shops left, selling fishing equipment and other small items. Judging by the old buildings and the wide streets in the locality, it seems that this island must have been quite prosperous in the past. Incidentally, the grave of the navigator William Baffin (1584–1622), after whom a bay in North America is named, is believed to be located there. There is also a Portuguese fortress in Hormuz, which is larger than the one situated in Larak. The main export of the locality is ferric oxide; and there is also a small village with a school. The district of Minab can be considered as a type of annex to these islands. It is called the India of Persia, because bananas and mangos, sold in Tehran, grow there.

A few decades ago, the people of all the neighbouring islands lived by smuggling but the government's crackdown on contraband made them poor. There was a famine in Bandar-i Abbasi itself and many other places in southern Persia. I stayed in a hotel and could often see how the servants threw out rubbish, and then immediately as if from nowhere a few children would rush to it in search of something edible. Then came dogs, then goats and finally some melancholic cows chewing paper and whatever else they could find. And as in Kerman, there were many beggars there. My friends advised me not to give them any money, since everything would be taken away by their parents and spent on opium. So usually I gave money to a baker instructing him to give bread to the beggars.

Meanwhile, I was waiting for a steamer which normally arrived quite regularly. But the Sheikh of Bahrain had now hired it for his family to go to Karachi and delayed its arrival. The company's agent told the passengers to wait on the spot for the steamer. I handed over my luggage to the company and took my place in a boat that would take me to the ship when it arrived. It was cool and quiet and the boat rocked slightly. All of a sudden local women and beggars jumped into the boat. They wanted to meet the arriving steamer and beg for water, which they would then be able to sell on their return. It is impossible to describe the nauseating smell which these representatives of womankind emitted – a mixture of fish odours with that of human sweat and dirty rags. The steamer arrived at daybreak, and it was a great pleasure to take a bath when I finally got on board.

The Sheikh himself settled on the second-class deck where his attendant at once set up an enormous coffee pot, which was boiling all the time. Servants with much smaller pots would fill them from the giant pot and serve coffee to the members of his party. It was interesting to see that, among the people who appeared to be relatives of the Sheikh, quite a few were Negroid. Some of them spoke fluent Persian. This may give an idea of the peculiar Perso-Arab life and culture in the Persian Gulf. The employees of the company complained at first that these nouveau riches caused trouble, although they paid generously. That was the situation when oil had just been discovered. But gradually they became more accustomed to the new ways of life.

All of this provides a brief idea of life at the junctions of the Arab and Iranian worlds. The Iranian world that is alive and moving forward, and the backward Arab world which long ago lost its driving force.

Egypt

As I have mentioned above, my work in Bombay consisted of editing and translating genuine Ismaili texts, which earlier had not been available to scholars. Only a few printing houses in India had Arabic fonts. And they were always busy with the orders of their permanent customers. Thus, the only way to get the books published was to print them lithographically. But it was also difficult to find good and accurate scribes for that process, and the printing quality was not always satisfactory. Moreover, the cost was rather high and it was constantly increasing. At that time I corresponded with a very talented orientalist, a German Jew called Dr Paul Kraus,[25] who was very much interested in Ismailism. He was a

Paul Kraus

---

[25] Paul Kraus (1904–1944) was actually a Czech orientalist and one of the pioneers of modern Ismaili studies. He studied Oriental languages at the Deutsche Universität in his native Prague, before going to Palestine where he studied at the Hebrew University of Jerusalem. In 1927, he enrolled at the University of Berlin, where he embarked on Islamic studies under Carl H. Becker (1876–1933). Subsequently, working with Julius Ruska (1867–1949), Kraus became interested in the alchemist Jabir b. Hayyan (Geber of the Latins), and produced original studies on this enigmatic figure and his connection to Ismaili gnosis. Arguing that the Jabirean corpus of texts belonged to the Qarmati–Ismaili movement, Kraus paved the way for later breakthroughs in our modern understanding of early Ismailism. After a three-year stay in Paris, where he was mentored by Louis Massignon (1883–1962), Kraus went to Egypt in 1937 as a lecturer at the Universities of Cairo and Alexandria. Kraus committed suicide in Cairo in 1944 under mysterious circumstances. See Charles Kuentz, 'Paul Kraus (1904–1944)', *Bulletin de l'Institut d'Égypte*, 27 (1944–1945), pp. 431–441, and Joel L. Kraemer, 'The Death of an Orientalist: Paul Kraus from

lecturer in Semitic studies at the University of Cairo [earlier known as Fu'ad I University]. He informed me about a suitable printing house in Cairo and I suggested to my superiors that I should go to Egypt to investigate whether it was advisable to print our books there. All this happened in the spring of 1937.

Dr Taha Husayn

I arrived in Cairo and discovered that it was cheaper to print in Egypt than in India, and that the quality of printing was also much better there. At that time, Egypt was still under British rule and life there made a very good and encouraging impression. Cairo with its libraries, museums, antiquities and a good university was a unique place in the Middle East. I met the head of the university, Dr Taha Husayn,[26] and some other professors. In comparison with India, theirs was a much more civilised world. The programme of my tour also included a visit to Syria, to the places inhabited by the Ismailis and the Druzes. But I received a telegram telling me that I had to proceed to the 'Congress of Orientalists' in Paris, which was taking place at the end of July.[27] For some reason, the police refused to extend my residence permit, so I decided to go to Persia first and from there travel to Paris.

Prague to Cairo', in M. Kramer, ed., *The Jewish Discovery of Islam: Studies in Honor of Bernard Lewis* (Tel Aviv, 1999), pp. 181–223. A number of Kraus's Ismaili-related studies, including his writings on Abu Hatim al-Razi (d. 934), have been collected in his *Alchemie, Ketzerei, Apokryphen im frühen Islam*, ed. R. Brague (Hildesheim and New York, 1994).

[26] Taha Husayn Bey (1889–1973), Egyptian educator, historian, journalist and novelist, who lost his eyesight at the age of two. Educated at al-Azhar University and the University of Paris, Sorbonne, he emerged as a leading modernist and held various educational posts in Egypt, including the Minister of Education during 1950–1951. Similarly to many Egyptian intellectuals of his generation, Taha Husayn wrote extensively on a wide variety of subjects, including classical and modern Arabic literature as well as Islamic history. Taha Husayn received many honours and was also nominated for the Nobel Prize. See P. Cachia, *Taha Husayn: His Place in the Egyptian Literary Renaissance* (London, 1956), and his 'Taha Husayn', *EI2*, vol. 10, pp. 95–96.

[27] Due to the outbreak of World War II, the 21st International Congress of Orientalists did not convene until July 1948.

I chose to go via Palestine and took a train to Jerusalem. It was a return to the world of backwardness. After my Egyptian experience, Palestinian railways were unbearable. They had dirty cars infested with insects and no electric fans. The train moved at a snail's pace, stopping at every insignificant station for a long time under the scorching sun. It arrived in Jerusalem in the hot midday. It was all most irritating. Shabby hotels in Jerusalem were divided not only in accordance with different classes but also into 'decent' and 'not-decent' categories.

After Cairo, everything looked so shabby and miserable, even depressing. I was lucky to meet in Jerusalem my old friend, the former Russian Consul from Turbat Haydari in Persia. Now he was managing the property of the Russian Orthodox Palestinian Society, which had been established to assist the Russian pilgrims visiting the Holy Land. The Society had hostels, hospitals and other institutions. Some of them were rented out to British authorities. The famous local antiquities were shown to me, but I am afraid they evoked very little religious sentiment. They just reminded me of 'the hair from the beard of the Prophet', which was shown to me in Hyderabad in the Deccan. This object looked like hair, but it certainly was not human hair. It was about 15 cm long and at least one millimetre thick. I expressed my doubts to the custodian of the relic, saying that the Prophet was an Arab and Arabs usually have soft and curly hair. It would be difficult to imagine the Arab Prophet with a beard of such massive hair. 'If you do not believe, then I shall not show you anything', was the answer of the keeper. Many still remember riots in Kashmir provoked by a suspicion of the theft of the 'hair of the Prophet's beard'. Was it similar to that of Hyderabad? Anyway, holy places and relics do not inspire much trust.

On the same day that I arrived in Jerusalem, the police had introduced a curfew with its usual restrictions. I had time for a trip to Bethlehem only, and the next morning I took a bus to Damascus. I shall deal with this journey in the section on Syria, but now I would like to describe my second visit to Cairo in 1948.

It was finally decided to print the publications of the 'Ismaili Society' in Cairo, and I left for Suez in 1948 with four books which were ready to go to the printer.[28] Cairo remained as attractive as it was in 1937, the

---

[28] These books included items 116 and 117 in Appendix 1, Works of Ivanow, as well as Hamid al-Din al-Kirmani's *Rahat al-aql*, the first publication in the Ismaili

war had not touched it. But something strange was happening to the transport. It was only possible to get a wartime utility boat and the ticket from Bombay to Suez cost as much as the ticket from Bombay to Rotterdam, which was double the distance. Similarly, from Bombay to Suez one had to pay more than going from Bombay to Port Said. The world had entered the period of economic madness which is still progressing.

In Cairo, I tried to see everything that was worth seeing, all libraries, museums and medieval sites. I also gave five lectures on the history of Ismailism at the university. I was, in addition, invited to lecture at the so-called American University [of Cairo], but I refused. It was interesting to see 'the future of Egypt' at weekly tea parties in the Student Club where I was invited. I did not find any geniuses among the male students but I was introduced to some very talented young lady students. The niece of Professor M. Kamil Husayn,[29] who published dozens of books on Ismailism, really impressed me. She was a very well-read medical student, possessing the signs of genuine intellectuality remarkable not only for someone who yesterday had been a recluse of a Cairo harem but for any advanced lady student of a most progressive European nationality. I also remember another

Umm Kulthum in concert

Society's C series. On this work, representing al-Kirmani's major philosophical treatise, see Daniel de Smet, *La Quiétude de l'intellect: Néoplatonisme et gnose Ismaélienne dans l'oeuvre de Hamid ad-Din al-Kirmani (Xe/XIe s.)* (Louvain, 1995), and Paul E. Walker, *Hamid al-Din al-Kirmani: Ismaili Thought in the Age of al-Hakim* (London, 1999).

[29] Muhammad Kamil Husayn (1901–1961), Professor of Islamic studies at Cairo University. He also collected and edited a number of Arabic Ismaili texts of the Fatimid period, which were published in Cairo in his own well-known 'Silsilat Makhtutat al-Fatimiyyin' series. See Daftary, *Ismaili Literature*, pp. 117, 122–123, 125, 126, 127, 129, 130, 131, 144, 157, 299. The niece in question was Aisha Mohamed al-Hady Husayn, who became a psychiatrist.

talented lady student who sang at musical performances given during the tea parties. She sang in the style of the now famous Umm Kulthum.[30] It was not easy for a foreigner to admire her singing but among her own people she was a rare talent. It was also very interesting and enjoyable to attend the lectures of the former Iranian ambassador to Egypt, Dr Ghasem Ghani,[31] who was an outstanding expert on Sufi literature. His early death was a great loss for Iranian intellectual circles.

The University of Cairo, founded not so many years ago, invited many good foreign professors. In fact, they formed 50 per cent of the university's teaching faculty. Therefore the university had acquired an excellent reputation. Its medical faculty was the best

---

[30] Umm Kulthum (ca. 1904–1975), famous Egyptian singer. Born Umm Kulthum Ibrahim al-Sayyid al-Baltaji into a poor rural family, she learned to sing Muslim devotional songs by imitating her father, the imam of a village mosque. By the 1930s, Umm Kulthum was one of the most sought after artists in Cairo, also participating in musical films. In the 1950s, she became linked with Gamal Abd al-Nasir's government, singing in support of the charismatic Egyptian president. Umm Kulthum eventually became a quasi-mythical figure, appealing to Arabs of different social classes and countries. See V. Danielson, 'Umm Kulthum (1904? –1975)', in *Encyclopaedia of Islam and the Muslim World*, ed. Richard C. Martin (New York, 2004), vol. 2, pp. 706–707, and Laura Lohman, *Umm Kulthum: Artistic Agency and the Shaping of a Legend* (Middletown, CT, 2010).

[31] Ghasem Ghani (1893–1952) was a physician, diplomat and an eminent scholar of Persian literature and history. He received his medical degree in 1919 from the American University of Beirut; and later, in the early 1920s, he received specialised medical training in Paris. While practising his medical profession in his native Khorasan, from 1928 Ghani also began his literary activities as a scholar, editing a number of Persian texts and helping Muhammad Qazwini (1877–1949) in producing the critical edition of Hafiz's *Diwan* of poetry in 1941. His last publication was *Bahthi dar tasawwuf* [A Discourse on Sufism] (Tehran, 1952). From the mid-1930s, Ghani also entered politics, serving several times as a parliamentary representative for Mashhad in the Majlis. In 1947, Ghani was appointed as Iranian ambassador to Egypt; and then in August 1948 as ambassador to Turkey. He spent his final years in America and died in San Francisco in 1952. Ghani was a prolific writer and corresponded with many eminent political and literary figures of the time. His diaries, notes and letters have been collected in twelve volumes under the general editorship of his son, Cyrus Ghani; see *Yaddashtha-yi Doktor Qasem Ghani* (London, 1980–1984); *A Man of Many Worlds: The Memoirs and Diaries of Dr. Ghasem Ghani*, ed. C. Ghani (Washington DC, 2006), and Abbas Milani, 'Ḡani, Qasem', *EIR*, vol. 10, pp. 276–278.

in the East. But eventually the old Eastern traditions of nepotism, favouritism and general deterioration got the upper hand. It is interesting to note that women, the so-called 'influential wives', played the main part in the advance of nepotism. I myself, although a foreigner and only an occasional visitor to the university, knew of many such cases.

In spite of all this, the differences between Cairo University and Indian universities, in terms of their standards, atmosphere and mentality of the students, were colossal. It is necessary to note though that at the University of Cairo all teaching was done in Arabic, the native language of the students, with foreign languages playing only an auxiliary part, while by contrast, the complex linguistic composition of India had forced them to adopt a foreign language – English – as their language of tuition. The negative impact [of this] on the students' mentality was inevitable.

Syria

Merje Square, Damascus, ca. 1920

In 1937, Syria had not yet disintegrated into miniature states incapable of feeding or defending themselves. It was still under the French protectorate. As I have already mentioned above, I went from Cairo to Jerusalem, and [thence] to Damascus. I liked Damascus. Unlike Cairo, and especially Tehran, it preserved so much of 'the spirit of the East'. Hills and a belt of gardens surrounded the city, which is often compared to Isfahan. Certainly there is some similarity but the oasis of Isfahan is much bigger. My bus arrived in Merje Square at sunset, and I took a room in a comparatively modest hotel, not the main hotel on the square itself, since experienced people had advised me against it. As everywhere in Asia, Damascus has its own modern part of the city with straight streets and cinemas. In India it is called the cantonment. In Damascus it is as unpleasant as everywhere. But the old part of Damascus, with its crooked and narrow streets and old city walls, is really lovely. In a few days I saw everything that a tourist should see – the Omayyad Mosque, bazaars and the 'street called straight', which was mentioned in the Bible. I visited the library near the bazaar and a few modest bookshops. I also went to the residence of the Orthodox Patriarch, where I met several Arab monks speaking fluent Russian and found the address of a shop where I could buy rye bread. It was a rarity; I saw it only in Qazwin during my early travels to Persia.

I made the acquaintance of Professor M. Kurd Ali,[32] a well-known historian, whom I later revisited many times. I also travelled to Suwayda, the Druze capital.[33] It is a small and poor town with the ruins of Byzantine columns and mosaics. I wanted to contact some learned Druzes to discuss some unclear points

M. Kurd Ali

---

[32] Muhammad Farid Kurd Ali (1876–1953), Syrian journalist, scholar, author and Minister of Public Education. Of Kurdish origins from Sulaymaniyya, Iraq, the Kurd Ali family had migrated to Syria. Muhammad Kurd Ali travelled extensively, also spending some time in Egypt, where he attended the al-Azhar lectures of Muhammad Abduh (1849–1905), the eminent Muslim theologian and Egyptian modernist, on Koran commentary. In 1919, Kurd Ali founded the Arab Academy of Damascus and served as its president until his death. Author of numerous works on the history and literature of the Arabs, he also published his memoirs entitled *Mudhakkirat* (Damascus, 1948–1951), 4 vols. See S. Dahan, 'Muhammad Kurd Ali (1876–1953). Notice biographique', in *Mélanges Louis Massignon*, vol. 1, pp. 379–394, and Ch. Pellat, 'Kurd Ali', *EI2*, vol. 5, pp. 437–438.

[33] The Syrian Druzes live mainly in the Hawran and Suwayda provinces, whose capital city is also called Suwayda, situated some 80 km south-east of Damascus. The Druzes represent a Muslim religious community that evolved out of the Ismaili community of the Fatimid period around 1017. The Druzes, who call themselves the Muwahhidun or Unitarians, live in various regions of Syria and Lebanon, with smaller numbers in Israel and in countries outside the Middle East. The Druzes guard their sacred literature and doctrines secretly, and do not permit conversions. See Nejla M. Abu-Izzeddin, *The Druzes: A New Study of their History, Faith and Society* (Leiden, 1984), and Kais M. Firro, *A History of the Druzes* (Leiden, 1992), focusing on the more recent history of the community.

from de Sacy's *Exposé*.³⁴ However, the people I was directed to appeared to be of miserable education. It is not surprising since, as the Syrian chargé d'affaires in Karachi, himself an educated Druze, later explained to me, the Druze religious authorities belong to a special caste and their position is secured by birth rather than education. I returned to Damascus and from there travelled to Homs and Hama. The latter seemed to be the most picturesque town in Syria. Then I went to Salamiyya, which is a dusty and hot place with nothing to see apart from the Ismaili sacred relics and a new agricultural college.³⁵ I was the guest of the local elder who was an Ismaili of the Aga Khani branch.

Life in Salamiyya was very typical of Syria. Middle-class people worked in the morning, then took their meals and slept. At 4 p.m. they went to the post office to see who had received letters. They quite unceremoniously opened newspapers sent to other people to see what

---

³⁴ A. I. Silvestre de Sacy, *Exposé de la religion des Druzes* (Paris, 1838; reprinted, Paris and Amsterdam, 1964), 2 vols. Antoine I. Silvestre de Sacy (1758–1838) devoted several decades to the study of the Druzes working from the Druzes manuscripts then available in European libraries. As a by-product of his Druze studies, de Sacy also contributed to the study of the early Ismailis as well as the Nizari Ismailis of the Alamut period. See E. Chassinat, ed., *Bibliothèque des Arabisants Français*. Première série: *Silvestre de Sacy* (Cairo, 1905), vol. 1, and H. Derenbourg, *Silvestre de Sacy (1758–1938)* (Paris, 1895). See also note 14 in Chapter 2, and note 75 in Chapter 3.

³⁵ Salamiyya is a town in central Syria in the district of Orontes about 40 km south-east of Hama. An ancient city, Salamiyya was conquered by the Arabs in 636. Soon after their victory, a number of Abbasids settled down in Salamiyya. The town played an important role in the history of the early Ismailis as the location for several decades (until 902) of the secret headquarters of their *daʿwa*. A mausoleum, known locally as the Maqam al-Imam, erected in the early 11th century, and still *in situ*, is believed by the Syrian Ismailis to contain the tombs of some early Ismaili Imams. A new phase in the history of Salamiyya, which had become entirely deserted, began in the middle of the 19th century, when a local Ismaili leader successfully petitioned the Ottoman authorities to settle the Syrian Ismailis in the locality. Sultan Muhammad Shah Aga Khan III, the 48th Imam of the Nizari Ismailis, organised the Ismailis of Salamiyya and built several schools for them as well as an agricultural institution there. With a population of around 100,000, the great majority of whom are Nizari Ismailis, Salamiyya now accounts for the largest concentration of Arab Nizari Ismailis in the Middle East. See H. Halm, 'Les Fatimides à Salamya', in *Mélanges offerts au Professeur Dominique Sourdel*; being *Revue des Études Islamiques*, 54 (1986), pp. 133–149, and J. H. Kramers and F. Daftary, 'Salamiyya', *EI2*, vol. 8, pp. 921–923.

was in them. After that they all went to the house of the Sheikh, where I was staying. Chairs were taken to the courtyard and the guests were served with coffee from a white teapot accompanied by a small white cup. The cup was filled and offered to a guest who would drink it and return it to a servant. He did not bother to wash it and simply put it together with the teapot under the chair. So, this was the practice and, when I noticed it, I began to decline coffee saying that I had heart palpitations and therefore could not drink it. However, they tried to persuade me and offered me the cup. When I nevertheless declined, they poured the coffee into the teapot to save it for the next guest. After spending two days there, I returned to Hama and then proceeded to Masyaf, which was also home to an Ismaili community, but they were Jaʿfaris, not Aga Khanis. It must be explained that the Ismailis split at the end of the 11th century into two groups. One of them, the Mustaʿlians, continued their allegiance to the later Fatimid Imams, and another, the Nizaris, followed another branch of the Fatimids.[36] In the 14th century, the Nizari sect was divided into two branches: the Muhammad-Shahis [or Muʾminis], now called Jaʿfaris, and the Qasim-Shahis, now known as the Aga Khanis.[37] According to the census undertaken by the French authorities in 1937, there were only about 4,000 Jaʿfaris left in Masyaf and Qadmus, while the Aga Khanis formed the majority.

I had letters of recommendation for the administrator of Masyaf, a young Syrian brought up in the French style. He was very polite and kind and entrusted me for housing and food to a wealthy businessman who had an office in the town. It also served as a kind of club where people came to chat. The most important local figure was a policeman, a Circassian by origin whose ancestors had emigrated from Russia to Ottoman Turkey a century earlier. He was a tall man always carrying a Russian Cossack sabre and behaving like a tyrant with everybody. He at once asked me whether I had seen captain so-and-so (I forget his name), a very polite and intelligent French officer, most probably a

---

[36] See Daftary, *The Ismaʿilis*, pp. 241–243.

[37] Ivanow was the first European scholar to refer to this schism; see items 9 and 82 in his Bibliography. See also Daftary, *The Ismaʿilis*, pp. 413–415, 452–456, and his 'Shah Tahir and Nizari Ismaili Disguises', in T. Lawson, ed., *Reason and Inspiration in Islam: Theology, Philosophy and Mysticism in Islamic Thought, Essays in Honour of Hermann Landolt* (London, 2005), pp. 395–406.

The castle of Masyaf

member of the security services. I went to see him, presented my documents, and he did not bother me after that. Apparently he told the Circassian to leave me alone.

Now Masyaf is a small town with very little commercial activity. It has a castle dating back to the time of the Crusades when it was an important place, the centre of the resistance of the legendary Old Man of the Mountain – Rashid al-Din Sinan, the leader of [the Syrian] Ismailis.[38] According to legend, he sent his disciples to murder his enemies. These murders were committed in most difficult circumstances where the assassins faced certain death. There are many legends about these exploits, probably just figments of the imagination.[39] The Old Man of the Mountain's castle, which now looks like a

---

[38] Sinan led the Syrian Nizari Ismailis to the peak of their power and glory for some three decades until his death in 1193. See Daftary, *The Ismaʿilis*, pp. 367–374; his 'Sinan and the Nizari Ismailis of Syria', in D. Bredi et al., ed., *Scritti in onore di Biancamaria Scarcia Amoretti* (Rome, 2008), vol. 2, pp. 489–500; his 'Rashid al-Din Sinan', *EI2*, vol. 8, pp. 442–443, and H. Halm, *Kalifen und Assassinen. Ägypten und der Vordere Orient zur Zeit der ersten Kreuzzüge 1074–1171* (Munich, 2014), pp. 250–254, 325–329.

[39] For the genesis of these so-called Assassin legends, which culminated in the version popularised by the Venetian traveller Marco Polo (1254–1324), see F. Daftary, *The Assassin Legends: Myths of the Ismaʿilis* (London, 1994), especially pp. 88–127.

very big house with none of the usual towers, was besieged many times. At the time of my visit there, the castle was under the protection of the Department of Archaeology, and it was possible to inspect it only with the Department's permission.[40] Permission was usually granted to tourists but it was very difficult to find the keeper of the key. The castle was small, beyond any comparison with the grand fortresses of Alamut and Lamasar in Persia. Not too far from Masyaf stood Qadmus,[41] an old settlement on the top of a low hill, which was still inhabited. There was nothing to see there, no antiquities and buildings of fame were left, only a few sacred spots, which according to legend are associated with Rashid al-Din Sinan, the Old Man.

There was nothing more to study, and I continued my journey to Tartus on the seashore. It is an ancient site, which has been preserved since the time of the Phoenicians who inhabited these shores. The only island along the Syrian coast, called Ra'd, is situated close to this place. There are some cyclopean structures, probably Phoenician, on this island. I stayed in the only local 'hotel', which deserves a few lines of description. It stood on the seashore and had a single room for guests as well as a billiards room, which was also occasionally rented out. Behind it, there was a bathroom with a single sink with no tube attached to it, thus dirty water ran all over the trousers of the person using the sink. Next to it there was a toilet.

I had a good view of the sea from my window and at sunset I could see the sharp promontory of Cyprus when the rocks, which were invisible at daytime, could be seen against the sun. I could also see the road winding along the shore. There was some space between it and

---

[40] The fortress and town of Masyaf are situated in central Syria, about 45 km to the west of Hama. In 1140, the Nizari Ismailis seized the fortress of Masyaf, their most important stronghold in Syria, from the Banu Munqidh of Shayzar. Masyaf, with a number of Arabic epigraphs from its Nizari Ismaili period, is one of the best preserved castles of the medieval Nizaris. In recent times, the citadel of Masyaf has been restored and conserved through the efforts of the Aga Khan Trust for Culture (AKTC). See M. Braune, 'Untersuchungen zur mittelalterlichen Befestigung in Nordwest-Syrien: Die Assassinenburg Masyaf', *Damaszener Mitteilungen*, 7 (1993), pp. 298–326; Willey, *Eagle's Nest*, pp. 220–227; Halm, *Kalifen und Assassinen*, pp. 329–335, and Maytham Hasan, 'Introduction to the Citadel of Masyaf', in S. Bianca, ed., *Syria: Medieval Citadels Between East and West* (Geneva, 2007), pp. 181–214.

[41] See Willey, *Eagle's Nest*, pp. 228–230, and Halm, *Kalifen und Assassinen*, pp. 206–208, 333 ff.

the sea, and a table was placed there. A group of young men sat at this table all day, animatedly discussing something or other, probably politics.

I remember that before my departure from Cairo, Dr P. Kraus, mentioned above, introduced me to one of his students, Muhammad Tartusi, who was a native of this place and owned a village in the vicinity. He spoke plausible English and he rendered a great service to me; without him I would have been rather helpless. He introduced me to Sheikh Muhammad, a member of the Syrian parliament, who most kindly invited me to his estate nearby, called Uqr Zayti. On an agreed day we met in Tartus and when Sheikh Muhammad arrived from Damascus we went to his estate. It was a group of houses occupied by the Sheikh's family and his brother. The name Uqr Zayti was given to the estate because of the olive trees on the nearby hill. These trees have strong thorns, and riding through the undergrowth is very unpleasant because the thorns tear one's clothes to pieces. Sheikh Muhammad, who was about 40 years of age, enjoyed great respect among the local farmers who often asked him to resolve their disputes. It was done in a very patriarchal way, and I took some photographs of the scenes.

The Sheikh had a blonde wife and four blonde children. This is a Syrian peculiarity when children are born blonde and then turn dark as they grow older. Syrians also have an amusing fashion to give women names in the form of the infinitive of what grammatically is called the eighth root of a verb. Thus, in the Sheikh's family, there were Izdehar ('flowering'), Intesar ('helping') and Ibtisam ('smiling'). Another feature of Syrian family life was notorious discords and feuds.

The Sheikh's house stood on a spur of the ridge, and on the next similar spur, called Khurbat al-faras ('Spine of the Horse') because of its shape, stood the house of his close relative, Sheikh Abdullah. I was personally invited by Sheikh Muhammad to his estate, but later discovered that it would be considered impolite if I did not visit Sheikh Abdullah. Therefore, I went for a few days to his place. Sheikh Abdullah was much less urbanised than his neighbour, but he was a nice old man of simple ways of life and said what he felt. Considering the religious books he showed me, he apparently was a Ja'fari Ismaili. However, he concealed his beliefs. I can still remember how, after a hot day, we sat at the door of Sheikh Abdullah's house with the host

himself, his son, an old relative and two Nusayri farmers present.⁴²
The moon was full and it was quiet. Suddenly both Nusayris stood up
and said that someone was calling from Uqr Zayti. Sheikh Abdullah
angrily shouted, 'Do not reply!' But the Nusayris heard the message
and said that they were asking about the guest, i.e., me. Sheikh
Abdullah again shouted, 'Do not reply!', but one of the Nusayris cried
back in his powerful voice that the guest was still there. I still do not
know what to admire, the power of the farmer's voice or the childish
irritation of the Sheikh. Next morning, the Sheikh very seriously tried
to persuade me not to call at Uqr Zayti but to go via the village of Melki
on my way back. It was a large village, which I would have really liked
to see, but I did not want to offend Sheikh Muhammad who had been
so kind to me.

The Syrians were a very mixed people, with a great proportion of
misfits and degenerates. I was surprised to see the physique of the
peasants, amongst whom were many lame people and midgets, who
were obviously weak and defective. Probably it was caused by
malnutrition, as there was little [arable] land around. These people
sharply contrasted against the well-nourished feudal family of the
Sheikh. After returning to Tartus, I took a bus to Halab (Aleppo), thus
travelling through the native land of the famous poet Abu'l-Ala.⁴³

Halab is a large town with many relics of antiquity. Plenty of
antiquities allegedly from ancient ruins on the banks of the Euphrates
were sold in its bazaar. In fact, they were fakes manufactured locally.
I bought a few, a clay lamp allegedly from Carchemish among them.
When I dropped it, the handle fell off and proved to be made of
cigarette ends covered with clay. From Aleppo I went to see an ancient
place, now called Lataqiyya [Latakia], which is a small ancient port
town. From there I moved to Beirut, passing again through Tartus.
I have heard that Beirut has changed considerably. It has been
modernised and grown in size. In 1937, I was still able to witness this

---

⁴² The Nusayri Shiʿis, who changed the name of their community to Alawis (or the followers of Ali) in the early 1920s, are concentrated in the north-western province of Latakia in Syria, with smaller communities in northern Lebanon and southern Turkey. See F. Daftary, *A History of Shiʿi Islam* (London, 2013), pp. 175–190, and H. Halm, 'Nusayriyya', *EI2*, vol. 8, pp. 145–148.

⁴³ Abu'l-Ala Ahmad b. Abd Allah al-Maʿarri (973–1058), famous Arab poet who lost his eyesight at an early age. See P. Smoor, 'al-Maʿarri', *EI2*, vol. 5, pp. 927–935.

interesting period of change from old to new. I wanted to visit the Catholic University, but it was closed because of the holidays. There was nothing more to see and I left for Damascus to say goodbye to my friends and have a last look at the city.

Two Syrian merchants travelling to Baghdad offered me a place in their car. Since the road was not safe, we had to start our journey at 2 a.m., in a convoy of cars accompanied by a military vehicle with a machine gun. The ground was remarkably hard and we were travelling at about 100 km per hour – I was sitting by the driver watching the speedometer. It did not take long to reach the halfway point between Syria and Baghdad, the Rutba-Wells, with its modest airport where old-fashioned planes had to be refuelled. There was also a restaurant for passengers and many Bedouins camped nearby. After this town, the road became worse, with patches of sand and pit holes. By evening we reached Ramadi and at 10 p.m. we were in Baghdad. My old friend P. I. Mashmeer, who worked for the Iraq railways, received me warmly. Dinner was served but I wanted to take a bath first. It proved impossible because the tap water was too hot. Day temperatures were 122° F, and the water tanks on the roof were overheating. Because of administrative procrastination, I had to spend all of August in Baghdad. It was the hottest time of the year when a temperature of 108° F is considered cool. But I often had to walk to the Persian Consulate. The police classified me as a journalist rather than a tourist in my passport and at that time the Persian government did not like journalists. I had to spend £8 on telegrams before I got a visa. Eventually, it was granted and I left for Iran.

But my time in Baghdad had not been wasted. I made a tour of the Shi‘i sacred places in southern Mesopotamia, Karbala and Najaf. There was nothing exciting there; they cannot be compared to the religious buildings in Meshhed and Qum in Iran. I walked in the cemeteries of Najaf

Karbala, ca. 1948

and read inscriptions on tombstones, but there were no old dates. Graves are rented out there and when the relatives of the deceased stop their payments, the headstones are removed and the place is rented out to somebody else. Thus it is hopeless to look for any historical materials there.

At last it was time to go. Departure by car was fixed for 3 a.m. Before that, I had a long talk with Mashmeer recollecting our life in Rayagada. It was our last meeting. Soon after my departure he fell ill, left for France and died there. A few weeks later, I went by bus from Tehran to Meshhed and then to Duzdap, which had not yet been renamed Zahidan, and from there by train to Bombay for the new year of 1938, bringing my friends tins of caviar from Tehran.

India

When I was living in Birjand, I subscribed to the *Journal of the Royal Asiatic Society*, published in London, as well as the *Journal of the Asiatic Society of Bengal*. At that time, they were both quite respectable periodicals but now their standards have hopelessly deteriorated. When I arrived in Calcutta in 1914, I wanted to visit the Asiatic Society of Bengal. As I have mentioned above, I was kindly invited to stay at the Russian Consulate. It was close to the Asiatic Society where I regularly went to work in the library. The Society was housed in an old-fashioned two-storey building with Masonic emblems. Later a high modern house replaced it.

I think some impressions of my first visit to the Society might be of interest, since the things I saw foreshadowed the future. First, I came to the large hall with an oval table in the middle. Portraits of eminent men were hanging on the walls, almost all of them in the style of crude bazaar painting. I cannot remember anything of artistic value. Moreover, there were sculptures of various gentlemen in some sort of bathing costume. The smell of rotting paper was everywhere.

Having presented myself as a member, I asked for a certain manuscript which I wanted to consult. I was directed to a young Muslim of chocolate brown hue. I gave him the order slip with the book's shelf mark. He asked me to sit at the table and wait for the

Wladimir Ivanow in India

manuscript. I sat down, noting for the sake of curiosity, the time. It took just about 20 minutes to fetch the book. At last a procession entered from a side door. At the head was the young Muslim of Indian origin, followed by a bearded co-religionist, followed by a *chaprasi* who, in turn, was followed by a sweeper, all of them stepping in a slow ceremonial pace like a military unit in a funeral procession.[44]

I sat there infuriated and fighting the urge to shout, '*jaldi karo!*' (move on). Then the sweeper handed over the book to the *chaprasi*, who gave it to the bearded Muslim, the latter to the chocolate man, and eventually he ceremonially laid it in front of me. It was all very stupid and irritating. When I gave the young man my next order he wanted to find servants first. I told him that I would take the book personally and went with him. And it took us only three minutes. The young man wrote Persian poetry under the pen name of Lulu (the pearl). I often saw him sitting and doing nothing, apparently waiting for poetic inspiration. Later on, I heard that he had died the following year.

The Hindu clerks (library *baboo*s) were more urbanised and quicker in their work. The most unpleasant member of the staff was the 'paid secretary'. He was called so in order to distinguish him from the 'learned' secretaries, who were elected but did not receive any pay. He was a Eurasian, that is, of mixed origin, half-European and half-Indian, what in modern language is called 'coloured' in America and South Africa. Eurasians formed some kind of distinct class or caste, convinced that they had been wronged. There were many charitable institutions that picked up such 'unwanted children', educated them and gave them names in honour of various celebrities, such as Nelson, Newton, etc. This one was Elliot. He was an elderly man who claimed that, having served with the society for 35 years, he knew everything better than anyone else. He never missed a chance to do something unpleasant, especially to newcomers, by exhuming from his memory some long forgotten rules and regulations invariably restricting and prohibiting something. He was very subservient to both European and Indian members of the Council. But he was not devoid of ambition

---

[44] *Chaprasi* is a Hindi term meaning the bearer of *chapra*s, a badge with the name of the office of the bearer inscribed on it. In British India, and subsequently, the term popularly denoted an office messenger bearing such a badge.

since he worked on an alphabetical index of papers published in the Journal of the Society since its inception. One can imagine what a man of so little education could do with it. The Council accepted the index, gave the author 500 rupees (for so many years of labour, as he complained to everybody) and threw his work away.

These things did not help to improve the general atmosphere, which sharply contrasted with that of the Asiatic Museum. It is worthwhile mentioning another typical person, the doorkeeper, who was a tall and robust middle-aged retired Hindu soldier, always polite and reliable. It was amusing to watch him when an occasional female visitor came to see me. He approached my desk and whispered, looking like a conspirator: '*Ek ta memsaheb*' (a lady).

Once or twice a month there were seminars for members when scholarly papers were presented. At the beginning, I regularly attended them but very soon I found them to be very dull and absolutely uninteresting. It was quite different in the past when even the governor of Bengal graced them with his presence. On such occasions, the visitors were previously required to wear white tie. But it never happened during my nine-year tenure there.

One of the most unpleasant features of local life was the astonishing lack of honesty among the local *iskolars* (from the English 'scholar'). For my work, I needed the well-known *Geschichte der arabischen Litteratur* by C. Brockelmann.[45] Despite its numerous errors and defects, it was indispensable for my research. I was horrified to see that pages in the middle were clearly torn out! The *iskolars* who had perused it did not make notes, they simply cut out entire pages! Apparently it was not a single individual who did this, since pages were missing in some other books, which were much in use. The library *baboos* were hopelessly lazy and careless in not detecting the damage. When I began to work with manuscripts, I discovered that many valuable miniatures had also been cut out. Moreover, relying on Sprenger's catalogue, I tried to trace many rare manuscripts, undoubtedly belonging to the Society, in European libraries. Sprenger was a German physician interested in Oriental studies, who in about 1854 prepared a catalogue of Persian manuscripts in

---

[45] Carl Brockelmann (1868–1956), *Geschichte der arabischen Litteratur* (Weimar, 1898–1902; 2nd ed., Leiden, 1943–1949); *Supplementbände* (Leiden, 1937–1942).

Northern India, including at the Asiatic Society of Bengal.[46] I tried to introduce micrometrical measurements of the elements of letters and thickness of paper but the lazy clerks found it too sophisticated and abandoned this practice. One of the most deplorable losses was the theft of Jami's autograph,[47] cut out from the collection of the autographs of the members of Mir Ali Shir Nawa'i's entourage by one of the rascal *iskolars*.[48] It has not yet been recovered and it is quite possible that it has been lost forever.

The collection of European reference books in the academic library of the Asiatic Society resembled the stock of a second-hand bookdealer. There was no system at all. In order to buy a book it was necessary to apply to the Council, which did not always allow the purchase. Thus, I often wrote directly to the authors in Europe and many of them were kind enough to send me their books free of charge. The late E. G. Browne,[49] Nicholson,[50] and some other scholars were among them.

---

[46] Aloys Sprenger (1813–1893), *A Catalogue of the Arabic, Persian and Hindustany Manuscripts of the Libraries of the King of Oudh*, vol. I (Calcutta, 1854).

[47] See items 61 and 92 in Appendix 1, Works of Ivanow. Abd al-Rahman Jami (1414–1492) was a Persian poet and Sufi; see P. Losensky et al., 'Jami', *EIR*, vol. 14, pp. 469–482.

[48] Mir Ali Shir Nawa'i (1441–1501), eminent Chaghatai Turkish poet and political figure of Central Asia during the Timurid period. He patronised the activities of numerous artists, poets and literati. See Maria Eva Subtelny, 'Mir Ali Shir Nawa'i', *EI2*, vol. 7, pp. 90–93.

[49] Edward Granville Browne (1862–1926), eminent British orientalist and doyen of Iranologists. Browne's life was spent almost entirely at the University of Cambridge, where he was the Sir Thomas Adams Professor of Arabic from 1902 until his death. He played a key role in promoting Persian studies in Europe. Browne's *A Literary History of Persia* (London and Cambridge, 1902–1924), 4 vols., based on original sources, remains a classic in the field. Browne also edited and translated a number of major Persian texts, published in the E. J. W. Gibb Memorial Series, in addition to cataloguing a number of manuscript collections at Cambridge; he also variously promoted Oriental studies at Cambridge. See R. A. Nicholson, 'Introduction, including Memoir and Bibliography', in E. G. Browne, *A Descriptive Catalogue of the Oriental Mss. Belonging to the late E. G. Browne*, ed. R. A. Nicholson (Cambridge, 1932), pp. vii–xxii; Arberry, *Oriental Essays*, pp. 160–196; C. Edmund Bosworth, 'Edward Granville Browne', in C. E. Bosworth, ed., *A Century of British Orientalists 1902–2001* (Oxford, 2001), pp. 74–86, and G. M. Wickens, 'Browne', *EIR*, vol. 4, pp. 483–485.

Unfortunately, *iskolar*s, *baboo*s and *maulvi-saheb*s were not the only dishonest people. One example speaks volumes. For nine years, despite all my requests, I was working without any contract or formal agreement. Presidents of the Society were appointed every January. They were elected with a total disregard to their suitability for this position. A person could be elected 'because he is a jolly good fellow', another because earlier he had helped to elect his friend. Often a wealthy speculator or profiteer was 'honoured' with the presidency in expectation of his financial donation to the Society. But in the case I want to describe I was dealing with a real *pukka* (to use an Indian idiom) academic.[51] I think he was a geologist with a very distinguished career and reputation. I went to him and explained what I wanted. He listened to me politely (such people are awfully polite), and said, 'My dear fellow, I fully realise your plight. But I have just been elected and first have to settle down and then I shall do for you what I can.' So far, so good. But four days later I read in a newspaper that Sir so-and-so had left for Europe for his ten-month leave and would not be returning because he was due to retire. So why did he lie to me? Why could he not tell me he was about to retire? These false promises are the worst kind of dishonesty. He was under no obligation to help me and if he could not do anything, what was the point of deceiving me? This was not an isolated incident, there were many even more serious cases in my life. Obviously these things did not inspire any respect for those concerned. But let us leave Calcutta, as there are people of the same spirit and conditions in other places.

---

[50] Reynold Alleyne Nicholson (1868–1945), British orientalist and outstanding scholar of Islamic mysticism. He studied Persian at Cambridge with E. G. Browne, and eventually succeeded his master at Pembroke College. Nicholson spent a lifetime studying Jalal al-Din Rumi (d. 1273), the greatest mystic poet of Islam and the Persian language. In 1907, Nicholson published his *A Literary History of the Arabs*, a companion to Browne's work on Persian literature. Subsequently, Nicholson wrote a number of works on Islamic mysticism. From 1920, Nicholson collected materials that led to his *magnum opus*, a complete edition and annotated translation of Rumi's *Mathnawi*, in eight volumes, published between 1925 and 1940 in the E. J. W. Gibb Memorial Series. See Arberry, *Oriental Essays*, pp. 197–232.

[51] *Pukka:* a Hindi term meaning 'genuine', 'authentic' or 'properly constructed'.

Eastern India

I have already mentioned that in 1930, due to some difficulties with the Asiatic Society of Bengal, I had to stop my work there. It was a great relief finally to get on the train and go to see my friend P. I. Mashmeer. I was travelling through a flat and swampy country with an occasional grove of coconut palms. The landscape is quite similar to that of western India. The railway went far from the seashore town of Poori, which is famous for the plague that started there as well as an old Hindu temple, which is often misspelled by foreigners as Jagernavat. It must read as Jagannath, which means 'The Lord of the World'. Everyone knows that during a certain holiday, which falls in mid-July, a temple chariot carries the statues of Hindu gods in a special procession. It is also told that some devotees throw themselves under the wheels of the huge vehicle to be crushed to death, believing that it will deliver them to Paradise. This is the result of ignorance and misunderstanding. I have never been to Poori and never seen this chariot myself but my friends tell me that similar vehicles, although smaller in size, may be found in every village temple in this part of Orissa. It seems that all these stories about people throwing themselves under the wheels are foreign fairy tales. The natives are very fond of alcohol and it is quite possible that all these martyrs are just drunkards falling under the chariot by accident. In any case, the Hindu concept of Paradise is quite different from European and Muslim ideas. I saw a similar chariot, or rather a cart, in Rayagada where I was staying with Mashmeer. There was a large crowd of people but no one threw himself under the wheels. It was very interesting to see the onlookers. They were Gonds, who are fairly dark in complexion.[52] On festive occasions, they paint their faces with something like a paste made of pounded sandalwood, leaving only large 'spectacles-like' circles around the eyes, which makes them look quite eerie. The chariot, which is a primitive vehicle the size of a big

---

[52] Representing the largest tribal groups in South Asia, the Gonds are scattered in many parts of central India, especially in the hills of Madhya Pradesh, where they established kingdoms. They are also found in eastern Maharashtra, Chhattisgarh, northern Andhra Pradesh and western Orissa. Their language is Dravidian, related to Tamil and Kanada. The designation of Gond, meaning hill, is used by outsiders; they refer to themselves as Koitur or Koi.

lorry, is usually kept in a shed. It is displayed only on such festivals. And the local Gonds are habitual drunkards, intoxicating themselves with fermented toddy juice.

Further south, the railway reaches the principality of Vizianagram. It is an interesting place to see, but it is necessary to obtain a permit to visit it. Near this locality, there is the seaport of Vishakhapatam, which is an important centre of shipbuilding. From this port the railway to Raypur begins. At that time, it was still under construction and there was only one daily train which I eventually took. The locals were Gonds but different from the Gonds of Baster in the north. There were also more urbanised groups of Telugu-speakers.[53] The Gond village is worth seeing. It looks like a long corridor with huts on both sides with their walls made of the panels of interwoven palm leaves. Thus, one can hear everything that is going on along this corridor.

At that time, Mashmeer was staying at the next station after Rayagada, called Satikona or Chatikona. To get there, it was necessary to cross the Nagavali River, which could become a serious obstacle during the rainy season. Since the bridge had not yet been built, we had to cross the river on a raft. Satikona was a picturesque place but not very comfortable to stay in because of the danger of the so-called black water fever or malaria. Like ordinary malaria, it spreads by anopheles mosquitoes but it also affects the bladder, causing bleeding. After the urine turns black because of the blood, death is inevitable within four hours since there is no cure. Because of that, all staff accommodation was protected with mosquito nets and by the orders of special malaria-protection doctors, kerosene was poured into swamps and ponds in order to kill the mosquitoes. It was a very quiet and hot place. Eventually, we were ordered to move to Rayagada, in order to keep as little workforce as possible in Satikona. The train, which was our only link with civilisation, came at 4 o'clock, bringing mail, newspapers and occasionally the railway authorities, for whom a special guestroom was kept in the building. The railway rented a house built by a missionary organisation. Their experiment in salvation failed since alcoholism and poverty were on the rise. But the missionaries were built solidly, ate plenty and dressed well. The contrast with their pauperised, under-

---

[53] Telugu belongs to the Dravidian family of languages, and is spoken predominantly in the state of Andhra Pradesh.

nourished converts, clad in rags, was especially striking when they talked of brotherhood.

Native men were of no use at the construction site since they were too lazy and usually sent their women to work. They worked as porters but carried very little in their hands. The following story can illustrate the local morals. On a very hot day, I stood with a Punjabi contractor in the shadow of a tree. Under the neighbouring tree, a large group of children was visibly suffering in the heat. I said to the contractor, who had been living in this locality for a long time, that it was rather stupid of these women to bring their children with them in such heat. He replied that it was not stupidity but rather a necessity. All these children were girls and their mothers were afraid to leave them behind fearing that drunkards would rape them. The people there became real brutes. They would send their women to work and when the women brought home their hard-earned money, the men took it by force and beat their wives. Missionary activity did not improve anything. Very often drunkards tried to stop cars and extort money for alcohol by standing in the middle of the road with their arms wide open. Everything looked hopeless. Physical degeneration was very visible, especially among women, who, despite their undernourishment, began to give birth very early, even at the age of nine. Here is, in reality, the fairyland of India.

I spent my time in Rayagada working and waiting for the decision on my future employment. During that time I prepared a considerable portion of my work for publication. Since it was too hot it was impossible to go for a walk during the daytime. But it was necessary to return home before dark because of dangerous snakes that crawled on every path in the evening. These snakes are deaf and they do not move away when you approach them, but then can attack a passer-by. And their venom is deadly. The following story was quite popular in that time. An engineer and his wife had a party. The lady went to her room and noticed a thin stick on her dressing table. She tried to pick it up but suddenly the stick started to move. She screamed, the guests rushed in but failed to find the snake. Of course, there were also many bigger snakes. There were also plenty of termites, also called 'white ants', although they are not ants. They build hollow structures looking like Gothic cathedrals, which the snakes often used as their nests.

I had many similar and quite fantastic impressions. Soon after we had moved from Satikona to Rayagada, I saw Mashmeer in a really agitated state. I asked him what was the matter and he replied, 'This damned black panther again. One more guard just resigned.' There was a bridge less than one kilometre from the station and it was necessary to keep a guard there. A house with a walled courtyard was built by the bridge and a guard with his family had settled there. Soon after that, the guard began to complain that at night it was impossible to go outside to answer the 'call of nature', since a dangerous black panther scoured the area. Several guards had already resigned and now one more had just left his job.

I saw a black panther, even two, in Bombay zoological garden. It is a rare beast, even in India, and it seems to be larger than the ordinary leopard which mainly hunts dogs. Nearby there were extensive groves of wild mango trees. It was a great nuisance since ripe fruit fell to the ground and stuck to one's soles. Besides, they attracted swarms of flies and monkeys, which greatly damaged the adjacent fields. Monkeys, snakes, rats and some other obnoxious animals are sacred to the Hindus if somebody kills them it may cause a great row. But the greatest wreckers are domestic cows, which are let loose for religious reasons. They are simply everywhere and they ruin crops and damage everything. But since they are considered sacred, to slaughter them for their meat is a great offence.

However, people may become accustomed to anything, even this zoological entourage. During my six-month stay in this wilderness, I began to feel very much at home there. So when the time came to return to 'civilisation', I began packing with some regret at leaving for Bombay. A big city with all its traffic, noise and shops appeared an unpleasant prospect.

Of all the Indian cities which I had visited, Bombay was undoubtedly the cleanest and, in a sense, the most picturesque. The surrounding landscape, the sea and comparatively prosperous appearance of its inhabitants, incomparable with that of the people of Calcutta, contributed to Bombay's beauty. Both Bombay and Calcutta are tremendous ethnological museums, each of them corresponding to its own part of India. There is a fascinating variety of human types among the 4.5 million inhabitants of Bombay. There are people from all parts of India and even from neighbouring countries. An observant ethnologist may find a profusion of material for his research. However, it is rather difficult to really get to know everything and find something that is really interesting. This task requires a long residence and good contacts. I stayed there for almost 30 years, from the beginning of 1931 until April 1959, and occasionally I was lucky to find something rare and interesting, such as spoken dialects from the Persian Gulf islands or the southern provinces of Persia, or even Afghanistan. It was possible in Bombay to meet people from Badakhshan,[54] and Hunza,[55] as well as from some other faraway place.

Calcutta is full of eastern Indians. There is even a Chinatown in the city with traditional shoemakers, shops, restaurants and Buddhist priests, as well as old customs such as binding women's feet. Fortunately, the latter custom is now discarded in China itself. One could even find Tibetans, Lepchus,[56] Nepalese, Assamese and Burmese in Calcutta. Nowadays, after the Chinese aggression against India, Chinatown has disappeared and its inhabitants have been expelled. I tried to establish contacts with the members of these minority groups but eventually I found it very difficult and time-consuming, since the people I was interested in were always shy and suspicious. They were

---

[54] Badakhshan is the name of a region in Central Asia situated between the Upper Amu Dayra, or Oxus, to the north, the Hindu Kush to the south and the Konduz River to the west. At present, Badakhshan is divided, along the Oxus, between Tajikistan and Afghanistan. The majority of the Persian-speaking inhabitants of Badakhshan belong to the Nizari branch of Ismailism. See X. de Planhol's 'Badakšan. i. Geography and Ethnography', *EIR*, vol. 3, pp. 355–360. See also note 76 in Chapter 3.

[55] Hunza is the name of a region in the extreme west of the Karakoram range of mountains, lying between Gilgit in the south, Iskhoman in the west, Afghan Wakhan in the north and Chinese Turkestan (or Xinjiang) in the east. Hunza was ruled independently for several centuries, by a family of *mir*s who had their seat in Baltit (now renamed Karimabad), until 1974, when the region became part of the federal state of Pakistan. The Hunzakuts have, since the 1820s, belonged to the Nizari branch of Ismailism, calling themselves Mawla'is. See W. Holzwarth, *Die Ismailiten in Nordpakistan* (Berlin, 1994), especially pp. 19–78; F. M. Hunzai, 'A Living Branch of Islam: Ismailis of the Mountains of Hunza', *Oriente Moderno*, NS, 23 (2004), pp. 147–160, and S. Bianca, ed., *Karakoram: Hidden Treasures in the Northern Areas of Pakistan* (Geneva, 2005).

[56] Lepchus, more correctly Lepchas, or the Lepcha people, are the indigenous people found mainly in the Indian state of Sikkim. They are also found in western Bengal, and in the neighbouring regions of Bhutan, Tibet and eastern Nepal.

unable to understand the very concept of academic interest free of any political or commercial objectives. Thus, they always suspected a hidden agenda. Occasionally, I came across some colourful figures like a certain turbaned Sheikh Kazem in Bombay, who was jokingly described by his friends as the head of the pirates and smugglers of the Trucial coast. He even published a navigation map of the Persian Gulf giving its depths and other useful information. It was undoubtedly compiled from British maps and simply translated into Persian. I also met people of faraway and isolated Kafiristan, known as the Safid-push [or white attired] Kafirs. In order to find these people and approach them without frightening them away one needs a long 'training' and plenty of time. However, the results are very often unrewarding. India provides an enormous field of study, which is difficult to manage single-handedly, despite the abundance of statistical and reference literature published by the British government.

It is interesting just to stop in a street and watch the crowd passing by. Bombay is situated on a group of small basalt islands with the gaps between them filled with soil. Thus it is a relatively small place and the bulk of its four and a half million people live in numerous suburbs connected to the city by electric railways. Trains arrive every three to five minutes at the central station, bringing crowds of working people every morning and taking them away every afternoon. A Persian friend of mine, who saw it for the first time, was convinced that he was witnessing an enormous political rally where all types of dress, colour of skin and general outlook were displayed. A tremendous proportion of the people bear the signs of degeneration. It especially applies to the Parsis, known as fire-worshippers, namely Indians of allegedly Persian [Zoroastrian] origin.[57] According to the statistical data, there are

---

[57] The name Parsi, meaning Persian, is given to those descendants of Zoroastrians who migrated to India, chiefly to Gujarat, from the 10th century. From the 17th century, with the arrival of European traders in western India, the Parsis emerged from their obscurity to positions of considerable wealth and high educational standards. Henceforth, the Parsis became leaders in Indian industrial development and politics. However, the Parsi community in South Asia has been on the decline; according to the 1981 census, they numbered only around 70,000 throughout India. Parsi communities now also exist on all continents. See John R. Hinnells, 'Parsis', *EI2*, vol. 8, pp. 273–275, and his 'Bombay. i. The Zoroastrian Community', *EIR*, vol. 4, pp. 339–346.

approximately 100,000 of them mainly in the Bombay area. About 15 per cent of them are lunatics, and there are also many people approaching lunacy. The community is fully aware of this and those who can afford it sometimes take steps to 'improve the race'. Under British rule, wealthy families often tolerated young wives having affairs with young European police officers, who 'fertilised' them. The results appeared to be good – children looking like southern Europeans.

Occasionally, one could witness strange things. I would like to describe here something which I never saw again. I was sitting waiting for the proofs of a lithographed Persian text. I could see a passage between some tall buildings inhabited by poor families. It was hot and the place was dirty with pools of smelly liquid and rags hanging from the windows. In such a place I suddenly saw a little girl, six or seven years old, who came to look at the stranger – me. I had never seen such a beautiful human being, everything in the child was absolutely perfect from the aesthetical point of view. I terribly regretted that I had no camera with me. She was such a flower growing on a heap of rubbish. Of course, I could not ask her about her caste or parents. Generally speaking, Indians are not very handsome people. They look better only in places where they have mixed with Iranians, like the Punjabis and in general people of the western provinces.

I have already written about the foundation of the 'Islamic Research Association'. One of its founding members was Asaf Ali Asghar Faizi [Fyzee], a Sulaymani Bohra by religion (an Ismaili, but belonging to a different branch from the Aga Khan's followers). He was a lawyer by profession and a graduate of the University of Cambridge. He belonged to the large family of intellectuals known as Tayabji-Hydari-Faizi. In their own western part of India they played the same role as the family of the famous poet Rabindranath Tagore played in Bengal in the east.[58] The mother of A. Faizi was one of the eight daughters of Justice Badruddin Tayabji, the Chief Justice of Bombay and one of the founders of the Indian Congress [Party]. Later on, Asaf Faizi himself became the Indian ambassador to Egypt and then the Vice-Chancellor of the University of Kashmir and Jammu [in Srinagar]. He is retired now but still continues his work on Ismaili law. He owns a house and

---

[58] Rabindranath Tagore (1861–1941), Bengali poet and writer who won the Nobel Prize for literature in 1913.

estate on the opposite shore of the Bay of Bombay, near the fishing village of Kihim. This is probably the most charming and admirable place that I had the chance to see in India. Faizi's house stands in a magnificent area surrounded by reefs. At high spring tides, the waves almost reach the veranda of Faizi's house, but this happens only when the tide is higher than 16 feet. The owner would often invite me to his enchanting place, and sometimes I would go in summer to stay there alone and work on my books.[59]

The whole atmosphere of that homely corner was saturated with the spirit of Ivan Turgenev's [1818–1883] novels describing old and restful estates. I can vividly remember our quiet conversations on the veranda with the sound of the tide in the background. From time to time our conversation would be interrupted by a definitely 'sarcastic' shout, 'Eghe!' It was a small bird of the owl family, which had a nest in the bushes of the garden. But during my later visits I did not hear this sarcastic voice again – the bird was gone. But such idyllic moments were quite rare in my life in Bombay. About 3 km from us, one could see in the mountains, inside the jungle, the Hindu temple of Maheshwari, which was often visited by pilgrims. But at night it was impossible to see the temple. Quiet and peaceful Kihim was an escape from hectic life, for the Faizi family and guests alike.

Northern India

During my student years, I was very interested in India and for three years I studied Sanskrit with Professor F. Shcherbatskoi, who later became a Member of the Academy of Sciences, and Professor Baron A. A. von Stael-Holstein.[60] After the Russian Revolution, the latter went to China and became a professor at Peking University specialising in the Sanskrit language. The Sanskrit literature is too rich to be

---

[59] On A. A. A. Fyzee (Faizi), see note 91 in Chapter 3.

[60] Alexander von Stael-Holstein (1877–1937), Russian scholar of Sanskrit, Sinologist and expert in the study of Buddhist texts. A lecturer in Sanskrit at St Petersburg University, he left Russia permanently for China during World War I. He taught Sanskrit at Peking University during 1918–1929, also serving as a visiting professor for a stint at Harvard University. See S. Elisséeff, 'Stael-Holstein's Contributions to Asiatic Studies', *Harvard Journal of Asiatic Studies*, 3 (1938), pp. 1–8.

comprehensively studied. Because of the sheer quantity of written material, which is not always of high quality, it does not matter how much work you do, there always remains something unstudied. I must mention that India was one of the things that compelled me to take up Oriental studies. I can vaguely remember from the years of my early childhood how my mother, herself a good student of Russian history, told me the story of the Russian medieval merchant Afanasii Nikitin from the city of Tver, who in 1466–1472 travelled to India via Persia, just as I did myself. Unlike me, he went to southern India, the area I was not very much interested in. However, I visited some of the places he mentioned in his book *Khozhdenie za tri moria* (A Journey Beyond Three Seas). Like Nikitin, I saw Gulbarga and some other places in central India. I read his travelogue published by the late Professor I. P. Minaev many times.[61]

Benares, the *ghats* on the River Ganges, late 19th century

At the end of July 1914, I started my tour from Calcutta to Benares, the holy city of the Hindus, seeing all its wonders and antiquities. Benares, the ancient city of Kashi, is for the Indians like Mecca for the Muslims. The most interesting part of the city is the riverfront with its *ghats*,[62] steps leading to the holy bathing places in the Ganges River. Perhaps the Dashashwamedh and the Manikarnika Ghats can be considered as architectural sites, whereas others are just tumbles of steps. The site should be visited with a good guide, someone who can recount the legends related to every *ghat*. At the time of my visit, such guides did not exist. The bazaars are also quite fascinating.

---

[61] Ivan Pavlovich Minaev (1840–1890), Russian orientalist and leading pioneer of Indian studies in Russia. Minaev conducted research in India, Nepal and Burma on the cultures, languages, literatures, ethnography and folklore of the South Asian peoples. See his collected works entitled *Ivan Pavlovich Minaev: Sbornik statei*, ed. G. G. Kotovskii (Moscow, 1967).

[62] *Gat*, more appropriately *ghat*, a Hindi term referring to the point where water meets the shore. Usually *ghats* have steps leading down to a body of water, particularly in the case of the holy rivers, such as the famous *ghats* of Benares.

They should be seen at dusk when the shops are lit and you can see everything inside. During one such walk, I saw a ceremonial procession headed by a *maharani* (princess) returning from a temple. I have never seen anything like that again. Nowadays princesses prefer motorcars to walking.

Generally speaking, Benares is not a particularly beautiful place and in daytime it looks rather dull and grey. I hired a boat and went to see the city and all its sacred buildings from the river, but nothing caught my eye. I hunted for books and was told to search for them in the Muslim part of the city. There were many Muslims and the absurd minarets of the mosques built by the sadist Awrangzib towered above the shrines.[63] This was my only visit to Benares. From there I went to Lucknow. The glories of this city have often been described and photographed. My first impression faded since after that I revisited the city many times when I went there to buy manuscripts. Because of its architecture and lifestyle, it looks like a Muslim city rather than a Hindu one. It might be interesting to describe my experiences during these book-buying missions.

When I went on my initial book-buying mission, first of all I had to go to the bazaar. The main bazaar of Lucknow, Chandni Chowk, is not very large. It is uncovered, with two-storey houses where the ground floors are occupied by shops; many of them are bookshops, while the upper floors are taken by prostitutes. This is a common Indian combination. After some rather rude refusals to show me manuscripts, I eventually found one and thus started my 'trade'. I did not buy much during my first visit but later I managed to obtain many good books there.

This is what I remember about the year 1927. The booksellers did not consider me a serious buyer. Accidentally, I came across a stationery shop, which had one manuscript, a collection of prayers. I paid good money for it and the trade started. The next day two men began to follow me. They were *dallals*, or brokers. Finally, they asked where I was staying and next morning they were waiting at the

---

[63] Awrangzib was the only Mughal emperor of India to launch major waves of persecution against the Ismailis and other Shi'i Muslims, both during his governorship of Gujarat and after ascending to the Mughal throne in 1658. He died in 1707. See W. Irvine and M. Habib, 'Awrangzib', *EI2*, vol. 1, pp. 768–769.

door of my hotel. One of them was a young Muslim who called himself a Pathan, obviously lying, and the other one was an old Hindu with one of his legs swollen by elephantiasis [gross enlargement due to lymphatic obstruction]. They had already found some private sellers and were anxious to take me there in order to get their commission. We took a taxi to a narrow back street, where my guardian angels began to knock at the door of a new house. The owner opened the door and invited us to an empty room without a single chair. He disappeared for a long time. I felt irritated but the 'angels' assured me that a chair would be brought soon. Then the owner came back, still without a chair, and invited us to another room. In the corner there was a heap of rubbish and debris. The owner disappeared again but soon came back with a long stick! It was really very annoying, but suddenly the owner began to dig out manuscripts from the heap with his stick. There were some interesting finds and so my visit was not wasted.

We went to a suburb to an old, dilapidated house. My guides took me to a heap of earth and started shouting. A girl, approximately eight years old, appeared on the roof. She was wearing a very long *chador*, the veil worn by Muslim women when they go out, and enormous slippers, which on her feet looked like skis. She came to the edge of the roof and invited us to climb to the roof where it was safer. Then she took us to an empty room with a single *charpay*. This is what the Indians call a sort of bed or bench with the seat made of interwoven rope. The girl in her mantle with a train and ski-like slippers went behind the curtain into the next room and brought out a small bundle of papers. Everything around looked so hopelessly poor and I began to examine the papers, determined to buy something if it was possible. Unfortunately, what she brought was complete rubbish – fragments, as the booksellers call them. I regretfully gave the papers back to the girl; she dived behind the curtain and returned carrying something small in her hands. It was a manuscript copy of the Koran, fairly modern and not worth buying. It was the last thing these people could offer for sale. The wind swept the curtain away – there stood an exceptionally tall old woman, the *bibi*. Apparently the girl put on her *chador* and slippers. I took out a five-rupee note and prepared to leave. My guides quite unashamedly rushed to the old woman to demand their 'commission'. It was an extremely unpleasant scene to watch.

Our next visit was to the doctors. It was a clean house with a large tidy room, and the floor was covered with a good carpet where there were placed several small low tables and desks. Several serious-looking men in decent dark clothes were sitting squatted on the floor. They began to produce books for sale. The books were clean, not worm-eaten, well bound, everything appeared respectable and serious. However, the books themselves were not interesting. But I asked for a price – 'Four hundred rupees', was the answer. It was ridiculous.

'And this?'

'Two hundred.'

And it went on and on like that. I rose and politely told them that I had no time for joking. They protested:

'You want to go without buying anything?'

'All right, I shall take something.'

And I picked up a lithographed brochure without even looking at it. Then I saw that I did not have it in my collection.

'How much?'

The doctors looked at each other, whispering and nodding their heads. The oldest of them said:

'Sixty rupees.'

'All right, goodbye.'

'No, no. You say how much you want to pay.'

'A quarter of a rupee.'

'Only that little?'

'Yes, the original price is printed here and it is half a rupee. It is a second-hand book. So I am offering you half the original price.'

'It is not fair', they whispered among themselves. 'All right, let us reconsider.'

Now the books were reasonably priced and I bought quite a good lot of them without overpaying.

We continued our journey and stopped in front of a big old house with a monumental gate. My guides told me that the owner's father and grandfather had been men of high rank. One of the halves of the gate opened and revealed a tiny girl. She was absolutely naked with only a silver chain on her belly. She looked at us and ran away into the house. Then came out a respectably dressed Hindu, and invited us to come in. The room, or rather hall, was absolutely empty and the man left to bring his books. It looked as if we were wasting our time. He returned with a textbook of official correspondence styles. It did not even have a cover and it had been lithographed many times.

'How much?'
'Six thousand rupees.'
'Thank you!'
'My grandfather copied it.'
'Keep it as a family relic.'

Everything can happen when you buy books from very different people. Once I even bought books from a blind man who came to my hotel. He was a member of the nobility, apparently in need of money. He brought me a few manuscripts and one of them was quite interesting. He correctly recognised individual manuscripts, apparently by their size, and I bought the interesting one at a reasonable price. But sometimes ridiculous things could also happen. Somebody can bring a handwritten textbook of geometry and ask for a fantastic price claiming that the drawings are 'miniatures'.

North-western India

Let us travel back in time to July 1914. Having visited Benares and Lucknow, I then went to Agra. Its famous architecture has been photographed and described many times. The most famous building there, the Taj Mahal, was popularised in millions of soapstone replicas sold in the bazaars. Yet it was still necessary to take a personal look at it, in order not to regret it later. So I thought, being sure that it was my first and last visit to India. I arrived in Agra in the morning. The monsoon rain was falling so strongly that it was difficult to get to the hotel. But after lunch the skies cleared up and I went sightseeing. I was most impressed by the Moti Masjid, the 'Pearl Mosque', in the fort. The rain had washed it thoroughly and I could see it in all its splendour and glory. It was a relatively small building of white marble. It displayed such a noble simplicity unspoilt by ornamentation that it looked like a

Agra, early 20th century

sculpture, a real jewel. It began to rain heavily again and I had to seek refuge in the hotel. Next morning, I headed to the nearby Muttra (it should be spelled Mathura), a sacred place near the famous site of Brindiban, where Krishna worked the miracle of 'dancing' simultaneously with 500 *gopies*, women tending to cows. Of course, the word 'dance' is used euphemistically. Summing it all up, there was nothing interesting and I went on to Delhi. At that time, Delhi, or New Delhi, was not yet regarded as the capital. The [British] viceroys stayed in Calcutta in the winter and Darjeeling in the summer. During my stay in India, I revisited Delhi on many occasions, mainly to attend some allegedly learned gatherings. The medieval sites in the vicinity of Delhi were much more interesting than the city itself. For example, the place called Nizamuddin,[64] which is the shrine of a medieval Sufi saint who died in 1325. I intended to write something about him. There, I met an interesting man called Hasan Nizami, a notable Urdu writer, who claimed to be a descendant of the saint. I do not know whether he is still alive. At that time, he was young and could speak understandable Persian. We met again during my subsequent visits to Delhi. I saw him for the last time in 1944.

Before World War I, Delhi was an important centre for the lithographic publishing of popular books in Persian and Urdu, mainly biographies of saints, poetry and so forth. One could find much of this stuff in the shops of the smelly street parallel to the main artery, Chandni Chowk. Now they are all gone. Apparently Delhi was never famous for its cleanliness. The Jum'a Masjid – the Friday Mosque – opposite the Red Fort, is worth seeing but half of it is hidden behind the dirty small shops of the sellers of old rugs and every other kind of rubbish. During one of my visits to Delhi, I met the city's 'mayor' at a party. I bluntly asked him why his municipality could not do something about this scandalous state of affairs. He was a businessman. In India, this implies education no higher than that of primary school. And he told me that 'this filth' brings the city 1,000 rupees

---

[64] Nizam al-Din Awliya (d. 1325) was a venerated master of the Chishti Sufi order. He expanded this Sufi *tariqa* in India and transformed it for mass spiritual culture. His mausoleum or *dargah* in Delhi is visited annually by large numbers of Muslims, Hindus and followers of other religions. See K. A. Nizami, *The Life and Times of Shaykh Nizam al-Din Awliya* (Delhi, 1991); his 'Nizam al-Din Awliya', *EI2*, vol. 8, p. 68, and L. Dhaul, *The Dargah of Nizamuddin Auliya* (New Delhi, 2006).

every year. It was amazing and I asked him whether it was impossible to find enough wealthy and patriotically minded people who could raise 1,000 rupees to get rid of this disgraceful situation. But obviously to discuss this issue with him was a waste of time. I have heard from recent visitors to Delhi that everything remains as it was in 1914.

I visited Lahore and Amritsar several times. Lahore was an important centre of lithographic printing and before World War I its products, as well as those of Bombay, were sold as far as Tashkent. To an extent, books are still printed there but on a more modest scale and rarely in Persian. When I was there in 1914, I visited a local celebrity called Iqbal,[65] an advocate, who at that time was gaining popularity for his philosophising versification in Persian. Initially, I took him quite seriously and wanted to discuss with him matters of Indian Sufism and Sufi literature, but eventually I found him to be very poorly informed on these subjects. He wanted to discuss politics and asked me why the Russians persecute the Muslims. I asked him where he had come across this information. He replied, 'We also read newspapers.' I told him it was nonsense to talk about mass persecution since there were many Muslims of high military rank [in Russia] and what was written in his newspapers was obviously British propaganda. He was not convinced and we parted. My impression of Lahore was that of a second-hand market, huge and crowded at the time. I have been there a few times and have bought from there an attractive collection of manuscripts, even after I was told that the local university had bought all the available manuscripts.

I was always very interested in Multan, because it was the earliest centre of general Islamic and Fatimid Ismaili propaganda in India.[66]

---

[65] Muhammad Iqbal (1877–1938), leading Persian and Urdu poet of India in the first half of the 20th century. He studied philosophy and law at Cambridge University, and subsequently spent most of his life in Lahore as a lawyer. Iqbal's ideas were instrumental in the formation of Pakistan, as he was interested in awakening the self-consciousness of Muslims. Iqbal was a prolific author, and there is also an extensive corpus of works on him. See D. Tailleu, ed., *A Descriptive Bibliography of Allama Muhammad Iqbal (1877–1938)* (Louvain, 2000); Annemarie Schimmel, *Gabriel's Wing: A Study into the Religious Ideas of Sir Muhammad Iqbal* (Leiden, 1963), and her 'Iqbal', *EIR*, vol. 13, pp. 197–200.

[66] See Samuel M. Stern, 'Isma'ili Propaganda and Fatimid Rule in Sind', *Islamic Culture*, 23 (1949), pp. 298–307; reprinted in his *Studies in Early Isma'ilism* (Jerusalem

I went there and was put up in a Eurasian boarding house, where I apparently caught malaria. I must point out that this was July 1914 and things at that time were quite different. It was terribly hot and Multan is notorious for its heat. At once I went looking for dervishes who could understand Persian. I did not know their local dialect and they did not speak Urdu. I came across one of them, who could understand Persian a little. He was an old man wearing only a heavy iron chain and a piece of cloth in front. He owned an interesting *risala*, a collection of poems and prose notes on Sufi matters. It was very tempting to buy it for the Asiatic Museum but although the saint did not mind my inspection of the book, he flatly refused to sell it. Instead, he insisted on displaying his 'miraculous power'. Actually he played some childish tricks by piercing his tongue and cheeks in the places where he already had some old holes.

I was told there was a wealthy man in the city who owned a good library, which he was gradually selling. I took the address and went to see him. He was an elderly man speaking fluent English, apparently a retired official. He received me warmly and showed his treasure but there was nothing exciting in it. From the way he was talking, I got the sense that his prices would be awfully inflated. To make things smoother, I decided to use some diplomacy and said something flattering about his books. Then I told him that I had something urgent to do, and might return the next day. He replied that he was very upset at not being able to entertain me properly. 'As you know,' continued my host, 'it is the month of Ramazan and nothing was cooked today. So we shall do it like that,' and he took out his purse and put ten silver rupees on the table, one by one. It was quite a substantial sum at the time. Then he turned to me and said, 'Please, take the money and go to the best restaurant and have a meal on me.' I began to explain that I perfectly understood his position and highly appreciated his feelings but the food in my boarding house was quite good, and I could not accept his money.

---

and Leiden, 1983), pp. 177–188; A. Hamdani, *The Beginnings of the Isma'ili Da'wa in Northern India* (Cairo, 1956); Ansar Z. Khan, 'Isma'ilism in Multan and Sind', *Journal of the Pakistan Historical Society*, 23 (1975), pp. 36–57, and Derryl N. Maclean, *Religion and Society in Arab Sind* (Leiden, 1989), pp. 126–140.

Such expressions of hospitality are, or rather were, quite common in India. Several years later in Hyderabad (Deccan), I invited several local learned Ismailis to tea in my hotel. I offered them tea and sweet cakes and they seemed to enjoy these quite well. When they left I went downstairs to pay for their tea. To my astonishment, the cashier refused to take my money, saying that my guests had already paid for the tea! I went to one of them to protest but he replied that they were local people and I was their guest. Therefore, they had to entertain me, not the other way around. And they resolutely refused my offer of a reimbursement.

A little more about Multan. I returned there in 1934. It had changed beyond recognition. The dervishes were gone, modern buildings had appeared and a cinema had opened. Many traces of the past had disappeared. I particularly wanted to find some information about the ruins of ancient Multan. However, I managed to see only the small, and obviously very modern, temple of Keshavpuri, the ancient Indian solar deity Kasyapapuri, whose qualities had been transferred to Shams-i Tabrizi,[67] a Sufi saint who is the protagonist of many fantastic legends. No trace of the ancient grand centre of worship could be found.

As already mentioned, my original plans to return to Russia via Multan and Colombo, and then by a Russian boat travelling from Vladivostok to Odessa, were changed by the war. Instead, I went to Karachi and from there travelled by train to St Petersburg via Bushir [Bushihr], Tehran and Turkestan. I returned to Calcutta only at the

---

[67] Shams-i Tabrizi is the name given to an enigmatic mystic who served as the spiritual guide of Jalal al-Din Rumi (d. 1273), the celebrated Persian mystic and poet. Shams met Rumi in Konya in the mid-1240s. Shams disappeared mysteriously, perhaps murdered, in 1247. Shams-i Tabrizi has been claimed as a co-religionist by the Ismailis, and a shrine under his name exists in Multan. However, the Shams buried in Multan may be identified with an Ismaili *pir*, Shams al-Din. See W. Ivanow, 'Shums Tabrez of Multan', in S. M. Abdullah, ed., *Professor Muhammad Shafi Presentation Volume* (Lahore, 1955), pp. 109–118; Tazim R. Kassam, *Songs of Wisdom and Circles of Dance: Hymns of the Satpanth Isma'ili Muslim Saint, Pir Shams* (Albany, NY, 1995), pp. 75–116; Z. Moir, 'The Life and Legends of Pir Shams as Reflected in the Ismaili Ginans: A Critical Review', in F. Mallison, ed., *Constructions hagiographiques dans le monde Indien. Entre mythe et histoire* (Paris, 2001), pp. 365–384; I. K. Poonawala, 'Pir Shams or Shams al-Din', *EI2*, vol. 8, p. 307, and Annemarie Schimmel, 'Shams-i Tabriz', *EI2*, vol. 9, p. 298.

end of 1920, and stayed there until June 1930. During these ten years I had the chance to visit many Indian cities and in 1928 even travelled to Persia. Thus ended my 'voyage beyond the seas', the Derbent (Caspian Sea), Hormuz (Persian Gulf) and the Hindustan Sea (Arabian Sea of the Indian Ocean), which had been visited by Afanasii Nikitin. But my own voyage did not stop at that point, for I again went to Persia and India.

I have already described my impressions of Lucknow and Hyderabad. Just a few words about some Hyderabadi customs. In 1926, I went to Hyderabad to buy books and a friend of mine invited me to meet some local intellectuals. I arrived on time and went through the exchange of all sorts of saccharine complimentaries. Then suddenly all 20 guests left. Only the host, his relative and myself remained. I asked what the matter was. They assured me that nothing had happened, the guests had drunk their tea and therefore had left. Nevertheless, this appeared strange to me and I made enquiries. It transpired that according to the Hyderabadi 'protocol', the guests invited to tea should take only one cup and then must clear away; to remain longer is considered impolite. When I protested that all over the world people gather together to meet each other and exchange opinions, not just to have a cup of tea, he replied that these were their ways and they could not change it. So never again did I accept an invitation to a tea party!

I also had an interesting experience in Kalimpong in the foothills of the Himalayas. Being exhausted by the terrible climate of Calcutta, I went there to recuperate for almost three months as a 'paying guest' in St Andrew's Colonial Homes. It was a grand charitable and missionary institution looking after, and educating, approximately 600 'accidental children' ranging from babies to 16-year-old adolescents. Scottish missionaries, Dr Graham and his wife, spent their lives founding and running this institution. It should be noted that the principal suppliers of these homes were the neighbouring tea plantations where women worked. Dr Graham routinely toured the nearby plantations and demanded contributions from the owners towards the maintenance of his institution. Everything was excellently organised. Apart from the school, there were a hospital, a farm and workshops. After graduation, students of both sexes were sent to Australia by special arrangement, where they were given jobs. Only five old men were employed there, but 82 women, mainly old Scottish spinsters, worked at the homes. So the amount of gossip and intrigue was colossal. The small market-town of Kalimpong is the last Indian outpost on the way to Tibet via the small principality of Sikkim [situated between Nepal and Bhutan], which neighbours China. The natives of this locality are known as the Lepchu, who speak not an Indian but an Indo-Chinese language. The general atmosphere there is Buddhist and there are many goods imported from China. Darjeeling, a town some 30 km away, at that time was gradually Westernising.

I rented a good room from the family of one of the few married teachers in the homes. From my window I could see Bhutan, another small Himalayan principality. Unlike Sikkim, it was closed to foreigners with the only exception being for high-ranking British Indian officials on official visits. The elevations in the area vary dramatically. While Kalimpong is at an altitude of only 4,000 feet, which is the same as Tehran, Darjeeling is at 7,000 feet. All the hills are covered with thick forests looked after by the Forestry Department. Without the department's permit, one could not even cut a tree in one's own garden. The landscape was as beautiful as any mountain landscape can be, but there were no flowers and fruit trees. There were some wild orchids, but not many of them. It was also the realm of leeches. They were everywhere in the grass. When a leech is on you, you cannot feel it, but it was rather normal to find on returning from a walk that your socks were soaked in blood. When a leech sucks enough of your blood, it falls off, but the tiny wound caused by it continues to bleed for some time. It is said that there are poisonous leeches whose bites cause inflammation, but I have never seen them.

There are also enormous varieties of insects, especially the [transparent-winged large insects] of the cicada family. According to Lepchu folklore, some of them 'shout' 're-re-re' and some 'ri-ri-ri'. Of course, they do not 'shout' but rather make a specific noise, like crickets. There is also an abundance of snakes, both poisonous and not, as well as a great variety of animals, but surprisingly there are no termites or ants, apparently due to the soil conditions, which are quite different from those of eastern India. There is a peculiar local bird called 'brain fever'. It was named so because its singing resembles this phrase and to hear it is considered a bad omen. Fine Chinese porcelain cups and silk as well as some other exotic objects were sold in the bazaar of Kalimpong. The city also had a Buddhist temple, and Buddhist monks were often seen on the streets.

Western India

My move to western India gave me the opportunity to meet the people who had remained under Islamic influence for a longer time, while at the same time being initially moulded by original Hinduism. It resulted in an interesting combination. I succeeded in what only a few could achieve, that is, establishing lasting contacts with various sects like the Ismailis and the Shaktis,[68] who usually do not welcome strangers. In doing this, I always followed the rule 'if the mountain does not come to Mahomet, then Mahomet can come to the mountain', as formulated by the founder of experimental methodology Sir Francis Bacon (1561-1626). All previous writings on the history and doctrines of the Ismailis were based on hearsay or the partisan accounts where deliberate lies were repeated for 'the glorification of God'. This 'pious' work has not stopped and the original sources of the sect are still labelled as 'propaganda'. Therefore, the Ismailis require that their adepts must not reveal their religious beliefs, literature and way of life. Due to favourable circumstances, I was very lucky to do what had never been done before, that is, to gain access to a substantial portion of secret Ismaili literature. Two prominent persons, themselves Ismailis belonging to two different branches, rendered me invaluable help. The first was the head of the Khoja Ismaili sect, the late Sir Sultan Muhammad Shah, Aga Khan [III], a man of creative mind and excellent education. He realised the harmful effects of retaining traditional secrecy in modern times and therefore abolished it.[69] The other outstanding Ismaili was a Sulaymani Bohra, Sir Akbar

---

[68] In Sanskrit, Shakti means 'power', or 'energy'. In Hindu tradition, Shakti symbolises the Goddess in her variegated forms, depicted sometimes as the divine consort of a particular god. The term Shaktas refers to the devotees of Shakti.

[69] On the reform policies of Aga Khan III, see M. Ruthven, 'Aga Khan III and the Isma'ili Renaissance', in Peter B. Clarke, ed., *New Trends and Developments in the World of Islam* (London, 1998), pp. 371-395; M. Boivin, *La rénovation du Shi'isme Ismaélien en Inde et au Pakistan. D'après les écrits et les discours de Sultan Muhammad Shah Aga Khan (1902-1954)* (London, 2003), and his *L'âghâ khân et les Khojah* (Paris, 2013). See also note 80 in Chapter 3.

Hydari,[70] the Prime Minister of Hyderabad, who was able to do for me what nobody of a lower rank would have been able to do. He introduced me to certain Bohra intellectual circles which strove for reforms aimed at liberating the Ismaili community from the obscurantism of the priestly clique. All of them made my work possible, and I have to express my profound gratitude to them.

However, there were always people who smelled danger for their selfish interests in the work of this kind, and they did not spare any effort to derail it. These were active saboteurs, but apart from them, there were so many people who realised the necessity of the advancement of knowledge but at the same time did nothing, being too lazy to lift a finger.

I have already described my visit to Multan in 1914. In 1934, I went there again. This time, I also visited the neighbouring places in the principality of Bahawalpur. There, I found some shrines of sectarian saints. According to tradition, they were the founders of the local religious community. However, it seems there are no historical grounds to substantiate these claims. Unfortunately, the locals do not always understand Urdu. They speak a variety of northern Punjabi and this was a serious obstacle to the study of their religious folklore. I collected materials on little-known sects, such as the Satpanth,[71] which to a certain extent consider themselves a form of Ismailism; and I also attempted to identify the role of Sufism in the formation of this sect. I started from Multan and its castle of the Khojas, who call themselves Sunars (the goldsmiths). I was very interested in their books, but it seemed there were no more old books to be found amongst them.

---

[70] See note 64 in Chapter 3.

[71] Satpanth, or the 'true path', is the technical Indian designation for the indigenous Ismaili tradition of the Nizari Khojas of South Asia. Drawing on a multitude of regional concepts and motifs prevalent in the Indian Muslim context of South Asia, this particular Nizari Ismaili tradition evolved over time. The eclectic Muslim–Hindu teachings of the Satpanth tradition are abundantly reflected in the *ginans*, the devotional literature of the Nizari Khojas. Certain splinter groups, such as the Imam-Shahis who later became Sunni or Twelver Shi'i, also referred to their religious tradition with the designation of Satpanth. See Ali S. Asani, *Ecstasy and Enlightenment: The Ismaili Devotional Literature of South Asia* (London, 2002), and his 'From Satpanthi to Ismaili Muslim: The Articulation of Ismaili Khoja Identity in South Asia', in Daftary, ed., *A Modern History of the Ismailis*, pp. 95–128. See also note 86 in Chapter 3 and notes 83 and 84 below.

Their spiritual thirst was evidently satisfied by the literature printed in Gujarati in Bombay. The linguistic problem of working with numerous local dialects greatly complicated any attempt to conduct research among them. For this reason, I decided to continue studying the ways of the Sufis, which were more accessible to foreigners.

In the Middle Ages, this place was a refuge for Sufi orders. Even now its main settlement, called Uchchh the Holy – Uchchh-i Sherif, is divided into two sections called Qaderi[72] and Chishti,[73] named after the two Sufi orders which are quite popular in India. Members of these two orders occupied separate parts of the settlement. I shall not deal with their history and doctrines since it

A page from the Khojki manuscript *Kalam-e Mawla*

---

[72] The Qaderi Sufi order is named after Abd al-Qadir al-Jilani, or Gilani (d. 1166), teacher and mystic who was the principal of a *madrasa* as well as a *ribat* or Sufi hospice in Baghdad. Gilani's heirs and disciples established different branches of this Sufi order in Egypt, Syria, Anatolia, North Africa, Afghanistan and India, amongst other regions. Indeed, the Qaderis represent the largest Sufi order in Islamic history. This order has developed some fifty branches, in Asia, Africa and Europe, including the Junaydiyya found in India. See Khaliq A. Nizami, 'The Qadiriyyah Order', in S. H. Nasr, ed., *Islamic Spirituality: Manifestations* (New York, 1991), pp. 6–25.

[73] Enjoying much influence in India, the Chishti Sufi order is named after a town, Chisht, east of Herat. In contrast to the Suhrawardi order, which spread mainly in Punjab and Bengal, the Chishti order spread all over India. With the establishment of the shrines (*dargah*) at tombs of well-known Chishtis venerated as saints, Sufi devotion was transferred from living sheikhs to dead saints or *pirs*. This transference led to the development of hereditary succession among the male descendants of a saint's family, occupying the position of *sajjada-nishin*, next to the line of the spiritual successors of the sheikhs. See S. Athar A. Rizvi, 'The Chishtiyyah', in Nasr, ed., *Islamic Spirituality: Manifestations*, pp. 127–143 and G. Böwering, 'Češtiya', *EIR*, vol. 5, pp. 333–339.

will take up too much time and space. Instead I shall describe only my visit there in 1934.

The road to the holy place from the railway station goes through the desert. There is also a short-cut from the station but it belongs to the local *nawab*, and it is necessary to obtain his permission to use it. It is not really necessary since it is simpler to hire a *tonga* – a two-wheeled cab, which can take you to the town. You arrive in a sort of square with a small bazaar. I arrived there in the autumn and the air was full of wasps. Meat was hanging in bags in the shop windows and layers of wasps covered these bags. I asked where I could stay and the passers-by directed me to a small shop which served as the office of a smart young municipal clerk. He told me there was no hotel in the town but both the Chishtis and Qaderis had their own guesthouses. Since the Qaderi *makhdum*, or head, had just gone hunting it would be better to approach the Chishtis. The clerk gave me a guide who took me to the place. A man was sent to inform the chief manager. Meanwhile, a respectable old man came in. He was a local doctor who very kindly and willingly helped me. The Chishti manager arrived too. He was a very tall old man, who from the very beginning declared that he could speak Persian but it proved that he did not understand it and was even unable to speak Urdu. The doctor most obligingly began to interpret – he spoke good English. The guesthouse was a one-storey building with a small hall and an oval table surrounded by a dozen chairs of various forms.

The inevitable tea was served, and I was asked what I would like to have for supper. The old manager confided in me that the Qaderi head was a very unpleasant man and it would be better to be very formal and polite with him. Therefore, it would be advisable to go to his place after tea and await his return from his falcon hunting excursion. Falconry is still fashionable in Punjab. So we went there and sat down, waiting and talking to the falconers. It was getting dark and we sent somebody to find out when the 'Lord' was expected back. But no one knew anything. So we returned home.

The supper was good; the cook had been reasonable with the spices, so I did not burn my mouth. I was desperate to stretch out on the bed. But this was not my destiny that evening. The tall man appeared, accompanied by a teenager with an unpromising face. He introduced him to me, and said that he was the *sajjada-nishin* – the heir-apparent and successor to the head of the order – and that he had invited me to join them in the *zikr* ceremony (it should be properly spelled *dhikr*, and this is recitation and singing of prayers). Well, there was nothing I could do and we all moved to another bigger hall. I was given the place of honour on the right-hand side of the young head of the order, and the music started, with the accompaniment of a *daf* (tambourine). The musicians and the singer were all good, but I cannot say that all this was pleasant for an unaccustomed listener. I felt overpowered with drowsiness. So I found a moment to whisper to the obliging doctor asking him to arrange for my departure. So he did, very diplomatically.

In the morning, we strolled to the 'city', namely the bazaar. The most interesting building was the house of the Qaderi *makhdum* (head). It was surrounded by walls and low buildings. Sticks were fixed over a narrow passage at human height. It was done in order to prevent people from riding near the Sufi's house, which would be considered a great discourtesy and a sign of disrespect. The doctor said that the Qaderis had many *tabarrukat* – religious memorial relics. He advised me to wait patiently for the head and ask him to show me the relics. The Chishtis were prepared to show me their relics immediately. They had a parchment copy of a genuine Kufic Koran and claimed that Imam Hasan himself,[74] who was the elder son of Hazrat Ali,[75] had copied it. I never specialised in Kufic manuscripts, but I had an impression that the book was not that old. I bitterly regretted that I had not brought with me a special camera to photograph it. They also showed me other manuscript copies of the Koran, but of much later dates. Then they displayed some clothes,

---

[74] Al-Hasan b. Ali (625–669), an early Shi'i Imam, who also ruled briefly as caliph in 661 before resigning. Thereupon, Mu'awiya established the Omayyad dynasty (661–750). See W. Madelung, 'Hasan b. Ali', *EIR*, vol. 12, pp. 26–28.

[75] Ali b. Abi Talib (d. 661), cousin and son-in-law of the Prophet Muhammad, also the first Shi'i Imam and the fourth of the 'rightly-guided caliphs'. Ali is highly revered by the Shi'is, who believe that the Prophet nominated him under divine command as his successor to the leadership of the nascent Muslim community. The literature on Ali's life and thought is vast. Ali's sermons, letters and sayings were subsequently collected by Sharif al-Radi (d. 1015) in a work entitled *Nahj al-balagha* (Way of Eloquence). See I. K. Poonawala and E. Kohlberg, 'Ali b. Abi Taleb', *EIR*, vol. 1, pp. 838–848, and the comprehensive multi-authored entry 'Ali b. Abi Talib', in *EIS*, vol. 3, pp. 477–583.

which allegedly belonged to the Prophet himself and the garments of the last head of the order. A man was sent to find out whether the Qaderi head was back. The answer was that he had returned very late and was still in bed. I decided to go there at 2 o'clock. When I arrived he was still in bed. I returned at four – he had gone out. This amounted to a deliberate insolence. In the evening, there was music again and I said that I would leave on the bus the following day.

As it is the usual practice all over the East, the village bus driver had his own concept of time. The bus was due to leave at six in the morning and the passengers were waiting but the driver did not arrive until nine. It was all right with me since I still had plenty of time before the train I wanted to catch. When my luggage was already in the bus, a man appeared who, in a rather impolite way, told me that the Qaderi head wanted me to stay in his guesthouse for three days. With the diplomatic help of the doctor, I told him to go to hell. Such arrogant religious magnates are usually very insolent, and it is good to teach them a lesson since they do not like affronts.

Summing up my impressions, the visit was interesting and instructive. However, the religious atmosphere of the past was no longer there. Only the holy names reminded me of religion and Sufism. Now, everything had disappeared without a trace. With regard to this, I may mention an insignificant but nevertheless symbolic event. When we were saying goodbye to each other near the bus, the old manager gave me a sugar cane, apparently the only 'fruit' that grew there. It was necessary to squeeze out the unpleasant and slightly sweet juice with the help of a rolling machine or to have horse's teeth. I wanted to throw it out but forgot it and the cane was put together with my luggage. At the railway station, the porter took it but I told him to throw it away. He asked me, 'You do not want it?'

'No.'

'May I take it?'

'Please.'

And he added, seemingly touched, *'tabarruki'* – blessed, coming from the holy place. Such was the difference in the sentiments of those who run 'the sacred institution' and those who still believe there is something 'holy' in it.

Both of these Sufi orders, Qaderi and Chisti, present in the holy city of Uchchh, are Sunni orders, which in medieval times played important roles in the lives of many people. Unfortunately, they did not have the custom of mentioning the construction dates at the sites on the shores of the Sutlej, which are now half ruined together with the old city. But it is interesting that the tombs belonging to Shi'i sects, such as the Satpanth, about which I wrote in my 1936 article on the sect of Imam-Shah in Gujarat,[76] are scattered there. About 2 km from Uchchh, is located the tomb of Hasan Kabir al-Din;[77] and, 22 km away, there is the tomb of Pir Sadr al-Din.[78] Their chronology is terribly confused, but there is no doubt that these Shi'i sects appeared here when the old Sufi orders already had many followers in the locality. In such a way, perhaps, the ideological struggles in the histories of Sufism, Shi'ism, Sunnism and the local Sunni-Muslim popular sects end.

Indeed, western India is full of various sectarian groups where the original Hinduism became mixed with Islamic, and mainly Sufi, ideas, such as in the case of the Satpanthis, all sorts of Penjpiriyya,[79] Haftpiriyya,[80] and so forth. They remained almost completely unstudied, but it would be interesting to consider them from the point of view of religious psychology. However, because of the eclectic nature of these groups and their cross-influences with all possible sectarian movements, it was difficult to study them. Therefore statements that a group was based on Sufi or even broad Islamic ideas were inevitably too vague. Besides, this phenomenon was still

---

[76] Reference to item 70 in Appendix 1, Works of Ivanow.

[77] Hasan Kabir al-Din (d. ca. 1470), a *pir*, or Satpanth Nizari preacher-saint, in India. He was the eldest son of Pir Sadr al-Din and succeeded his father to the leadership of the Nizari Khojas around 1416. He travelled extensively before settling down in Uchchh, which then served as the seat of the Satpanth mission in India.

[78] Sadr al-Din, one of the earliest Satpanth preacher-saints or *pirs* in India, converted large numbers of Hindus and gave them the name of Khoja. Based in Uchchh, he is reported to have died sometime between 1369 and 1416; his shrine is located near Jetpur, in the vicinity of Uchchh and to the south of Multan.

[79] A compound Persian term referring to the followers of the 'five *pirs*' (*panj pir*). The exact identity of these *pirs* varied for different groups and in different regions. Currently, their followers found mainly in the Indian state of Uttar Pradesh and in Punjab, in Pakistan, drawing people from different religious traditions.

[80] A compound Persian term referring to the followers of the 'seven *pirs*' (*haft pir*); in some accounts the term also has reference to *Haft-tan*, another Persian term meaning seven bodies.

rather unexplored. In my own attempts to analyse Sufi, or rather dervish, beliefs and folklore, I found that very often there are no historical facts to deal with, just figments of the imagination. Their genealogies, either historical or spiritual, lack any sense of chronology and association with history. It is impossible to find even some common sense in them. One of the most interesting, and at the same time most difficult, fields of research is the order of *qalandar*s [or wandering dervishes], if it is possible to describe it as an order. Everything is shrouded in mystery with this movement, including the etymology of its name and even its place of origin. Throughout my life, I tried to find some reliable information on the *pir* of the Sindhi *qalandar*s, La'l Shahbaz Qalandar.[81] Accidentally, I visited the centre of his worship in the ancient and now visibly decaying town of Sehwan, not far from the archaeological site of Mohenjo Daro. I read all the Sufi hagiographies in Persian starting from the most ancient and ending with some quite modern ones, but I was unable to find anything. Learned Sufis always treated *qalandar*s as beggars, not as members of one of the Sufi *tariqa*s. Looking for information on the Satpanthi saints, I jumped at the opportunity to visit Sehwan.

In Karachi, I met a Sindhi doctor who was a native of that place. He had a house in Sehwan and he offered to let me stay there. So I spent several days in this place. There was the shrine of the saint built in a grand style, which was looked after by his alleged direct descendant. The mausoleum was built by one of the Great Mughals of Delhi,[82] Shah Jahan (1628–1659), who also built the famous Taj Mahal in Agra as a burial place for his wife Mumtaz Mahal. In fact, she died in Burhanpur where the site of her original grave is still shown, but her body was exhumed and transferred to Agra. It is interesting to note that in Sehwan the local tradition holds that Shah Jahan himself was buried in the shrine of La'l Shahbaz Qalandar. This is not confirmed by the historical accounts.

---

[81] For a detailed discussion of this enigmatic Sufi saint, who may have been connected to the Ismaili movement in Sindh, and his shrine at Sehwan, at the site of an old Shaivite sanctuary, see M. Boivin, *Artefacts of Devotion: A Sufi Repertoire of the Qalandariyya in Sehwan Sharif, Sindh, Pakistan* (Karachi, 2011).

[82] The Mughal emperors of India, who were Sunni Muslims, ruled from Delhi and Agra, from 1526 till 1858. Generally speaking, the Mughal emperors of India were tolerant towards religious minorities in their dominions.

The site itself was grand, there was no inscription on the saint's tomb and the only dated stone was a portion of probably an old tombstone stuck in the wall by the entrance to the burial chamber. It bears the date of AH 723, approximately AD 1324 [AD 1323]. Shah Jahan died more than 300 years later. Of course, there are many examples of princes being buried in the shrines of the saints who lived long before them. But certainly the construction of such a grand building should have been noted in the annals of history. As the proof that the shrine was also the resting place of Shah Jahan, the locals point to the kettle drums kept there. Usually they are displayed only at the places of royal residence or burial. Also, a leopard, which the locals call a 'lion', is kept in a cage there as if it befits the royal burial place. It may be noted that these kettle drums are used in ceremony, resembling the Persian *naqara-khana* at sunset and sunrise, which is also associated with the royal residence. At the same time, it is interesting to note the survival of Hindu elements. There is a bunch of bells over the entrance. It is typical for Hindu temples but usually cannot be found in Muslim shrines. The only difference that I could observe was that those entering the shrine did not toll the bells like the Hindus do. At sunset, the *qalandar*s came to the compound and blew their traditional horns, accompanied by the roar of the kettle drums. It was quite a majestic spectacle.

The gates to the shrine were open for 24 hours, but at 11 o'clock [in the morning] the doors leading to the burial chamber were closed with special prayers for 15 minutes and then reopened in the same way by the *sajjada-nishin*, the supposedly direct descendant and successor of the *pir*. As far as I know, this is not an Islamic custom, but it is practised on certain ceremonial dates for washing the tomb with milk in the Satpanthi shrine of Satgur Nur in Navsari.[83] Around the

---

[83] The commencement of Nizari, or Satpanth, Ismaili tradition in India is associated with an enigmatic figure known as Satgur Nur, meaning 'true teacher'. Based on the Satpanthi tradition, as reflected in the *ginan* literature of the Khojas, Satgur Nur was probably sent from Daylam (Persia) to Gujarat, where he allegedly converted the local Rajput king, Siddharaja Jayasingha (1094–1133), who actually died as a devout Hindu. A shrine at Navsari, near Surat in Gujarat, ascribed to him, mentions 1094 as the date of the saint's death. See A. Nanji, *The Nizari Isma'ili Tradition in the Indo-Pakistan Subcontinent* (Delmar, NY, 1978), pp. 50–96, and I. Poonawala, 'Nur Satgur', *EI2*, vol. 8, pp. 125–126.

entrance hall, there are rooms for *qalandars*. Again this is not typical of Islamic shrines. I tried my best to see the rooms and find out how their occupants lived but could not find anyone speaking Urdu to show me around. The *sajjada-nishin* himself was an elderly man with sick eyes, and apparently of not much learning. It was difficult to obtain any information from him. I tried to ask him about his supposed ancestor, the *pir* buried there, but he was unable to tell me anything.

An interesting thing about the leopard, or lion as they called it, was that a middle-aged woman who did not cover her face looked after it. A crowd of local men were joking with her, quite indecently at the uproar of laughter. She asked me for some money to feed 'the lion'. Being interested in *qalandars*, I did everything to find somebody who could speak Persian or at least Urdu, but I failed completely. But once a young man looking like an ordinary *qalandar* addressed me in good English. He said that he had a BA degree but had become a *qalandar*. I at once invited him to my place for an interview but he said that he had something to do and would come at 2 o'clock; however I never saw him again. I made enquiries about him but no one had ever heard of him. Was he a police spy or a disappointed intellectual?

Once I was taken to a Sufi *pir* who was not a *qalandar*. He proved to be a Pathan who could not speak Urdu fluently. There was something strange about him and his disciples. My suspicions strengthened when I offered to photograph them – dervishes usually liked it, but they vigorously protested, all of them.

Sehwan was an extremely poor locality, with miserable bazaars and empty shops. During my stay there I did not see a single book. The general impression was that the place had seen better days, and then, fairly recently before my visit, things had changed for the worse. Was it due to the decline of pilgrimage to the shrine? Nobody could give me any sensible information. A general loss of interest in saints and famous shrines could be noticed everywhere. It can be explained by the worldwide economic crisis and the immense rise in the cost of living when people have nothing to spare for charity. I have already described this phenomenon in my paper on the Imam Shah sect.[84]

---

[84] Reference to item 70 in Appendix 1, Works of Ivanow. The Imam-Shahis, also known as Satpanthis, were a group of dissenters who seceded from the Nizari Khoja

Decay and impoverishment were spreading everywhere. One of the typical examples is the formerly fairly wealthy stronghold of Satpanthism at Pirana, on the way from Ahmadabad to Cambay. Afanasii Nikitin refers to it in his book but apparently he never visited the place. This locality became poor because the Khoja and Satpanthi customs of bringing children to the shrine of Imam Shah had ceased to exist. Previously, the hair of a child was cut off, then it was weighed and the parents gave its weight in gold or silver to the shrine. Many other similarly old customs have disappeared. A few words about the Bohras who penetrated Gujarat at an earlier time. They still have a very interesting library in Surat, which is under the control of their Mullaji, the Head Priest.[85] As a few anti-Mullaji Bohras who had had a chance to visit this institution have told me, the books coming to the library are simply piled up. They are never sorted, cleaned or registered. Another library, which together with a school was

---

community in Gujarat. Nar (Nur) Muhammad seceded from the Khoja community in 1513 on the death of his father, Imam Shah, the eponym of the splinter group. Nar Muhammad (d. 1533) acquired many followers in Gujarat, who became also known as Satpanthis and Pirana Panthis. The adherents of this syncretist sect have tended to revert back towards Hinduism. See Dominique-Sila Khan and Z. Moir, 'Coexistence and Communalism, the Shrine of Pirana in Gujarat', *South Asia*, Special Issue, 22 (1999), pp. 133–154. The complex question of identities, and shifting identities in India, is analysed in Dominique-Sila Khan's *Crossing the Threshold: Understanding Religious Identities in South Asia* (London, 2004).

[85] Ivanow is referring here to the religious leader, known as *daʿi mutlaq* (or *daʿi* with absolute authority), of the Daʾudi Tayyibi Ismailis, who are a community of around one million, concentrated mainly in Gujarat and Bombay. The Tayyibi Ismailis are known locally as Bohras in South Asia. In the absence of their Imams, who have remained in concealment since 1130, the Bohras have been led by *daʿi mutlaqs*, who in practice now effectively operate as Imams and designate their successors. The main educational institution of the Daʾudi Bohras is located at Surat, in Gujarat, and is known as Jamiʿa Sayfiyya. The library of this institution contains vast collections of Ismaili manuscripts, which continue to remain inaccessible to scholars and researchers. At the time of Ivanow's visit to Sehwan, the *daʿi mutlaq* of the Daʾudi Bohras was Tahir Sayf al-Din (d. 1965) who had succeeded to office in 1915. Tahir Sayf al-Din's son and successor, Muhammad Burhan al-Din, died in 2014 at the age of 102; and his succession was disputed between his brother and one of his sons. See Daftary, *The Ismaʿilis*, pp. 282–295; A. A. A. Fyzee, 'Bohoras', *EI2*, vol. 1, pp. 1254–1255, and M. Abdulhussein, 'Bohras', in *The Oxford Encyclopaedia of the Islamic World*, vol. 1, pp. 354–356.

managed by a dissenting party in Burhanpur, was for years the subject of litigation.

An Accident in the Jungle

Completing the section on my impressions of India, I would like to describe an incident which fortunately did not end tragically, but under less favourable circumstances could have developed into something very unpleasant. As mentioned above, in 1930 my friend P. I. Mashmeer, who worked as an engineer in the construction of a portion of the Visakhapatnam–Raypur railway in eastern India, invited me to stay with him as a guest. His section was more than 100 miles long and it went beyond the station of Ambadola or Ambodala, which was 57 miles from the station of Rayagada where he had his residence. Foreigners rarely visited this part of India, and therefore it was very interesting for me. One afternoon, Mashmeer came from his office for tea and said, 'You wanted so much to go to Ambadola. Here is a good chance for you; I have to send my assistant Toby (a young engineer from London) there. Again, something is wrong with the air compressors at the blast works. But you have to start before sunrise in order to be back on the same day.' I was certainly very glad and the next morning we left for Ambadola.

We travelled in a battered Ford, which despite its old age was still in service. Many parts of the car were missing; no roof or self-starter, the handles on the doors were replaced with hooks, only one light in front and no tail lights. But the most remarkable thing was the huge handle for starting the engine. I have never seen anything like it in my life. No one knew where it came from and what machine it originally belonged to. It was almost a metre long and quite heavy. We covered the distance without any trouble by seven in the morning and had a very tasty breakfast offered by the local engineer, a Muslim from Rawalpindi. Then the engineers went to see the air compressors and I went sightseeing. The place was a broad opening in the forest cleared for rice fields with ditches and footpaths suddenly going under water. The only interesting thing was the elephant belonging to the local landlord. This was the first time I saw this animal not in a zoo but working.

By one o'clock, the engineers had returned and we sat down to lunch and later started on our way back in the best of spirits.

Everything was going well, but suddenly our Ford began to 'cough'. We had to go uphill but the car belched steam and finally stopped. Toby examined it and found that no water had been poured into the radiator. He had told the foreman at the blast works to do it but apparently the worker had forgotten about it. What should we do? The nearest village was several kilometres away. Toby remembered that there was a pond nearby and volunteered to bring some water from there in oil tins, which we had with us. I wanted to go with him but he protested saying that it would be better if I stayed with the car guarding it armed with the freakish handle. Toby told me that the pond was only half a mile away. Alas! It was more than that and I spent a long time sitting in the car in the absolute silence of the declining day. It seemed to me that I heard people talking somewhere but I did not pay any attention to it. At last I saw Toby emerging from behind a corner, with his hat on the back of his head and his shirt sticking to his sweating body. I moved to jump off the car, and ran to help him and at that very moment, I heard a blood-freezing human shout. Toby put the tins on the road and taking out his pistol from the pocket rushed to the bushes where the cries came from. I caught the handle and heard two pistol shots. I also rushed through the bushes, and saw that there was a clearing overgrown with grass and shrubs. On my left Toby was aiming his pistol at something. I shouted, 'What's the matter?' He replied, 'A tiger was chasing a woman with a child. Come, let us see – I think I hit him.' I protested that with a small pistol it was impossible to kill a tiger and it would be very dangerous to come close to a wounded animal.

'But where is the woman?'

'She probably fell in the grass, stumbling as she ran. I clearly heard the voice of a child crying.'

Soon, we found a prostrated woman, who apparently had fainted, and a crying baby wrapped in rags.

We came closer and touched the woman. She did not move. It was impossible to leave them there, so we decided to carry them to our car. Toby picked up the woman, remarking that she was as light as a twelve-year-old girl, and I lifted the baby and the monstrous handle. We squeezed ourselves through the dusty bushes and laid down the woman and her baby near the car. Toby went to pour water into the radiator and I took out the thermos flask with ice, which we had with us and put a piece of ice on the woman's forehead. It worked, she opened her eyes and then probably frightened by the disfigured reflection of her own face in the shiny thermos, screamed and rushed towards the forest. But I managed to catch her by the hand. She at once lost her vigour and I put her on the back seat of the car and gave her the baby. Everything was ready and we started to move.

We covered approximately 2 km and it was getting dark. Suddenly Toby shouted, 'Good gracious! Elephants!' He started blowing the horn but with no effect. We turned on the headlamp and discovered that it was a crowd of people carrying bundles of dry wood on their backs. Suddenly our passenger started to talk to them and the people on the road answered her. I then shouted in Urdu, 'Hey you people, have you got anyone who can speak Urdu?' An old man with white hair came up and I asked him whether he knew the woman we had brought. He replied that he knew her since she was his daughter. I told him to ask her whether she wanted us to drive her to the village or if she preferred to join the crowd. She said something and the old man translated that she wanted to go with them. We helped her to get out, handed her child to her and she walked away.

We returned at about 10 o'clock. Mashmeer was already worrying. He gave us dinner and we ate with the proud feeling that we had just saved some human beings from imminent death. However, very often when you help somebody with the best of intentions, the matter turns against you, causing much trouble in recompense for your assistance. About a week later, Mashmeer as usual came for tea from his office, gave me an envelope and said, 'These are your adventures'. The official letter, marked 'strictly confidential', said that according to the report of the district police, two European employees shot a native woman and carried her corpse away in a motor car. Investigate the matter and take the necessary steps. This certainly was a very unpleasant thing. As an old Indian judge I knew in Bombay used to say, 'It is always better not to have anything to do with Indian justice'. And now we were right in the middle of a criminal investigation. I suggested to Mashmeer that I should type my report and that it should be submitted to the authorities. Toby must also do the same. Mashmeer approved this and our statements of evidence went to those concerned. A week later, a letter arrived saying that the police had proved that our evidence was absolutely false. Mr So-and-So, the district magistrate, had been appointed to investigate the case on the spot. Give him all necessary assistance. The date of his arrival would be telegraphed.

Mashmeer was excited; it was obvious that the police wanted to get a bribe from the railway administration! He at once wrote a detailed letter to his superiors and began waiting for the investigator. I do not remember how much time had passed before at last a telegram was received saying that he was on his way. Apparently to demonstrate his integrity and lack of any affiliation to the railway, he came not by the daily train but in a police lorry, bringing with himself several policemen, clerks and an interpreter. Mashmeer greeted him politely and offered to let him stay in our guestroom, but he refused and instead stayed in the dirty and bug-infested *kuchari*, the village's building for official and court sittings. The official was a middle-aged Madrasi (a Tamil from southern India). He spoke good English and Urdu but did not know the local language. As it later emerged, his interpreter did not understand the local people either. After taking some rest, he summoned both Toby and myself and questioned us separately, definitely assuming we had committed a crime. He kept us until 10 o'clock and then dismissed us with the announcement that we all, including Mashmeer, should proceed to the murdered woman's village. Next day we all went there.

As far as I can remember after the more than 20 years that have elapsed, the ceremony was going according to the usual 'protocol' of similar proceedings. The judge sat under a shady tree, the crowd assembled around him, we stayed near our car. Interrogation was conducted in many languages – the magistrate spoke English, Urdu and his native Tamil, and we could understand only bits and pieces of what he asked and what answers were given. When everything was over, the magistrate told us that he had been quite shocked when in reply to his question regarding the name of the deceased, he heard the name of the woman, and, then, the man who was speaking pushed a miserable-looking woman forward and said, 'And here she is herself.' And she firmly asserted that she was shot 'many times' and was dead. But one of the 'whites' had brought a *mantar* (magic object) and revived her. The judge asked where the bullet hit her, she pointed to the upper part of her chest but there was no mark of a wound there. To make everything clear, the magistrate asked, 'How could it happen that a woman with a child could be found alone in a forest in the evening?' The answer was that she was not alone, there were also her relatives and her husband. The old head of the village, the only man who understood Urdu, pulled out an emaciated Gond and said, 'This is her husband'.[86] The judge asked us whether we had ever seen this man. Both of us replied, 'No, we did not see any one there'. The judge asked the Gond where he was. The man pointed upwards – in the tree.

'Why did you go there?'

'I was afraid that the *gora-log* would shoot me.'[87]

'But why should the *gora-log* shoot you?'

The man mumbled something. The magistrate asked the headman whether he was present there at the time.

'No, he was far away'.

'But did he hear the shots?'

'Yes.'

'How many?'

'Oh! Very many!'

The judge asked us, 'How many shots were made?'

Toby replied, 'Only I was shooting and I fired only twice because the tiger hid himself in the bushes'. I said, 'May I show the *mantar* about which they are talking?'

'Yes, show it.'

I brought the thermos flask from the car. The 'murdered' woman saw it, screamed and rushed away in terror. The judge wrote something. Then he asked, 'Are you sure there was no tiger?'

Chorus: 'No tiger.'

The judge said to me: 'Did you see the tiger?'

I replied, 'No, because it had disappeared when I came'.

The judge said to Toby, 'Are you absolutely sure you saw the tiger?'

Toby replied, 'Yes, absolutely, otherwise there would have been no need to shoot'.

By our car stood a tall, heavily moustached policeman. He angrily spat on the ground and told me in good Urdu, 'How stupid are these

---

[86] See note 52 above.

[87] *Gora-log: a* Hindi term meaning 'white' (*gora*) 'people' (*log*). Thus, *gora-log* had referred to the white Englishmen in British India.

people! *Pagli-log*.⁸⁸ Certainly there was a tiger but they are afraid to admit it. They fear that the tiger will know this and will come to kill all of them. This interpreter *baboo* does not understand them and they do not understand him, and he only misleads the judge.'⁸⁹ I said, 'Do you understand their language?' 'Yes,' he replied, 'I have lived here for a long time. These people are so stupid, they believe in anything.'

When the judge finished his scribblings, I asked for his permission to say something important and told him what I had just heard from the policeman. He called the policeman and started talking to him in Tamil; finally he was convinced that we were right. He turned towards us and said in English, 'Gentlemen, I am sorry for having caused you so much inconvenience. It is now perfectly clear that there was no murder or attempted murder. We Indian judges quite often have to consider cases in which superstition plays a major part. I will stop the prosecution at once and you will soon receive an official document to this effect. You may go now.'

So, this absurd episode was over owing to the judge's intelligence. In the hands of somebody else prone to meaningless litigation or bribery, this matter could have turned into a very vexatious affair. But lawyers play tricks and manipulate the law, not just in India. We all went to our car. The judge accepted our hospitality and enjoyed a fried chicken, although being a Hindu he was supposed to be a strict vegetarian. After lunch, he dismissed his police lorry and departed at 6 o'clock on the returning train.

---

⁸⁸ A Hindi term meaning 'mad' (*pagal*) 'people' (*log*), or madmen. Thus, *pagli-log* refers to madmen or crazy people.

⁸⁹ See note 49 in Chapter 3.

Appendices

by

Farhad Daftary

Appendix 1

Bibliography of the Works of Wladimir Ivanow

List of abbreviations

IRA	Islamic Research Association, Bombay
JCOI	Journal of the K. R. Cama Oriental Institute
IS	The Ismaili Society, Bombay
JASB	Journal and Proceedings of the Asiatic Society of Bengal
JBBRAS	Journal of the Bombay Branch of the Royal Asiatic Society
JRAS	Journal of the Royal Asiatic Society of Great Britain and Ireland
NS	New Series

1914

1. 'On the Language of the Gypsies of Qainat (in Eastern Persia)', *JASB*, 10 (1914), pp. 439–455.

1915

2. 'Neskol'ko obraztsov persidskoi narodnoi poezii' [Several Specimens of Persian Popular Poetry], *Zapiski vostochnogo otdeleniia Imperatorskogo Russkogo arkheologicheskogo obshchestva*, 23 (1915), pp. 33–59.

1917

3. 'A Biography of Shaykh Ahmad-i-Jam', *JRAS* (1917), pp. 291–365.

4. 'Ismailitskie rukopisi Aziatskogo Muzeia. Sobranie I. Zarubina, 1916 g.' [Ismaili Manuscripts in the Asiatic Museum. Collection of I. Zarubin, 1916], *Izvestiia Rossiiskoi Akademii Nauk*, Petrograd/*Bulletin de l'Académie (Impériale) des Sciences de Russie*, 6 Series, 11 (1917), pp. 359–386. English summary and review in E. Denison Ross, 'Ismaili MSS in the Asiatic Museum, Petrograd 1917', *JRAS* (1919), pp. 429–435.

1918

5. 'Kratkaya opis' materialov dlya izucheniya persidskikh nariechii i govorov, sobrannikh v 1912-1914 godakh v Persii' [Summary List of Materials for Studying Persian Dialects Collected in Persia in 1912-1914], *Izvestiia Rossiiskoi Akademii Nauk*, Petrograd/*Bulletin de l'Académie des Sciences de Russie*, 6 Series, 12 (1918), pp. 411-412.

1920

6. 'Further Notes on Gypsies in Persia', *JASB*, NS, 16 (1920), pp. 281-291.
7. 'A Notice on the Library attached to the Shrine of Imam Riza at Meshed', *JRAS* (1920), pp. 535-563. Errata in *JRAS* (1921), pp. 248-250, by F. Krenkow, and p. 480, by W. Ivanow.

1922

8. *Ismailitica*, in *Memoirs of the Asiatic Society of Bengal*, 8 (1922), pp. 1-76. Contains: I. *Book on the Recognition of the Imam*, an edition of the Persian text and English translation of Khayrkhwāh-i Harātī's *Faṣl dar bayān-i shinākht-i imām* (pp. 3-49); and II. Notes on the Ismailis in Persia (pp. 50-76). Russian translation, 'Zametki ob ismailitakh Persii', in no. 159, pp. 167-177. See also nos. 110, 116, 144.

Muḥammad Riḍā b. Sulṭān Ḥusayn Ghūriyānī, better known as Khayrkhwāh-i Harātī, died not long after 1553. He was one of the earliest *dāʿī*s and authors of the Anjudān revival in the post-Alamūt history of the Nizārī Ismailis. He was a prolific writer, as well as a poet, and his works, all written in Persian, are invaluable for understanding the Nizārī doctrine of the time.

9. 'An Ismailitic Pedigree', *JASB*, NS, 18 (1922), pp. 403-406.
10. 'An Old Gypsy-Darwish Jargon', *JASB*, NS, 18 (1922), pp. 375-383.
11. 'The Sources of Jami's *Nafahat*', *JASB*, NS, 18 (1922), pp. 385-402.
12. 'Letters of Mahru', *JRAS* (1922), pp. 579-580.

1923

13. 'Tabaqat of Ansari in the Old Language of Herat', *JRAS* (1923), pp. 1-34 and 337-382. Partial Persian translation by Muḥammad Nasīm Nakhat as 'Ṭabaqāt al-Ṣūfiyya-i Anṣārī dar lahja-yi qadīm-i Harāt', in *Adab*, 10 (1962), pp. 28-42.

14. 'Imam Ismail', *JASB*, NS, 19 (1923), pp. 305–310.

15. 'More on the Sources of Jami's *Nafahat*', *JASB*, NS, 19 (1923), pp. 299–303.

16. 'Note on an Early Persian Work on Ethics', *JASB*, NS, 19 (1923), pp. 295–298.

17. 'A "Witch-case" in Mediaeval India', *JASB*, NS, 19 (1923), pp. 43–50.

1924

18. *Concise Descriptive Catalogue of the Persian Manuscripts in the Collection of the Asiatic Society of Bengal.* Bibliotheca Indica, 240 (Calcutta: Asiatic Society of Bengal, 1924; reprinted, Calcutta: The Asiatic Society, 1985). pp. xxxvii + 934. This collection contains 1,781 titles.

19. 'Nouveaux documents persans concernant Al Halladj' [Abridged French translation of the English original by Louis Massignon], *Revue du Monde Musulman*, 58 (1924), pp. 261–267; reprinted in L. Massignon, *Opera Minora*, ed. Y. Moubarac (Paris: Presses Universitaires de France, 1969), vol. 2, pp. 40–45.

1925

20. 'Rustic poetry in the Dialect of Khorasan', *JASB*, NS, 21 (1925), pp. 233–313.

21. Review of Zhukosvky, V., *Matériaux pour l'étude de dialectes persans*, partie II, fasc. I, and partie III, fasc. I, Petrograd, 1922 (*Revue du Monde Musulman*, 60, 1925, pp. 235–237).

1926

22. *Concise Descriptive Catalogue of the Persian Manuscripts in the Curzon Collection, Asiatic Society of Bengal.* Bibliotheca Indica, 241 (Calcutta: Asiatic Society of Bengal, 1926). pp. xxxviii + 582.

Named the 'Curzon Collection' in honour of Lord George Nathaniel Curzon (1859–1925), the Viceroy of India (1899–1905), this collection contains some 756 manuscripts.

23. 'Notes on the Ethnology of Khurasan', *The Geographical Journal*, 67 (1926), pp. 143–158.

24. 'Two Dialects Spoken in the Central Persian Desert', *JRAS* (1926), pp. 405–431.

25. 'Muhammadan Child-killing Demons', *Man: A Monthly Record of Anthropological Science*, 26 (1926), pp. 195–199.

26. 'Le "baiser au mendiant" en Perse', *Revue du Monde Musulman*, 63 (1926), pp. 168–171.

1927

27. *Concise Descriptive Catalogue of the Persian Manuscripts in the Collections of the Asiatic Society of Bengal*. First Supplement. Bibliotheca Indica, 244 (Calcutta: Asiatic Society of Bengal, 1927), pp. xx + 160. This catalogue contains a description of 377 titles.

28. 'Notes on Khorosani Kurdish', *JASB*, NS, 23 (1927), pp. 167–236.

29. 'Some Persian Darwish Songs', *JASB*, NS, 23 (1927), pp. 237–242.

30. 'Jargon of the Mendicant Darwishes', *JASB*, NS, 23 (1927), pp. 243–245.

31. 'Some Poems in the Sabzawari Dialect', *JRAS* (1927), pp. 1–41.

32. 'Études sur les corporations musulmanes indo-persans, tr. A. M. Kassim', *Revue des Études Islamiques*, 1 (1927), pp. 249–272.

33. 'The Date of the Danish-nama-i-Jahan', *JRAS* (1927), pp. 95–96.

34. 'Pidar-sukhta', *JRAS* (1927), pp. 96–97.

35. 'Pro C. Salemann: A Letter to the Editors from W. Ivanow (Calcutta)', *Islamica*, 3 (1927), pp. 271–272; and Karl Hadank's reply, pp. 486–490.

1928

36. *Concise Descriptive Catalogue of the Persian Manuscripts in the Collections of the Asiatic Society of Bengal*. Second Supplement. Bibliotheca Indica, 248 (Calcutta: Asiatic Society of Bengal, 1928), pp. xxii + 137.

The bulk of the 164 volumes described in this supplement were purchased by Ivanow himself on behalf of the Asiatic Society, at Lucknow, in 1926.

37. 'Persian as Spoken in Birjand', *JASB*, NS, 24 (1928), pp. 235–351.

38. 'A Biography of Ruzbihan al-Baqli', *JASB*, NS, 24 (1928), pp. 353–361.

1929

39. 'Notes on the Dialect of Khūr and Mihrijān', *Acta Orientalia*, 8 (1929), pp. 45–61.

40. 'Exportation of Manuscripts from Persia', *JRAS* (1929), pp. 441–443.

41. 'Faraḥ-nāma-i-Jamālī', *JRAS* (1929), pp. 863–868.

42. 'Pro C. Salemann: A Second Letter to the Editors from W. Ivanow', *Islamica*, 4 (1929), pp. 109–112.

1931

43. 'The Dialect of Gozärkhon in Alamut', *Acta Orientalia*, 9 (1931), pp. 352–369.

44. 'Alamut', *The Geographical Journal*, 77 (1931), pp. 38–45.

45. 'An Ismailitic Work by Nasiru'd-din Tusi', *JRAS* (1931), pp. 527–564. The work in question, *Rawḍat al-taslīm*, is a comprehensive treatise expounding the Nizārī Ismaili teachings of the Alamūt period, compiled under al-Ṭūsī's supervision. This work is now attributed to Ḥasan-i Maḥmūd-i Kātib. See also no. 120.

46. 'A Specimen of Bashgali from Kamdesh', *Acta Orientalia*, 10 (1931), pp. 576–595.

47. 'Notes on Phonology of Colloquial Persian', *Islamica*, 4 (1931), pp. 576–595.

48. 'More on Biography of Ruzbihan al-Baqli', *JBBRAS*, NS, 7 (1931), pp. 1–7.

1932

49. 'An Ismaili Interpretation of the Gulshani Raz', *JBBRAS*, NS, 8 (1932), pp. 69–78. The work in question, *Baʿḍī az taʾwīlāt-i Gulshan-i rāz*, is comprised of esoteric interpretations (*taʾwīlāt*) of selected passages of the celebrated Sufi *mathnawī* poem composed by Maḥmūd-i Shabistarī (d. after 1339). The Ismaili author of this partial commentary may have been Shāh Ṭāhir al-Ḥusaynī al-Dakkanī (d. ca. 1549), the 31st Imam of the Muḥammad-Shāhī Nizārī Ismailis. This Persian text was subsequently edited and published, together with its French translation, by Henry Corbin (1903–1978), in his *Trilogie Ismaélienne*. Bibliothèque Iranienne, 9 (Tehran and Paris, 1961), text pp. 131–161, translation pp. 1–174.

50. 'Notes sur l'Ummu'l-kitab des Ismaëliens de l'Asie Centrale', *Revue des Études Islamiques*, 6 (1932), pp. 419–481. See also no. 67.

51. 'Petermann-Justi's Gabri-Übersetzungen', *Islamica*, 5 (1932), pp. 573–580.

52. 'Late Professor E. G. Browne's Specimen of the Gabri Dialect', *JRAS* (1932), pp. 403–405.

53. 'The Name of the Black Sea in Pre-Muhammadan Persia, by A. A. Freimann, translated from Russian by W. Ivanow', *JCOI*, 22 (1932), pp. 26–31.

54. 'Four Short Papers on Iranian Subjects, by A. A. Freimann', *JCOI*, 22 (1932), pp. 32–37. Notes on the contents of the papers, originally in Russian, by W. Ivanow. The papers include: 'List of Manuscripts acquired in Bukhara in 1915 by W. Ivanow on behalf of the Asiatic Museum of the Imperial

Russian Academy of Sciences. Part II. Jewish-Persian MSS'. The Cama Oriental Institute was established in 1916 in Bombay in memory of the Parsi orientalist, Kharshedji Rustamji Cama (1831–1909). The *Journal of K. R. Cama Oriental Institute* was published from 1922 until 1944.

55. 'Two Silver Dishes of Sasanian Times, by F. Rosenberg [Summary translation from Russian by W. Ivanow]', *JCOI*, 22 (1932), p. 38.

56. Review of Miller, V. F., *Ossetic Russian and German Dictionary*, ed. A. A. Freimann, Leningrad, 1927–1929, 2 vols. (*JCOI*, 23, 1932, pp. 92–96).

1933

57. *A Guide to Ismaili Literature*. Prize Publication Fund, XIII (London: Royal Asiatic Society, 1933), pp. xii + 138. Contains a description of some 691 titles by 148 authors. Paul Kraus (1904–1944) reviewed this work and provided additional bibliographical information in his 'La bibliographie Ismaëlienne de W. Ivanow', in *Revue des Études Islamiques*, 6 (1932), pp. 483–490. See also no. 150.

58. Editor of Khākī Khurāsānī, *Dīwān*, partial edition as *An Abbreviated Version of the Diwan of Khaki Khorasani*. IRA Series, 1 (Bombay: IRA, 1933). pp. ii + 20 (English) + 128 (Persian). Part of the *Dīwān* of poetry by Imām Qulī Khākī Khurāsānī (d. after 1646), a Persian Nizārī Ismaili poet of the Anjudān period in Nizārī history. It also includes this poet's *Nigāristān* (pp. 109–124), a lengthy *qaṣīda*, and *Bahāristān* (pp. 124–128), a *qaṣīda* of 79 verses on the eras of religious history.

59. Editor of *Two Early Ismaili Treatises: Haft-Babi Baba Sayyid-na and Matlubu'l-mu'minin by Tusi*. IRA Series, 2 (Bombay: IRA, 1933), pp. 9 (English) + 64 (Persian). This publication includes the anonymous *Haft bāb-i Bābā Sayyidnā* (pp. 4–42), a treatise on the declaration of the *qiyāma* in 1164 at Alamūt, evidently witnessed by this Nizārī author, who may have been Ḥasan-i Maḥmūd-i Kātib (d. after 1243). This work, wrongly attributed to Bābā Sayyidnā, viz., Ḥasan-i Ṣabbāḥ (d. 1124), was translated into English as *The Popular Appeal of the Qiyāma*, by Marshall G. S. Hodgson (1922–1968), in his *The Order of Assassins* (The Hague, 1955), pp. 279–324. The second work in this collection is the *Maṭlūb al-mu'minīn* (pp. 43–55), a short treatise written at the request of a noble lady from the household of the Nizārī Imam ʿAlāʾ al-Dīn Muḥammad (d. 1255), by Naṣīr al-Dīn al-Ṭūsī (d. 1274). A better edition, together with English translation, of the *Maṭlūb al-mu'minīn* is included in al-Ṭūsī, *Shiʿi Interpretations of Islam: Three Treatises on Theology and Eschatology*, ed. and tr. S. J. Badakhchani. Ismaili Texts and Translations

Series, 13 (London: I.B.Tauris in association with The Institute of Ismaili Studies, 2010), text pp. 19–29, translation pp. 33–43.

60. Editor and translator of Shihāb al-Dīn Shāh al-Ḥusaynī, *Risāla dar ḥaqīqat-i dīn*, published as *True Meaning of Religion (Risala dar Haqiqati Din)*. IRA Series, 3 (Bombay: IRA, 1933). pp. iii + 28 (English) + 37 (Persian). Intended for the general reader, the *Risāla dar ḥaqīqat-i dīn* contains a summary exposition of certain Ismaili teachings, with special reference to the doctrine of the imamate. Shihāb al-Dīn Shāh (d. 1884) was the eldest son of Āqā ʿAlī Shāh (d. 1885), the 47th Imam of the Nizārī Ismailis. See also nos. 108, 109, 132.

1934

61. 'Genuineness of Jami's Autographs', *JBBRAS*, NS, 10 (1934), pp. 1–7.

62. 'A New Arabic History of Ismailism' [Review of ʿAbd Allāh b. al-Murtaḍā al-Khawābī (1895–1936), *al-Falak al-dawwār fī samāʾ al-aʾimma al-aṭhār*, Aleppo, 1352/1933] (*Ismaili Africa Birthday*, no. 7, 13 June 1934, p. 6).

63. Review of Fyzee, Asaf A. A., *Ismaili Law of Wills*, Bombay, 1933 (*JBBRAS*, NS, 10, 1934, p. 79). This book contained the Arabic text and English translation of the *Kitāb al-waṣāyā*, an extract from al-Qāḍī al-Nuʿmān's *Daʿāʾim al-Islām*. See also no. 124.

1935

64. Editor and translator of Khayrkhwāh-i Harātī, *Kalām-i pīr*, published as *Kalami Pir: A Treatise on Ismaili Doctrine, also (wrongly) called Haft-Babi Shah Sayyid Nasir*. IRA Series, 4 (Bombay: IRA, 1935), pp. lxviii + 146 (English) + 117 (Persian). The *Kalām-i pīr* is apparently a plagiarised version of Abū Isḥāq Quhistānī's *Haft bāb*, produced by Khayrkhwāh-i Harātī (d. after 1553) and wrongly attributed to Shāh Sayyid Nāṣir, viz., Nāṣir-i Khusraw (d. after 1072). See also no. 141.

65. 'The Gabri Dialect Spoken by the Zoroastrians of Persia', *Rivista degli Studi Orientali*, 16 (1935), pp. 31–97; 17 (1937), pp. 1–39, and 18 (1939), pp. 1–58.

66. 'Three New Works on the History of Ismailism' [Reviews of Mamour, P. H., *Polemics on the Origin of the Fatimid Caliphs*, London, 1934; Ḥasan, Ḥasan Ibrāhīm, *al-Fāṭimiyyīn fī Miṣr*, Cairo, 1932; Shaykh ʿAbd Allāh b. al-Murtaḍā al-Khawābī, *al-Falak al-dawwār*, Aleppo, 1352/1933] (*JBBRAS*, NS, 11, 1935, pp. 71–74).

1936

67. Editor of *Ummu'l-kitāb*, in *Der Islam*, 23 (1936), pp. 1–132; reprinted in İsmail Kaygusuz, *Bir Proto-Alevi Kaynaği, Ummü'l-Kitab* (Istanbul, 2009), with Turkish trans. by A. Selman, pp. 121–258. Ivanow's edition was translated into Italian by Pio Filippani-Ronconi (Naples: Istituto Universitario Orientale di Napoli, 1966), pp. lv + 301. Written in archaic Persian and preserved by the Nizārī Ismailis of Central Asia, the *Umm al-kitāb* was originally produced in the 8th century in Arabic by the Mukhammisa (the Pentadists), an early sect of the Shiʿi *ghulāt*. This work does not contain any Ismaili doctrines even though it was adopted into the literature of the Central Asian Nizārī Ismailis.

68. Editor of Aḥmad b. Ibrāhīm al-Nīsābūrī, *Istitār al-imām*, and Muḥammad b. Muḥammad al-Yamānī, *Sīrat Jaʿfar al-ḥājib*, under the title of *Mudhakkirāt fī ḥarakat al-Mahdī al-Fāṭimī*, in *Majallat Kulliyat al-Ādāb, al-Jāmiʿ al-Miṣriyya/Bulletin of the Faculty of Arts, University of Egypt*, 4, part 2 (1936), pp. 89–133. English translations of these works by Ivanow in no. 104, pp. 157–183 and 184–223, respectively. The *Istitār al-imām* of the *dāʿī* al-Nīsābūrī (d. after 996) is an important historical source on the settlement of the early Ismaili Imams in Salamiyya, Syria, and the eventual journey of Imam ʿAbd Allāh al-Mahdī (d. 934) from Syria to North Africa. The *Sīra* is the autobiography of Jaʿfar b. ʿAlī, chamberlain (*ḥājib*) to the Fatimid Caliph-Imam al-Mahdī, compiled later; it contains unique details on al-Mahdī's long journey from Salamiyya to Ifrīqiya in North Africa.

69. *A Creed of the Fatimids (A Summary of the Tāju'l-ʿaqāʾid by Sayyid-nā ʿAlī b. Muḥammad b. al-Walīd, ob. 612/1215)*. (Bombay: Qayyimah Press, 1936), pp. viii + 82. A compendium of Ismaili doctrines, the *Tāj al-ʿaqāʾid* was intended for ordinary believers. The author was the fifth *dāʿī muṭlaq* (1209–1215) of the Ṭayyibī Mustaʿlian Ismailis in Yemen. The Arabic text of the *Tāj al-ʿaqāʾid wa-maʿdin al-fawāʾid* was edited by ʿĀrif Tāmir (Beirut, 1967; 2nd ed., Beirut, 1982).

70. 'The Sect of Imam Shah in Gujrat', *JBBRAS*, NS, 12 (1936), pp. 19–70. The Imām-Shāhīs were originally a group of dissenters who seceded from the Nizārī Khoja community in Gujarāt. The eponym of the Imām-Shāhīs was Imām Shāh (d. 1513), who had attempted in vain to be appointed by the Nizārī Ismaili Imam as the *pīr*, or leader, of the Nizārī Khojas in India.

71. 'Some Muhammadan Shrines in Western India', *Ismaili*, Golden Jubilee Number (21 January, 1936), pp. 16–23.

72. 'Rāshid al-Dīn Sinān', in *The Encyclopaedia of Islam*, ed. M. H. Houtsma et al. (Leiden: E. J. Brill, 1913–1936), vol. 3, pp. 1123–1124; reprinted in *E. J. Brill's First Encyclopaedia of Islam, 1913–1936* (Leiden: E. J.

Brill, 1987), vol. 6, pp. 1123–1124. Sinān (d. 1193) was the greatest of the medieval Nizārī Ismaili *dāʿīs* in Syria. The original 'Old Man of the Mountain' of the Crusader sources, Sinān played a prominent role in the regional politics of his time. He led the Syrian Nizārīs for some three decades to the peak of their power and fame until his death.

73. 'Ismāʿīlīya', in *The Encyclopaedia of Islam*, Supplement, ed. M. H. Houtsma et al. (Leiden: E. J. Brill, 1934–1938), pp. 98–102; German translation in *Handwörterbuch des Islam*, ed. A. J. Wensinck and J. H. Kramers (Leiden: E. J. Brill, 1941), pp. 222–227; English text reprinted in *Shorter Encyclopaedia of Islam*, ed. H. A. R. Gibb and J. H. Kramers (Leiden: E. J. Brill, 1953), pp. 179–183; also reprinted in *E. J. Brill's First Encyclopaedia of Islam, 1913–1936* (Leiden: E. J. Brill, 1987), vol. 9, Supplement, pp. 98–102.

74. Review of Arberry, Arthur J., *Catalogue of Arabic Manuscripts in the Library of the India Office*, vol. II (part) II *On Ṣūfism and Ethics*, Oxford, 1936 (*JBBRAS*, NS, 12, 1936, pp. 110–112).

75. Review of Sām Mīrzā Ṣafawī, *The Tuhfa i Sami* (Section V), ed. Mawlawi Iqbal Husain, Patna, 1934 (*JBBRAS*, NS, 12, 1936, pp. 112–114).

1937

76. 'A New Book on Ismaili History' [Review of Bouthoul, Betty, *Le grand maître des Assassins*, Paris, 1936] (*Ismaili*, Birthday Special, no. 14, 9 January 1937, pp. 1–6; reprinted in *Read and Know*, vol. 2, no. 3, November 1967, pp. 7–15).

77. Review of Ibn Yūsuf Shīrāzī, *Fihristi Kitāb-khāna-i Dānishkada-i Maʿqūl wa Manqūl dar Madrasa-i ʿĀlī-i Sipahsālār* (Catalogue of Persian and Arabic Manuscripts in the Library of the Faculty of Arts, Sipahsalar High School, Tehran), vol. 1, Tehran, 1315/1937 (*JBBRAS*, NS, 13, 1937, pp. 49–52).

78. Review of Wolff, Fritz, *Glossar zu Firdosis Schahname*, and Supplementband: *Verskonkordanz der Schahname-ausgaben von Macan, Vullers und Mohl*, Berlin, 1935 (*JBBRAS*, NS, 13, 1937, pp. 52–53).

1938

79. 'Some Ismaili Strongholds in Persia', *Islamic Culture*, 12 (1938), pp. 383–396. Russian translation, 'Nekotorye ismailitskie kreposti v persii', in no. 159, pp. 150–166. On the Nizārī Ismaili fortresses of Alamūt and Girdkūh in northern Persia.

80. 'Tombs of Some Persian Ismaili Imams', *JBBRAS*, NS, 14 (1938), pp. 49-62. Russian translation, 'Pogrebeniya nekotoryh persidskih ismailitskih imamov', in no. 159, pp. 129-149. On the tombs of some Nizārī Ismaili Imams at Anjudān and Kahak in central Persia.

81. 'An Ismaili Poem in Praise of Firdawis', *JBBRAS*, NS, 14 (1938), pp. 63-72. The Persian text and English translation of a poem in praise of the *fidā'īs* who killed Atabeg Qizil Arslān in 1191. The poem, originally attributed to Ra'īs Ḥasan Bīrjandī, is now considered to have been composed by Ḥasan-i Maḥmūd-i Kātib (d. after 1243); see his *Dīwān-i qā'imiyyāt*, ed. S. J. Badakhchani (Tehran, 2011), pp. 205-208.

82. 'A Forgotten Branch of the Ismailis', *JRAS* (1938), pp. 57-79. Russian translation, 'Zabytaya vetv ismailizma', in no. 159, pp. 109-128. On the Muḥammad-Shāhī (Mu'minī) branch of Nizārī Ismailism, also containing biographical information on Shāh Ṭāhir b. Raḍī al-Dīn al-Ḥusaynī, the 31st and the most famous Imam of that branch.

83. 'Mahallat', *Ismaili Weekly*, Special Welcome Number (11 December, 1938), pp. 1-4.

84. Review of Drower, E. S., *The Mandaeans of Iraq and Iran*, Oxford, 1937 (*JBBRAS*, NS, 14, 1938, pp. 80-81).

1939

85. *Catalogue of the Arabic Manuscripts in the Collection of the Royal Asiatic Society of Bengal*, Volume I, prepared by Wladimir Ivanow, and revised and edited by M. Hidayat Husain. Bibliotheca Indica, 250 (Calcutta: Royal Asiatic Society of Bengal, 1939), pp. xviii + 694. Contains the descriptions of some 1,200 manuscripts. This collection is particularly rich in terms of Twelver Shiʿi and Zaydi Shiʿi titles.

86. 'The Organization of the Fatimid Propaganda', *JBBRAS*, NS, 15 (1939), pp. 1-35; reprinted in Bryan S. Turner, ed., *Orientalism: Early Sources*, Volume I, *Readings in Orientalism* (London: Routledge, 2000), pp. 531-571. Russian translation, 'Organizaciya fatimidskoy propagandy', in no. 159, pp. 21-60.

87. 'Ismailis in Khorasan and Fars', *Ismaili Weekly*, Special Birthday Number (19 January, 1939), pp. 1-10.

88. Review of Donaldson, Bess Allen, *The Wild Rue: A Study of Muhammadan Magic and Folkore in Iran*, London, 1938 (*JBBRAS*, NS, 15, 1939, pp. 77-78).

89. Review of Palmer, E. H., *Oriental Mysticism: A Treatise on the Sufistic Philosophy of the Persians*, 2nd ed. by A. J. Arberry, London, 1938 (*JBBRAS*, NS, 15, 1939, pp. 78-79).

90. Review of Hitti, Philip et al., *Descriptive Catalogue of the Garrett Collection of Arabic Manuscripts in the Princeton University Library*, Princeton, 1938 (*Islamic Culture*, 13, 1939, pp. 516–519).

1940

91. 'Ismailis and Qarmatians', *JBBRAS*, NS, 16 (1940), pp. 43–85. Russian translation, 'Ismaility i karmaty', in no. 159, pp. 61–108. A study of the similarities and divergencies between the two branches of early Ismailism.

92. 'Another Autograph of Jami', *JBBRAS*, NS, 16 (1940), pp. 104–105.

93. 'Some Materials for the Study of Indian Dialects', in Mohammed Shafi, ed., *Woolner Commemoration Volume (In Memory of the Late Dr A. C. Woolner)* (Lahore: Mehar Chand Lachhman Das, 1940), pp. 113–115.

94. 'On Ismaili Missionaries', *Ismaili*, Special Golden-Platinum Jubilee Day Number (Dar-es-Salaam, n. d. [1940], pp. 18–20).

95. Review of Lewis, Bernard, *The Origins of Ismāʿīlism: A Study of the Historical Background of the Fāṭimid Caliphate*, Cambridge, 1940 (*JBBRAS*, NS, 16, 1940, pp. 107–110).

96. Review of Moghadam, M. E. and Y. Armajani, *Descriptive Catalog of the Garrett Collection of Persian, Turkish and Indic Manuscripts including some Miniatures in the Princeton University Library*, Princeton, 1939 (*JBBRAS*, NS, 16, 1940, pp. 121–122).

1941

97. 'Early Shiʿite Movements', *JBBRAS*, NS, 17 (1941), pp. 1–23.

98. 'Some Recent Russian Publications on Archaeological Research in Central Asia', *JBBRAS*, NS, 17 (1941), pp. 25–41. Contains reviews of *Transactions of the Oriental Section of the 'Hermitage Museum'*, vols. II and III, Leningrad, 1940; Trever, C., *The Monuments of Greco-Bactrian Art*, Moscow and Leningrad, 1940; *Papers Read at the Third International Congress of Persian Art and Archaeology, held in Leningrad, September, 1935*, Moscow and Leningrad, 1939.

99–103. 'Bohoras', 'Imām', 'Imām-Shāh', 'Khodja', 'Ṭāhir', in *Handwörterbuch des Islam*, ed. A. J. Wensinck and J. H. Kramers (Leiden: E. J. Brill, 1941), pp. 83–84, 206–208, 318–319, 713–714; English translation, with bibliographical revisions, in *Shorter Encyclopaedia of Islam*, ed. H. A. R. Gibb and J. H. Kramers (Leiden: E. J. Brill, 1953), pp. 64–65, 165–166, 167, 256–257, 560.

1942

104. *Ismaili Tradition Concerning the Rise of the Fatimids.* IRA Series, 10 (Bombay, etc.: Published for the Islamic Research Association by H. Milford, Oxford University Press, 1942), pp. xxii + 337 (English) + 113 (Arabic).

This work also contained extracts from a number of Ismaili texts, together with their English translations, published here for the first time. It contains extracts from the following Arabic Ismaili texts: al-Qāḍī al-Nuʿmān (d. 974), *Sharḥ al-akhbār* (pp. 1–34); al-Khaṭṭāb b. al-Ḥasan al-Ḥajūrī al-Hamdānī (d. 1138), *Ghāyat al-mawālīd* (pp. 35–39); al-Qāḍī al-Nuʿmān, *Iftitāḥ al-daʿwa* (pp. 40–46); Idrīs ʿImād al-Dīn (d. 1468), *Zahr al-maʿānī* (pp. 47–80); Jaʿfar b. al-Manṣūr al-Yaman (d. ca. 957), *Kitāb asrār al-nuṭaqāʾ* (pp. 81–106); Ḥātim b. Ibrāhīm al-Ḥāmidī (d. 1199), *Majālis* (pp. 107–113). It also contains the English translations of the following Ismaili texts or their extracts: Aḥmad b. Ibrāhīm al-Nīsābūrī (d. after 996), *Istitār al-imām* (pp. 157–183); Muḥammad b. Muḥammad al-Yamānī (fl. 10th century), *Sīrat al-ḥājib Jaʿfar b. ʿAlī* (pp. 184–223); al-Qāḍī al-Nuʿmān, *Iftitāḥ al-daʿwa* (pp. 224–231); Idrīs ʿImād al-Dīn, *Zahr al-maʿānī* (pp. 232–274); Jaʿfar b. al-Manṣūr al-Yaman, *Kitāb asrār al-nuṭaqāʾ* (pp. 275–304); Ḥātim b. Ibrāhīm al-Ḥāmidī, *Majālis* (pp. 305–313). The Arabic extracts of this collection have been reprinted as *al-Muntakhab min baʿḍ kutub al-Ismāʿīliyya*, ed. ʿAmmār al-Mīr Aḥmad, with an introduction by Ṣabbāḥ Jamāl al-Dīn (Beirut, Baghdad and London: Alwarrak Publishing, 2011), pp. 152.

105. 'On the Development of Urdu', in *Proceedings of the Third Session of the Idara-i-Maarif-i-Islamia*, held at Delhi under the Presidentship of Sir Shah Muhammad Sulaiman on 26, 27 and 28 December, 1938 (Lahore: Working Committee of the Idara-i-Maarif-i-Islamia, 1942), pp. 27–42.

1946

106. *The Alleged Founder of Ismailism.* IS Series [A], 1 (Bombay: Published for the Ismaili Society by Thacker and Co., 1946), pp. xv + 197.

This work, initiating the publications of The Ismaili Society, correctly identified the historical personality of ʿAbd Allāh b. Maymūn al-Qaddāḥ, who had been cited maliciously, as the founder of the Ismaili movement and the ancestor of the Fatimid caliphs, in the anti-Ismaili writings of the Sunni polemicists, starting with Ibn Rizām who flourished in the 10th century. See also no. 137. See F. Daftary, "ʿAbd Allāh b. Maymūn al-Qaddāḥ', in W. Madelung and F. Daftary, ed., *Encyclopaedia Islamica* (Leiden, 2008), vol. 1, pp. 167–169.

107. 'Some Wartime Russian Oriental Publications', *JBBRAS*, NS, 22 (1946), pp. 67–72. Contains reviews of I. Kratchkovsky, *While Studying Arabic Manuscripts*, Leningrad, 1945; V. A. Gordlevsky, *The Seljuq State in Asia Minor*, Moscow, 1941; *Sovietskoe Vostokovedenie* [Soviet Oriental Studies], Leningrad, 1941 and 1945, vols. II and III, respectively.

1947

108. Editor of Shihāb al-Dīn Shāh al-Ḥusaynī, *Risāla dar ḥaqīqat-i dīn*. Facsimile Edition of the Autograph Copy. IS Series [B], Ismaili Texts and Translations Series, 1 (Bombay: Published for the Ismaili Society by Thacker and Co., 1947), pp. xii (English) + 75 (Persian); reprinted as IS Series B, 8 (Bombay: The Ismaili Society, 1955), pp. xvi (English) + 75 (Persian). Gujarati translation, *Hakikate din yane dharammo kharo arth*, tr. V. N. Hooda. IS Series D – Gujarati, I (Bombay: Ismailia Association, 1951), p. 68; Urdu translation, *Risāla dar ḥaqīqat-i dīn*, tr. ʿAbbās Sabzavārī (Karachi: Ismailia Association Pakistan [1950]), p. 106.

109. Translator of Shihāb al-Dīn Shāh al-Ḥusaynī, *Risāla dar ḥaqīqat-i dīn* as *True Meaning of Religion*. IS Series [B], Ismaili Texts and Translations Series, 2 (2nd ed., Bombay: Published for the Ismaili Society by Thacker and Co., 1947), pp. xv + 51.

110. Translator of Khayrkhwāh-i Harātī, *Faṣl dar bayān-i shinākht-i imām* as *On the Recognition of the Imam*. IS Series [B], Ismaili Texts and Translations Series, 4 (2nd revised ed., Bombay: Published for the Ismaili Society by Thacker and Co., 1947), pp. 6 + 55. Gujarati translation, *Shanakhate imam yane imamni orkha(n)*, tr. V. N. Hooda. IS Series D – Gujarati, 2 (Bombay: Published for the Ismaili Society by Thacker and Co., 1947), pp. 6 + 55.

1948

111. *Studies in Early Persian Ismailism*. IS Series A, 3 (Leiden: Published for the Ismaili Society by E. J. Brill, 1948), p. 202. This work contains the following studies: I. Main Trends in the History of Shiʿism (pp. 1–31); II. Early Ismaili Terminology (pp. 33–49). III. The Book of Righteousness and True Guidance (*Kitāb al-rushd wa'l-hidāya*) (pp. 51–83); IV. The Book of the Teacher and the Pupil (*Kitāb al-ʿālim wa'l-ghulām*) (pp. 85–113); V. An Early Controversy in Ismailism (pp. 115–159); VI. Tenth Century Ismaili *Dāʿī* in Persia (pp. 161–180). See also no. 128.

The complete Arabic text of Jaʿfar b. Manṣūr al-Yaman's *Kitāb al-ʿālim wa'l-ghulām*, together with its English translation, has now appeared under the title of *The Master and the Disciple: An Early Islamic Spiritual Dialogue*, ed. and tr. James W. Morris. Ismaili Texts and Translations Series, 3 (London: I.B.Tauris in association with The Institute of Ismaili Studies, 2001), pp. xiii + 225 (English) + 180 (Arabic).

112. *Nasir-i Khusraw and Ismailism*. IS Series B, 5 (Bombay: Ismaili Society, 1948), p. 78. Persian translation, *Nāṣir-i Khusraw va Ismāʿīliyān*, tr. Yaʿqūb Āzhand, in his *Ismāʿīliyān dar taʾrīkh* (Tehran: Intishārāt-i Mawlā, 1984), pp. 403–463. Nāṣir-i Khusraw (d. after 1072) was the famous Persian poet, traveller and Ismaili *dāʿī*. He is considered by the Nizārī Ismailis of Badakhshān and other regions of Central Asia as the founder of their communities. See also no. 131.

113. Editor of *Collectanea*, Vol. 1. IS Series A, 2 (Leiden: Published for the Ismaili Society by E. J. Brill, 1948), pp. xii + 242. In addition to nos. 114 and 115, this collection contains the following: Some Specimens of Satpanth Literature, translated by V. N. Hooda (pp. 55–137); The Holy Shikshapatri, translated from Maratthi by Peer Syed Dewan M. Noor-Ali Shah (pp. 139–145); Fragments of the *Kitābu'r-Rushd wa'l-Hidāyat*, the Arabic text edited by Dr M. Kamil Hussein (pp. 185–213).

114. 'Satpanth', in no. 113, pp. 1–54.

Meaning 'true path', Satpanth is the designation for the indigenous Ismaili tradition of the Nizārī Khojas of South Asia. The eclectic Muslim–Hindu teachings of the Satpanth tradition are reflected in the *ginān*s, the devotional literature of the Nizārī Khojas.

115. 'An Ali-Ilahi Fragment', in no. 113, pp. 147–184.

1949

116. Editor of Khayrkhwāh-i Harātī, *Faṣl dar bayān-i shinākht-i imām, or, On the Recognition of the Imam*. IS Series B, 3 (2nd revised ed., Leiden: Published for the Ismaili Society by E. J. Brill, 1949), pp. xvi (English) + 28 (Persian).

117. Editor and translator of Nāṣir-i Khusraw, *Shish faṣl*, published as *Six Chapters, or, Shish Fasl, also called Rawshanaʾi-nama*. IS Series B, 6 (Leiden: Published for the Ismaili Society by E. J. Brill, 1949), pp. xii + 111 (English) + 47 (Persian). Gujarati translation, *Roshnainama yane shash fasle shah Nasir Khushru*, tr. V. N. Hooda, IS Series D – Gujarati, 4 (Bombay: Published for the Ismaili Society by V. N. Hooda, 1949), pp. 95.

This is a short Ismaili treatise on *tawḥīd*, God's word (*kalima*), the soul (*nafs*), the intellect (*'aql*), *nāṭiq*, *asās*, *imām*, as well as reward and punishment in the hereafter.

118. 'Noms bibliques dans la mythologie Ismaélienne', *Journal Asiatique*, 237 (1949), pp. 249–255.

This article examines some biblical names occurring in the Ismaili literature of the Fatimid period and complements Georges Vajda's 'Melchisédec dans la mythologie Ismaélienne', *Journal Asiatique*, 234 (1943–1945), pp. 173–183; reprinted in G. Vajda (1908–1981), *Études de théologie et de philosophie Arabo-Islamiques à l'époque classique*, ed. Daniel Gimaret et al. (London, 1986), article I.

119. '*Shish Faṣl or Rawshanā'i-nāma* by Nasir-i Khusraw', in *Actes du XXIe Congrès International des Orientalistes*, Paris 23–31 juillet, 1948 (Paris: Société Asiatique de Paris, 1949), p. 295.

1950

120. Editor and translator of Naṣīr al-Dīn al-Ṭūsī, *Rawḍat al-taslīm*, published as the *Rawḍatu't-taslim, commonly called Tasawwurat*. IS Series A, 4 (Leiden: Published for the Ismaili Society by E. J. Brill, 1950), pp. lxxxviii + 249 (English) + 160 (Persian).

A better edition of this work, based on older manuscripts (including one dated 1560), has now been produced by S. Jalal Badakhchani, in his *Paradise of Submission: A Medieval Treatise on Ismaili Thought. A New Persian Edition and English Translation of Ṭūsī's Rawḍa-yi taslīm*. Ismaili Texts and Translations Series, 5 (London: I.B. Tauris in association with The Institute of Ismaili Studies, 2005), text pp. 8–220, translation pp. 13–177. The edition prepared by Badakhchani, originally as part of his University of Oxford doctoral thesis, submitted in 1989, was translated into French by Christian Jambet, in his *La Convocation d'Alamût. Somme de philosophie Ismaélienne, Rawdat al-taslîm (Le jardin de la vraie foi)* (Lagrasse: Verdier, 1996), translation pp. 121–374. Khwāja Naṣīr al-Dīn Muḥammad b. Muḥammad al-Ṭūsī (d. 1274) was a prominent Shi'i scholar. He spent some three decades in the fortresses of the Nizārī Ismailis of Persia and converted to Ismailism. He also contributed significantly to the Nizārī thought of his time. The *Rawḍa*, the major Nizārī Ismaili work of the late Alamūt period, completed in 1243, was compiled under al-Ṭūsī's supervision. Ṣalāḥ al-Dīn Ḥasan-i Maḥmūd-i Kātib, also known as Ḥasan-i Ṣalāḥ-i Munshī (d. after 1243), may have been the actual compiler, or editor, of this work.

121. Foreword to Nāṣir-i Khusraw, *Kitāb gushāʾish va rahāʾish*, ed. S. Nafīsī. IS Series A, 5 (Leiden: Published for the Ismaili Society by E. J. Brill, 1950), pp. x–xi.

A new edition and English translation of this work, based on its unique manuscript found in the library of the late Iranian scholar and judge, Sayyid Naṣr Allāh Taqavī (1871–1947), and used in S. Nafīsī's edition, appeared as *Knowledge and Liberation: A Treatise on Philosophical Theology*, ed. and tr. Faquir M. Hunzai (London: I.B.Tauris in association with The Institute of Ismaili Studies, 1998), text pp. 1–75, translation pp. 23–114.

1952

122. *Brief Survey of the Evolution of Ismailism*. IS Series B, 7 (Leiden: Published for the Ismaili Society by successors of E. J. Brill, 1952), p. 92. Corrections in no. 157, pp. 83–85.

This is the first modern survey of Ismaili history in terms of its main phases, as identified by Ivanow himself.

123. 'Tarānahā-yi rustāʾī dar Īrān' [Rural Poetry in Iran], *Iran wa Hind*, 1 (1952), pp. 85–88.

124. Review of al-Qāḍī al-Nuʿmān b. Muḥammad, *Daʿāʾim al-Islām*, vol. 1, ed. Asaf A. A. Fyzee, Cairo, 1951 (*JBBRAS*, NS, 27, 1952, pp. 321–323).

The *Daʿāʾim al-Islām*, commissioned by the Fatimid Caliph-Imam al-Muʿizz (953–975), was composed around 960 in two volumes, with volume one on *ʿibādāt* (acts of worship) and volume two on *muʿāmalāt* (worldly affairs and transactions). This legal compendium served as the official code of the Fatimid state, and is still in use within the Ṭayyibī Ismaili community. The full text of the *Daʿāʾim* was edited by Asaf A. A. Fyzee (Cairo, 1951–1962); English translation by A. A. A. Fyzee, completely revised by I. K. Poonawala, as *The Pillars of Islam* (New Delhi, 2002–2004), 2 vols.

1953

125. Editor and translator of *Pandiyāt-i jawānmardī*, published as *Pandiyat-i Jawanmardi, or 'Advices of Manliness'*. IS Series A, 6 (Leiden: Published for the Ismaili Society by successors of E. J. Brill, 1953), pp. 19 + 97 (English) + 102 (Persian).

This work contains the sermons, or religious admonitions, of the 32nd (Qāsim-Shāhī) Nizārī Imam, Mustanṣir biʾllāh (d. 1480), and it is one of the earliest doctrinal works produced during the Anjudān revival in Nizārī Ismailism. These sermons or advices (*pandiyāt*) were compiled by an anonymous Nizārī author during the imamate of Mustanṣir bi'llāh's son and successor, Imam ʿAbd al-Salām Shāh.

126. Editor and translator of *The Truth-Worshippers of Kurdistan. Ahl-i Haqq Texts*. IS Series A, 7 (Leiden: Published for the Ismaili Society by successors of E. J. Brill, 1953), pp. xv + 246 (English) + 207 (Persian). The Persian text of this work, originally lithographed in this edition in 1950 in Bombay, was reprinted separately in 156 pages, in Tehran in 1960, and also together with the first printing of the English part.

127. Foreword and Index to Ḥamīd al-Dīn al-Kirmānī, *Rāḥat al-ʿaql*, published as *Rahatu'l-ʿAql, 'Peace of Mind'*, ed. M. Kamil Ḥusayn and M. Muṣṭafā Ḥilmī. IS Series C, 1 (Leiden: Published for the Ismaili Society by E. J. Brill, 1953), pp. xi–xiii, 1–48 (Index).

Completed in 1020 for advanced adepts, the *Rāḥat al-ʿaql* contains the metaphysical system of the *dāʿī* al-Kirmānī (d. after 1020). This work represents a unique syncretic tradition within the Iranian school of 'philosophical Ismailism'. Here, al-Kirmānī harmonises Ismaili theology (*kalām*) with Neoplatonism and other philosophical traditions. This work and its sources are thoroughly studied in Daniel de Smet's *La Quiétude de l'intellect: Néoplatonisme et gnose Ismaélienne dans l'oeuvre de Ḥamîd ad-Dîn al-Kirmânî (Xe/XIes)* (Louvain, 1995).

1955

128. *Studies in Early Persian Ismailism*. IS Series A, 8 (2nd revised ed., Bombay: The Ismaili Society, 1955), p. 157.

This is the 2nd edition of no. 111 above. In this edition the first chapter of the earlier 1948 edition is replaced by a new chapter entitled 'The Problem of Pre-Fatimid Ismailism' (pp. 1–8).

129. 'Shums Tabrez of Multan', in S. M. Abdullah, ed., *Professor Muḥammad Shafīʿ Presentation Volume, Armaghān-i ʿIlmī* (Lahore: The Majlis-e-Armughān-e-ʿIlmi, 1955), pp. 109–118.

130. 'Abū ʿAlī Sīnā va Ismāʿīliyān-i makhfī' [Avicenna and the Hidden Ismailis], in *Jashn-nāma-yi Ibn Sīnā/Le livre du Millénaire d'Avicenne*. Societé Iranienne pour la conservation des Monuments Nationaux, Collection du Millénaire d'Avicenne, 31 (Tehran: Anjuman-i Āthār-i Millī, 1955), vol. 2, pp. 450–454.

1956

131. *Problems in Nasir-i Khusraw's Biography*. Ismaili Society Series B, 10 (Bombay: The Ismaili Society, 1956), pp. xiv + 88.

132. Translator of Shihāb al-Dīn Shāh al-Ḥusaynī, *True Meaning of Religion, or, Risala dar Haqiqat-i Din*. IS Series B, 9 (3rd ed., Bombay: The Ismaili Society, 1956), pp. xix + 52.

133. *The Ismaili Society of Bombay: The Tenth Anniversary (16.2.1946-16.2.1956)* (Bombay: Ismaili Printing Press, 1956), pp. 13.

134. 'Ismaili Mission in Indo-Pakistan', *Imamat*, vol. 1, no. 2 (November, 1956), pp. 19–24.

135. 'Ismailis in Russia', *Imamat*, vol. 1, no. 2 (November, 1956), pp. 39–41; reprinted in *Read and Know*, vol. 1, no. 12 (1967), pp. 11–15.

136. Translator of N. V. Peegulevskaya [Nina Viktorovna Pigulevskaya], 'Economic Relations in Iran during the IV–VI Centuries A.D.', in *Short Communications of the Oriental Institute of the Academy of Sciences, USSR*, Moscow, 1955, vol. 14, pp. 46–57 (*JCOI*, 38, 1956, pp. 1–22).

1957

137. *Ibn al-Qaddah (The Alleged Founder of Ismailism)*. IS Series A, 9 (2nd revised ed., Bombay: The Ismaili Society, 1957), p. 162.

138. 'Peinture et poésie en Orient', *Orient*, 4 (1957), pp. 7–16.

139. 'Study Ismailism', *Imamat*, vol. 1, no. 3 (October, 1957), pp. 15–18; reprinted in *Platinum* (June 1961), pp. 5–6; reprinted as 'The Importance of Studying Ismailism', in *Ilm*, vol. 1, no. 3 (1975), pp. 8–9 and 20; reprinted also in *Roshni*, no. 5 (11 July, 1981), pp. 17–18; reprinted as 'Why Should we Study Ismailism', in *Ismaili Bulletin*, vol. 4, no. 9 (May, 1978), pp. 13–15; Portuguese translation, 'A importância do estudo do Ismailismo', *Jagruti*, no. 2 (December, 1979), pp. 7–8.

1958

140. 'Care for Book', in *Golden Jubilee Souvenir of the H. R. H. Prince Aga Khan Library and Reading Room, Kharadar* (Karachi, 1958), pp. 31–32.

1959

141. Editor and translator of Abū Isḥāq Quhistānī, *Haft bāb-i Abū Isḥāq*, published as *Haft Bab, or, 'Seven Chapters'*. IS Series A, 10 (Bombay: The Ismaili Society, 1959), pp. 27 + 85 (English) + 68 (Persian).

The *Haft bāb* of the Nizārī Ismaili *dāʿī* Abū Isḥāq Quhistānī (d. after 1498) is one of the earliest doctrinal texts produced during the Anjudān revival in Persian Nizārī Ismailism.

142. 'Taṣawwuf va *Chirāgh-nāma*' [Sufism and Ismailism: *Chirāgh-nāma*], *Majalla-yi Mardum-shināsī/Revue Iranienne d'Anthropologie*, 3 (1338/1959), pp. 13–17 (English summary), 53–70 (Persian).

This work contains the original text of the medieval *Chirāgh-nāma* (pp. 60–70), which is still used by the Nizārī Ismailis of Central Asia in their *Chirāgh-rawshan* ritual commemorating the dead. See H. Elnazarov, 'The Luminous Lamp: The Practice of *Chirāgh-i rawshan* among the Ismailis of Central Asia', in F. Daftary and G. Miskinzoda, ed., *The Study of Shiʿi Islam: History, Theology and Law* (London, 2014), pp. 529–541.

1960

143. *Alamut and Lamasar: Two Mediaeval Ismaili Strongholds in Iran – An Archaeological Study*. IS Series C, 2 (Tehran: The Ismaili Society, 1960), pp. xv + 105 + 16 plates. Persian translation of chapter four as 'Nukātī dar bāra-yi Alamūt', tr. Masʿūd Rajabniyā, in G. R. Riḍāzāda Langarūdī, ed., *Yādigār-nāma: majmūʿa-yi taḥqīqī taqdīm shuda bi ustād Ibrāhīm Fakhrāʾī* (Tehran: Nashr-i Naw, 1984), pp. 465–484.

These and other medieval Nizārī fortresses were subsequently studied over a four-decade period by Peter Willey (1922–2009); see especially his *Eagle's Nest: Ismaili Castles in Iran and Syria*. Ismaili Heritage Series, 10 (London: I.B.Tauris in association with The Institute of Ismaili Studies, 2005).

144. Editor of Khayrkhwāh-i Harātī, *Faṣl dar bayān-i shinākht-i imām*. IS Series B, 11 (3rd ed., Tehran: The Ismaili Society, 1960), pp. 11 (English), 44 + 7 (Persian).

145. Review of Bertel's, Andrey E., *Nasir-i Khosrov i ismailizm*, Moscow, 1959 (*Rahnema-ye Ketab*, 3, 1960, p. 551).

146. Review of Fidāʾī Khurāsānī, Muḥammad b. Zayn al-ʿĀbidīn, *Kitāb-i hidāyat al-muʾminīn al-ṭālibīn*, ed. A. A. Semenov, Moscow, 1959 (*Rahnema-ye Ketab*, 3, 1960, pp. 372–375). Fidāʾī Khurāsānī (d. 1923) was a Persian Nizārī historian and poet. This history of Ismailism, from its origins to modern times, which is permeated with errors, has been preserved by the Nizārīs of Badakhshān. Ivanow discovered that the final part of this history, on the Aga Khans, was apparently written in Bombay around 1910 by a certain Mūsā Khān Khurāsānī (d. 1937), who was in the service of the contemporary Nizārī Imams.

1961

147. Editor of Khayrkhwāh-i Harātī, *Taṣnīfāt-i Khayrkhwāh-i Harātī*. IS Series A, 13 (Tehran: The Ismaili Society, 1961), pp. 14 (English) + 151

(Persian). This publication includes Khayrkhwāh's *Risāla* (pp. 1-75); *Qiṭaʿāt* (pp. 77-111), and *Ashʿār-i Gharībī* (pp. 113-132), containing selected poems.

In his *Risāla*, originally lithographed by Sayyid Munīr Badakhshānī (1882-1957) as *Kitāb-i Khayrkhwāh-i muwaḥḥid waḥdat* (Bombay, 1915), the author expounds his ideas on the status and attributes of the ranks of *pīr* and *ḥujjat* in the *daʿwa* hierarchy of the Nizārīs, also providing valuable autobiographical information. In his poetry (*ashʿār*), Khayrkhwāh adopted the pen-name (*takhalluṣ*) of Gharībī, after the contemporary Nizārī Imam, Mustanṣir bi'llāh (d. 1498), who was also known as Gharīb Mīrzā.

148. *Foreword* to Nāṣir-i Khusraw, *Gushāʾish va rahāʾish*, ed. Saʿīd Nafīsī. IS Series A, 11 (2nd ed., Tehran: The Ismaili Society, 1961), pp. 011-012.

149. *Foreword* to Sayyid Suhrāb Walī Badakshānī, *Sī va shish ṣaḥīfa*, published as *Sī-u shish ṣaḥīfa (Thirty-Six Epistles)*, ed. Hūshang Ujāqī. IS Series A, 12 (Tehran: The Ismaili Society, 1961), pp. 09-015.

Sayyid Suhrāb Walī Badakhshānī (d. after 1452) was a Central Asian Nizārī author. A typical representation of the Badakhshānī Nizārī tradition, this work is also known as the *Ṣaḥīfat al-nāẓirīn*. On this author, who may have belonged to the Muḥammad-Shāhī branch of Nizārī Ismailism, see F. Daftary, 'Badakhshānī, Sayyid Suhrāb Walī', in W. Madelung and F. Daftary, ed., *Encyclopaedia Islamica* (Leiden, 2013), vol. 4, pp. 60-62.

1963

150. *Ismaili Literature: A Bibliographical Survey*. A Second Amplified Edition of 'A Guide to Ismaili Literature'. IS Series A, 15 (Tehran: The Ismaili Society, 1963), pp. xv + 245. This work contains some 929 titles.

This catalogue served as the standard work of reference in the field until the publication of Ismail K. Poonawala's *Biobibliography of Ismāʿīlī Literature* (Malibu, CA, 1977). Professor Poonawala is currently working on a revised, and much expanded, edition of this work.

151. *Foreword* to Shihāb al-Dīn Shāh al-Ḥusaynī, *Kitāb-i khiṭābāt-i ʿāliya*, published as *Supreme Admonitions, Khitabat-e ʿAliya*, ed. Hūshang Ujāqī. IS Series A, 14 (Tehran: The Ismaili Society, 1963), pp. ix-xv.

In these sixty-four *khiṭābāt* or sermons, written shortly before 1881, the eldest son of the 47th Nizārī Imam Āqā ʿAlī Shāh (d. 1885), who predeceased his father by a few months, discusses various doctrinal issues and religious duties, also mentioning certain historical events and the genealogy of the Nizārī Ismaili Imams.

1966

152. 'My First Meeting with Ismailis of Persia' (Dar-es-Salaam: Umoja Press, 1966), also in *Read and Know*, vol. 1 (1966), pp. 11–14; reprinted in *Ilm*, vol. 3, no. 3 (December, 1977), pp. 16–17.

1969

153. 'Hakim Nizari Kohistani', *Africa Ismaili*, vol. 2, no. 7 (19 December, 1969), pp. 6–8; reprinted in A. M. Sadaruddin, ed., *The Best of Africa Ismaili*, vol. 11 (n.d.), pp. 58–60.

1974

154. 'Spiski rukopisei Bukharskoi kollektsii (Predislovie i primechaniia Iu. E. Borshevskogo)' [List of the Manuscripts of the Bukhara Collection. Introduction and Notes by Yurii E. Borshchevskii], in *Pis'mennye pamiatniki Vostoka. Istoriko-filologicheskoe issledovaniia, Ezhegodnik 1970* [Written Monuments of the East. Historical and Philological Studies] (Moscow, 1974), pp. 407–436. This list was originally compiled by Ivanow himself during 1915–1918.

1975

155. 'Ismailism and Sufism', *Ismaili Bulletin*, vol. 1, no. 12 (Ramaḍān 1395/September 1975), pp. 3–6.

1985

156. 'al-ʿIrq al-mansī fi'l-Ismāʿīliyya', abridged and translated by ʿĀrif Tāmir (1921–1998), in *al-Bāḥith*, vol. 7, no. 1 (1985), pp. 75–81.

1999

157. *Correspondance Corbin-Ivanow. Lettres échangées entre Henry Corbin et Vladimir Ivanow de 1947 à 1966*, ed. Sabine Schmidtke, with a Preface by Christian Jambet. Travaux et mémoires de l'Institut d'études iraniennes, 4 (Paris: Institut d'études iraniennes; Louvain: Peeters, 1999), pp. 235. Persian translation, *Mukātabāt-i Henry Corbin va Vladimir Ivanow*, tr. ʿAbd

al-Muḥammad Rūḥbakhshān (Tehran: Mūza va Markaz-i Asnād-i Majlis-i Shūrā-yi Islāmī, 2003), pp. 336.

This collection contains some 88 letters exchanged between H. Corbin (1903-1978) and W. Ivanow, including nine letters written by Ivanow to Mrs Stella Corbin (d. 2003), and one letter written by L. Massignon (1883-1962) to Ivanow.

158. 'Autobiographical Information, ed. O. F. Akimushkin', *Peterburgskoe Vostokovedenie*, 10 (2002), pp. 446-458.

Ivanow provided this note as a draft for his own obituary, and sent it to Oleg Fedorovich Akimushkin (1929-2010), the Russian orientalist and cataloguer of Persian manuscripts in St Petersburg.

2011

159. *Ocherki po istorii ismailizma* [Essays on the History of Ismailism], ed. Hakim Elnazarov and Maryam Rezvan, with a Foreword by Farhad Daftary (St Petersburg: Izdo tel'stvo Zodchii, 2011), pp. 198.

A collection of Ivanow's works, translated into Russian by Nikolay Terletsky, and published under the auspices of The Institute of Ismaili Studies on the occasion of the 125th anniversary of Ivanow's birth. See nos. 8(II), 79, 80, 82, 86 and 91. F. Daftary's entry on 'Ivanow', which first appeared in *Encyclopaedia Iranica*, ed. E. Yarshater (New York, 2008), vol. 14, pp. 298-300, is reproduced here in the original English together with its Russian translation (pp. 11-20). Also, the bibliography of Ivanow's publications, originally compiled by F. Daftary and published in *Islamic Culture*, 45 (1971), pp. 55-67, is reproduced in this collection (pp. 178-186).

160. *Piat'desiat let na Vostoke. Vospominaniia*, translated into English by S. Andreyev, revised by S. Aksakolov, edited with annotations by F. Daftary as *Fifty Years in the East: The Memoirs of Wladimir Ivanow* (London: I.B.Tauris in association with The Institute of Ismaili Studies, 2014).

Notices on W. Ivanow

1. Afshār, Īraj. 'Wladimir Ivanow', *Rahnema-ye Ketab*, 13 (1970), pp. 469-471.

2. Daftary, Farhad. 'Bibliography of the Publications of the late W. Ivanow', *Islamic Culture*, 45 (1971), pp. 55-67; bibliography of Ivanow's Ismaili publications reprinted in *Ilm*, vol. 3, no. 4 (March, 1978), pp. 35-40; also reprinted in V. A. Ivanov, *Ocherki po istorii ismailizma* [Essays on the History

of Ismailism], ed. H. Elnazarov and M. Rezvan (St Petersburg: Izdotel'stvo Zodchiy, 2011), pp. 178–186.

3. ___ 'W. Ivanow: A Biographical Notice', *Middle Eastern Studies*, 8 (1972), pp. 241–244.

4. ___ 'Bibliography of W. Ivanow: Addenda and Corrigenda', *Islamic Culture*, 56 (1982), pp. 239–240.

5. ___ 'Wladimir Ivanow: ustādī dar Ismāʿīliyya-shināsī', *Ayandeh*, 9 (1983), pp. 665–674.

6. ___ 'Anjoman-e Esmāʿīlī', *Encyclopaedia Iranica*, vol. 2, p. 84.

7. ___ 'Ivanow, Vladimir Alekseevich', *Encyclopaedia Iranica*, vol. 14, pp. 298–300; reprinted, with Russian translation, in V. A. Ivanov, *Ocherkii po istorii ismailizma*, pp. 11–20.

8. ___ 'Wladimir Ivanow and Modern Ismaili Studies', in S. Prozorov and H. Elnazarov, ed., *Russkie uchënye ob ismailisme/Russian Scholars on Ismailism* (St Petersburg: St Petersburg State University, Faculty of Philology, 2014), pp. 24–37.

9. Firuzi, Javad. 'Ivanov, Vladimir Alekseevich', *Great Islamic Encyclopaedia*, ed. K. Musavi Bojnurdi (Tehran, 2001), vol. 10, pp. 721–722.

10. Fyzee, Asaf A. A. 'W. Ivanow (1886–1970)', *Indo-Iranica*, 23 (1970), pp. 22–27.

11. ___ 'Wladimir Ivanow (1886–1970)', *Journal of the Asiatic Society of Bombay*, New Series, 45–46 (1970–1971; published in 1974), pp. 92–97.

12. Husseini Qasemi, Sharif. 'Fehrest-e Asar-e Ivanof' [List of the Works of Ivanow], *Qand-e Parsi* (Delhi, 1986), pp. 165–187.

13. Jambet, Christian. 'Préface', in *Correspondance Corbin-Ivanow. Lettres échangées entre Henry Corbin et Vladimir Ivanow de 1947 à 1966*, ed. Sabine Schmidtke (Paris: Institut d'études iraniennes; Louvain: Peeters, 1999), pp. 5–10.

14. Öz, Mustafa. 'Ivanow, Wladimir', *Türkiye Diyanet Vakfı İslâm Ansiklopedisi* (Istanbul, 2001), vol. 23, pp. 487–488.

Appendix 2

Publications of the Islamic Research Association

1. *An Abbreviated Version of the Diwan of Khaki Khorasani*. Persian text, edited with an introduction by W. Ivanow. Islamic Research Association, No. 1 (1933).

2. *Two Early Ismaili Treatises: Haft-babi Baba Sayyid-na and Matlubu'l-mu'minin by Tusi*. Persian text, with an introductory note by W. Ivanow. Islamic Research Association, No. 2 (1933).

3. *True Meaning of Religion (Risala dar Haqiqati Din)*, by Shihabu'd-Din Shah al-Husayni. Persian text and English translation by W. Ivanow. Islamic Research Association, No. 3 (1933).

4. *Kalami Pir: A Treatise on Ismaili Doctrine, also (wrongly) called Haft-Babi Shah Sayyid Nasir*. Edited in original Persian and translated into English by W. Ivanow. Islamic Research Association, No. 4 (1935).

5. *Arabon ki Jahaz-rani (Arab Navigation)*, by Syed Sulaiman Nadwi (in Urdu). Islamic Research Association, No. 5 (1935).

6. *The Book of Truthfulness (Kitab al-Sidq)*, by Abu Saʿid al-Kharraz. Edited and translated from the Istanbul Unicum by Arthur John Arberry. Islamic Research Association, No. 6 (1937).

7. *al-Hidayatu'l-Amiriya, being an epistle of the tenth Fatimid Caliph al-Amir bi-ahkami'l-lah, and an Appendix, Iqaʿ Sawaʿiqi'l-irgham*. Edited with an introduction and notes by Asaf A. A. Fyzee. Islamic Research Association, No. 7 (1938).

8. *The Songs of Lovers (ʿUshshaq-Nama)*, by ʿIraqi. Persian text, edited and translated into verse by Arthur J. Arberry. Islamic Research Association, No. 8 (1939).

9. *A Shiʿite Creed, being a translation of the Risalatu'l-Iʿtiqadati'l-Imamiya of Ibn Babawayhi*, by Asaf A. A. Fyzee. Islamic Research Association, No. 9 (1942).

10. *Ismaili Tradition Concerning the Rise of the Fatimids*, by W. Ivanow. Islamic Research Association, No. 10 (1942).

11. *Islamic Research Association Miscellany*. Volume One, 1948. Edited by Asaf A. A. Fyzee. Islamic Research Association Series, No. 11 (1949).

12. *The Nuh Sipihr of Amir Khusraw*. Persian text, edited by Mohammad Wahid Mirza. Islamic Research Association Series, No. 12 (1950).

13. *Kitabu'l Kashf of Ja'far b. Mansuri'l Yaman*. Edited by R. Strothmann. Islamic Research Association Series, No. 13 (1952).

Appendix 3

Publications of the Ismaili Society
The Ismaili Society's Series of Texts, Translations and Monographs

Series A

1. *The Alleged Founder of Ismailism*, by W. Ivanow. Bombay, 1946, pp. xvi + 198.

2. *Collectanea*, Vol. I, 1948. Edited by W. Ivanow. Leiden, 1948, pp. xii + 242.

3. *Studies in Early Persian Ismailism*, by W. Ivanow. Leiden, 1948, pp. xii + 202.

4. *The Rawdatu't-Taslim commonly called Tasawwurat*, by Nasiru'd-din Tusi. Persian text, edited and translated into English by W. Ivanow. Leiden, 1950, pp. lxxxviii + 249 (English) + 160 (Persian).

5. *Kitab-i Gusha'ish wa Raha'ish (The Book of Unfettering and Liberation)*, by Nasir-i Khusraw. Edited in the original Persian by Dr Sa'id Nafisi. Leiden, 1950, pp. xix + 125.

6. *Pandiyat-i Jawanmardi or 'Advices of Manliness'*. Edited in the original Persian and translated into English by W. Ivanow. Leiden, 1953, pp. x + 20 + 97 (English) + 102 (Persian).

7. *The Truth-Worshippers of Kurdistan. Ahl-i Haqq Texts*. Edited in the original Persian and analysed by W. Ivanow. Leiden, 1953, pp. xv + 246 (English) + 212 (Persian).

8. *Studies in Early Persian Ismailism*, by W. Ivanow. Second revised edition. Bombay, 1955, pp. xii + 157.

9. *Ibn al-Qaddah (The Alleged Founder of Ismailism)*, by W. Ivanow. Second revised edition. Bombay, 1957, pp. xii + 162.

10. *Haft Bab or 'Seven Chapters'*, by Abu Ishaq Quhistani (written at the beginning of the 16th century). Edited in the original Persian and translated into English by W. Ivanow. Bombay, 1959, pp. xii + 27 + 85 (English) + 68 (Persian).

11. *Gusha'ish wa Raha'ish*, by Nasir-i Khusraw. Second edition of the original Persian text, by Sa'id Nafisi. Tehran, 1961, pp. xii + 108.

12. *Si-u Shish Sahifa (Thirty-Six Epistles)*, by Sayyid Suhrab Wali Badakhshani (written in AH 856/AD 1452). Persian text edited by Hushang Ujaqi, with a Foreword by W. Ivanow. Tehran, 1961, pp. xv + 84.

13. *Tasnifat-i Khayr-khwah-i Herati (Works of Khayr-khwah Herati)*. Edited in the original Persian by W. Ivanow. Tehran, 1961, pp. xiv + 151.

14. *Supreme Admonitions, Khitabat-e 'Aliya*, of Pir Shihabu'd-din Shah al-Husayni. Persian text edited by Hushang Ujaqi. Bombay, 1963, pp. xv + 82.

15. *Ismaili Literature: A Bibliographical Survey*. A second amplified edition of 'A Guide to Ismaili Literature', London, 1933, by W. Ivanow. Tehran, 1963, pp. xvi + 245.

Series B

1. Shihabu'd-Din Shah al-Husayni, *Risala dar Haqiqat-i Din or True Meaning of Religion*. Facsimile edition of the autograph copy, by W. Ivanow. Bombay, 1947, pp. xii + 75.

2. Shihabu'd-Din Shah al-Husayni, *True Meaning of Religion or Risala dar Haqiqat-i Din*. Translated into English by W. Ivanow. Second edition, Bombay, 1947, pp. xv + 51.

3. *Fasl dar Bayan-i Shinakht-i Imam or On the Recognition of the Imam*. Persian text edited by W. Ivanow. Second revised edition, Leiden, 1949, pp. xvi + 28.

4. *On the Recognition of the Imam (Fasl dar Bayan-i Shinakht-i Imam)*. Translated from Persian by W. Ivanow. Bombay, 1947, pp. xii + 60.

5. *Nasir-i Khusraw and Ismailism*, by W. Ivanow. Bombay, 1948, pp. 78.

6. *Six Chapters or Shish Fasl, also called Rawshana'i-nama*, by Nasir-i Khusraw. Persian text edited and translated into English by W. Ivanow. Leiden, 1949, pp. xii + 111 (English) + 47 (Persian).

7. *Brief Survey of the Evolution of Ismailism*, by W. Ivanow. Leiden, 1952, pp. 92.

8. Shihabu'd-Din Shah al-Husayni, *Risala dar Haqiqat-i Din or True Meaning of Religion*. Facsimile edition of the autograph copy, by W. Ivanow. Second impression, Bombay, 1955, pp. xvi + 75.

9. Shihabu'd-Din Shah al-Husayni, *True Meaning of Religion or Risala dar Haqiqat-i Din*. Translated into English by W. Ivanow. Third edition, Bombay, 1956, pp. xix + 52.

10. *Problems in Nasir-i Khusraw's Biography*, by W. Ivanow. Bombay, 1956, pp. xv + 88.

11. *Fasl dar Bayan-i Shinakht-i Imam (On the Recognition of the Imam)*, by Khayr-khwah pisar-i Khwaja Husayn Harati. Edited by W. Ivanow. Third edition, Tehran, 1960, pp. xvi + 11 + 44.

Series C

1. *Rahatu'l-ʿAql, 'Peace of Mind'*, by Sayyid-na Hamidu'd-din al-Kirmani (d. ca. AH 411 or AD 1021). Edited in the original Arabic by Dr M. Kamil Hussein and Dr M. Mustafa Hilmy. Leiden, 1953, pp. xiii + 48 + 438.

2. *Alamut and Lamasar: Two Medieval Ismaili Strongholds in Iran, An Archaeological Study*, by W. Ivanow. Tehran, 1960, pp. xv + 105 + 28 plates.

Bibliography

The following abbreviations are used in the footnotes to the text and the bibliography:

EI	*The Encyclopaedia of Islam*, first edition
EI2	*The Encyclopaedia of Islam*, new (second) edition
EIR	*Encyclopaedia Iranica*
EIS	*Encyclopaedia Islamica*
ZVORAO	*Zapiski vostochnogo otdeleniia Imperatorskogo Russkogo arkheologicheskogo obshchestva*, St Petersburg (Petrograd)

Abaev, Vasilii I. (ed.). *Iranskii Sbornik: k semidesiatiletiu professora I. I. Zarubina* [Iranian Collection: On the 70th Birthday of Professor I. I. Zarubin]. Moscow, 1963.

Abdulhussein, Mustafa. 'Bohras', in *The Oxford Encyclopaedia of the Islamic World*, ed. John L. Esposito. Oxford, 2009, vol. 1, pp. 354–356.

Abu Ishaq Quhistani. *Haft bāb*, ed. and tr. W. Ivanow. Bombay, 1959.

Abu-Izzeddin, Nejla M. *The Druzes: A New Study of their History, Faith and Society*. Leiden, 1984.

Actes du XXIe Congrès International des Orientalistes, Paris, 23–31 juillet 1948. Paris, 1949.

Aga Khan I, Hasan Ali Shah. *Ibrat-afza*. Bombay, 1862.

Aga Khan III, Sultan Muhammad (Mahomed) Shah. *The Memoirs of Aga Khan: World Enough and Time*. London, 1954.

—— *Aga Khan III: Selected Speeches and Writings of Sir Sultan Muhammad Shah*, ed. K. K. Aziz. London, 1997–1998.

Akimushkin, Oleg F. 'K istorii formirovaniia fonda musul'manskikh rukopisei Instituta Vostokovedeniia AN SSSR' [On the History of the Formation of the Collection of Islamic Manuscripts of the Institute of Oriental Studies of the USSR], *Pis'mennye pamiatniki Vostoka. Istoriki filologicheskie issledovania 1978–1979*. Moscow, 1987.

—— et al. *Persidskie i tadzhikskie rukopisi Instituta narodov Azii AN SSSR: Kratkil alfavitnyi katalog* [Persian and Tajik Manuscripts in the Institute of the Peoples of Asia, the USSR Academy of Sciences], ed. Nikolai D. Muklukho-Maklai. Moscow, 1964.

—— et al. 'The Triumph of the Qalam', in Petrosyan et al., *Pages of Perfection*, pp. 35–75.

Aksenov, Aleksandr I. et al. (ed.). *Ekonomicheskaia istoriia Rossii s drevneishikh vremen do 1917 goda* [Economic History of Russia from Ancient Times to 1917]. Moscow, 2008.

Alekseev, Vasilii M. 'Sergei Federovich Ol'denburg kak organizator i rukovoditel' nashikh orientalistov' [S. F. Oldenburg as Organiser and Leader of our Orientalists], *Zapiski Instituta Vostokovedeniia Akademii Nauk SSSR*, 4 (1934), pp. 31–57.

Allen, Thomas W. 'Arthur Ernest Cowley, 1861–1931', *Proceedings of the British Academy*, 19 (1933), pp. 351–359.

Anon. 'Assassins', *EI*, vol. 1, pp. 491–492.

Ansari, N. H. and Sharif H. Qasemi. 'Bengal. ii. Royal Asiatic Society of Bengal', *EIR*, vol. 4, pp. 141–143.

Arba rasaʾil Ismaʿiliyya, ed. Arif Tamir. Salamiyya, 1953.

Arberry, Arthur J. *Oriental Essays: Portraits of Seven Scholars*. London, 1960.

Asani, Ali S. *Ecstasy and Enlightenment: The Ismaili Devotional Literature of South Asia*. London, 2002.

—— 'From Satpanthi to Ismaili Muslim: The Articulation of Ismaili Khoja Identity in South Asia', in F. Daftary, ed., *A Modern History of the Ismailis: Continuity and Change in a Muslim Community*. London, 2011, pp. 95–128.

Assemani, Simone. *Ragguaglio storico-critico sopra la setta Assissana, detta volgarmente degli Assassini*. Padua, 1806.

Badakhchani, S. Jalal. '*Poems of the Resurrection*: Hasan-i Mahmud-i Katib and his *Diwan-i Qaʾimiyyat*', in Omar Alí-de-Unzaga, ed., *Fortresses of the Intellect: Ismaili and Other Islamic Studies in Honour of Farhad Daftary*. London, 2011, pp. 431–442.

Baffioni, Carmela (ed.). *Atti del Convegno sul centenario della nascita di Louis Massignon*. Naples, 1985.

al-Baghdadi, Abd al-Qahir b. Tahir. *al-Farq bayn al-firaq*, ed. M. Badr. Cairo, 1910. English trans., *Moslem Schisms and Sects*, part II, tr. A. S. Halkin. Tel Aviv, 1935.

Bartol'd, Vasilii Vladimirovich. 'Pamiati V. A. Zhukovskogo' [In Memoriam V. A. Zhukovskii], *ZVORAO*, 25 (1921), pp. 399–414.

—— *Turkestan Down to the Mongol Invasion*. London, 1928; ed. C. Edmund Bosworth, 3rd ed., London, 1968.

—— *La découverte de l'Asie. Histoire de l'orientalisme en Europe et en Russie*, tr. B. Nikitine. Paris, 1947.

—— *Sochineniia* [Collected Works]. Moscow, 1963–1977.

'Bartol'd, Vasilii Vladimirovich', in Sofia D. Miliband, ed., *Biobibliograficheskii slovar' Otechestvennykh vostokovedov s 1917 g* [Biobibliographical Dictionary of Native Orientalists from 1917]. Moscow, 1995, vol. 1, pp. 128–131.

Basu, Aparma. *The Growth of Education and Political Development in India, 1898–1920*. New Delhi, 1974.

Bawa, Vasant K. *The Last Nizam: The Life and Times of Mir Osman Ali Khan*. New Delhi, 1992.

Bertel's, Andrei E. *Nasir-i Khosrov i ismailizm* [Nasir-i Khusraw and Ismailism]. Moscow, 1959.

—— and M. Bakoev. *Alfavitnyi katalog rukopisei obnaruzhennykh v Gorno-Badakhshanskoi Avtonomnoi Oblasti ekspeditsiei 1959–1963 gg./ Alphabetic Catalogue of Manuscripts found by 1959–1963 Expedition in Gorno-Badakhshan Autonomous Region*, ed. B. G. Gafurov and A. M. Mirzoev. Moscow, 1967.

Bianca, Stefano (ed.). *Karakoram: Hidden Treasures in the Northern Areas of Pakistan*. Geneva, 2005.

—— *Syria: Medieval Citadels between East and West*. Geneva, 2007.

Blois, François de. *Arabic, Persian and Gujarati Manuscripts: The Hamdani Collection in the Library of The Institute of Ismaili Studies*. London, 2011.

Bobrinskoy, Aleksey A. 'Sekta Ismailiya v Russkikh i Bukharskikh predelakh Sredney Azii' [The Ismaili Sect in Russian and Bukharan Central Asia], *Etnograficheskoe Obozrenie*, 2 (1902), pp. 1–20.

Boivin, Michel. *La rénovation du Shiʿisme Ismaélien en Inde et au Pakistan. D'après les écrits et les discours de Sultan Muhammad Shah Aga Khan (1902–1954)*. London, 2003.

—— *Artefacts of Devotion: A Sufi Repertoire of the Qalandariyya in Sehwan Sharif, Sindh, Pakistan*. Karachi, 2011.

—— *L'âghâ khân et les Khojah*. Paris, 2013.

Bosworth, C. Edmund. *The New Islamic Dynasties: A Chronological and Genealogical Manual*. New York, 1996.

—— *Eastward Ho! Diplomats, Travellers and Interpreters of the Middle East and Beyond 1600–1940*. London, 2012.

—— (ed.). *A Century of British Orientalists 1902–2001*. Oxford, 2001.

Boucharlat, Rémy. 'France. xiii. Institut Français de Recherche en Iran', *EIR*, vol. 10, pp. 176–177.

Böwering, Gerhard. 'Češtiya', *EIR*, vol. 5, pp. 333–339.

Braune, Michael. 'Untersuchungen zur mittelalterlichen Befestigung in Nordwest-Syrien: Die Assassinenburg Masyaf', *Damaszener Mitteilungen*, 7 (1993), pp. 298–326.

Bregel, Yuri. 'The Bibliography of Barthold's Works and the Soviet Censorship', *Survey*, 24 (1979), pp. 91–107.

—— 'Barthold and Modern Oriental Studies', *International Journal of Middle East Studies*, 12 (1980), pp. 385–403.

—— 'Mangits', *EI2*, vol. 6, pp. 418–419.

—— 'Barthold', *EIR*, vol. 3, pp. 830–832.

—— 'Central Asia. vii. In the 12th–13th/18th–19th Centuries', *EIR*, vol. 5, pp. 193–205.

Brockelmann, Carl. *Geschichte der arabischen Litteratur*. Weimar, 1898–1902; 2nd ed., Leiden, 1943–1949; *Supplementbände*. Leiden, 1937–1942.

Browne, Edward G. *A Literary History of Persia*. London and Cambridge, 1902–1924.

—— *A Descriptive Catalogue of the Oriental Mss. Belonging to the late E. G. Browne*, ed. Reynold A. Nicholson. Cambridge, 1932.

Broxup, Marie. 'The Basmachi', *Central Asian Survey*, 2 (1983), pp. 57–81.

Bruijn, Johannes T. P. de. 'Hammer-Purgstall', *EIR*, vol. 11, pp. 644–646.

Cachia, Pierre. *Taha Husayn: His Place in the Egyptian Literary Renaissance*. London, 1956.

—— 'Taha Husayn', *EI2*, vol. 10, pp. 95–96.

Chakrabarty, Ramakanta. *The Asiatic Society 1784–2008*. Calcutta, 2008.

Chassinat, Emile (ed.). *Bibliothèque des Arabisants Français*. Première série: Silvestre de Sacy. Cairo, 1905.

Corbin, Henry. *Cyclical Time and Ismaili Gnosis*, tr. R. Manheim and J. W. Morris. London, 1983.

—— *History of Islamic Philosophy*, tr. L. Sherrard. London, 1993.

Correspondance Corbin-Ivanow. Lettres échangées entre Henry Corbin et Vladimir Ivanow de 1947 à 1966, ed. Sabine Schmidtke. Paris and Louvain, 1999.

Cortese, Delia. *Ismaili and Other Arabic Manuscripts: A Descriptive Catalogue of Manuscripts in the Library of The Institute of Ismaili Studies*. London, 2000.

—— *Arabic Ismaili Manuscripts: The Zahid Ali Collection in the Library of The Institute of Ismaili Studies*. London, 2003.

Daftary, Farhad. 'Bibliography of the Publications of the late W. Ivanow', *Islamic Culture*, 45 (1971), pp. 55–67, and 56 (1982), pp. 239–240.

—— 'W. Ivanow: A Biographical Notice', *Middle Eastern Studies*, 8 (1972), pp. 241–244.

—— 'Wladimir Ivanow: ustadi dar Isma'iliyya-shinasi', *Ayandeh*, 9 (1983), pp. 665-674.

—— 'Professor Asaf A. A. Fyzee (1899-1981)', *Arabica*, 31 (1984), pp. 327-330.

—— 'The Bibliography of Asaf A. A. Fyzee', *Indo-Iranica*, 37 (1984), pp. 49-63.

—— 'Marius Canard (1888-1982): A Bio-Bibliographical Notice', *Arabica*, 33 (1986), pp. 251-262.

—— 'Persian Historiography of the Early Nizari Isma'ilis', *Iran, Journal of the British Institute of Persian Studies*, 30 (1992), pp. 91-97.

—— *The Isma'ilis: Their History and Doctrines*. 2nd ed., Cambridge, 2007. Russian trans., *Ismaility: Ikh istoriia i doktriny*, tr. Leila R. Dodykhudoeva, ed. Oleg F. Akimushkin. Moscow, 2011. Persian trans., *Tarikh va sunnatha-yi Isma'iliyya*, tr. F. Badra'i. Tehran, 2014.

—— *The Assassin Legends: Myths of the Isma'ilis*. London, 1994. French trans., *Légendes des Assassins*, tr. Z. Rajan-Badouraly. Paris, 2007. Russian trans., *Legendy ob Assasinakh*, tr. Leila R. Dodykhudoeva, ed. Oleg F. Akimushkin. Moscow, 2009.

—— (ed.). *Mediaeval Isma'ili History and Thought*. Cambridge, 1996.

—— 'Hasan-i Sabbah and the Origins of the Nizari Isma'ili Movement', in Daftary, ed., *Mediaeval Isma'ili History and Thought*, pp. 181-204.

—— *A Short History of the Ismailis: Traditions of a Muslim Community*. Edinburgh, 1998. Russian trans., *Kratkaya istoriya isma'ilizma*, tr. Leila R. Dodykhudoeva and Lola N. Dodkhudoeva. Moscow, 2003.

—— 'Nasir al-Din al-Tusi and the Ismailis of the Alamut Period', in N. Pourjavady and Ž. Vesel, ed., *Nasir al-Din Tusi, Philosophe et savant du XIIIe siècle*. Tehran, 2000, pp. 59-67.

—— 'Bibliography of the Works of Wilferd Madelung', in F. Daftary and J. Meri, ed., *Culture and Memory in Medieval Islam: Essays in Honour of Wilferd Madelung*. London, 2003, pp. 5-40.

—— *Ismaili Literature: A Bibliography of Sources and Studies*. London, 2004.

—— *Ismailis in Medieval Muslim Societies*. London, 2005.

—— 'The "Order of the Assassins": J. von Hammer and the Orientalist Misrepresentations of the Nizari Ismailis', *Iranian Studies*, 39 (2006), pp. 71-81.

—— 'Ismaili History and Literary Traditions', in H. Landolt et al., ed., *An Anthology of Ismaili Literature: A Shi'i Vision of Islam*. London, 2008, pp. 1-29.

—— 'Sinan and the Nizari Ismailis of Syria', in Daniela Bredi et al., ed., *Scritti in onore di Biancamaria Scarcia Amoretti*. Rome, 2008, vol. 2, pp. 489–500.

—— (ed.) *A Modern History of the Ismailis: Continuity and Change in a Muslim Community*. London, 2011.

—— *Historical Dictionary of the Ismailis*. Lanham and Toronto, 2012.

—— *A History of Shiʿi Islam*. London, 2013.

—— 'Rashid al-Din Sinan', *EI2*, vol. 8, pp. 442–443.

—— 'al-Tayyibiyya', *EI2*, vol. 10, pp. 403–404.

—— 'Umm al-Kitab: 2. Among the Shiʿa', *EI2*, vol. 10, pp. 854–855.

—— 'Anjoman-e Esmaʿili', *EIR*, vol. 2, p. 84.

—— 'Carmatians', *EIR*, vol. 4, pp. 823–832.

—— 'Fedaʾi Ḵorasani', *EIR*, vol. 9, p. 470.

—— 'Hamid-al-Din Kermani', *EIR*, vol. 11, pp. 639–641.

—— 'Ismaʿilism. iii. Ismaʿili History', *EIR*, vol. 14, pp. 178–195.

—— 'Ivanow, Vladimir', *EIR*, vol. 14, pp. 298–300.

—— 'Abd Allah b. Maymun al-Qaddah', *EIS*, vol. 1, pp. 167–169.

—— 'Fatimids', in *Medieval Islamic Civilization: An Encyclopedia*, ed. Josef W. Meri. New York, 2006, vol. 1, pp. 250–253.

—— 'Assassins', in *The Oxford Encyclopedia of the Islamic World*, ed. John L. Esposito. Oxford, 2009, vol. 1, pp. 227–229.

—— and Zulfikar Hirji. *The Ismailis: An Illustrated History*. London, 2008.

Dahan, Sami. 'Muhammad Kurd Ali (1876–1953). Notice biographique', in *Mélanges Louis Massignon*. Damascus, 1956–1957, vol. 1, pp. 379–394.

Daniel, Victor et al. *Nikolai Markov: Architecture of Changing Times in Iran*. Tehran, 2004.

Danielson, Virginia. 'Umm Kulthum (1904?–1975)', in *Encyclopaedia of Islam and the Muslim World*, ed. Richard C. Martin. New York, 2004, vol. 2, pp. 706–707.

de Planhol, Xavier. 'Abadan. ii. Modern Abadan', *EIR*, vol. 1, pp. 53–57.

—— 'Badakšan. i. Geography and Ethnography', *EIR*, vol. 3, pp. 355–360.

—— 'Bandar-e Abbas(i)', *EIR*, vol. 3, pp. 685–687.

de Smet, Daniel. *La Quiétude de l'intellect: Néoplatonisme et gnose Ismaélienne dans l'oeuvre de Hamid ad-Din al-Kirmani (Xe/XIe s.)*. Louvain, 1995.

—— 'Henry Corbin et études Ismaéliennes', in M. A. Amir-Moezzi et al., ed., *Henry Corbin, philosophies et sagesses des religions du livre*. Turnhout, 2005.

Defrémery, Charles F. 'Nouvelles recherches sur les Ismaéliens ou Bathiniens de Syrie, plus connus sur le nom d'Assassins', *Journal Asiatique*, 5 Series, 3 (1854), pp. 373-421, and 5 (1855), pp. 5-76.

Dehérain, Henri. *Silvestre de Sacy 1758-1838. Ses contemporains et ses disciples*. Paris, 1938.

Derenbourg, Hartwig. *Silvestre de Sacy (1758-1938)*. Paris, 1895.

Dhaul, Laxmi. *The Dargah of Nizamuddin Auliya*. New Delhi, 2006.

Dickson, William E. R. *East Persia: A Backwater of the Great War*. London, 1924.

Digard, Jean-Pierre. 'Gypsy. i. Gypsies of Persia', *EIR*, vol. 11, pp. 412-415.

Dmitriiev, Nikolai K. 'V. D. Smirnov: A Memoir', *Journal of the Royal Asiatic Society*, 2 (1928), pp. 408-410.

Dumasia, Naoroji M. *The Aga Khan and His Ancestors: A Biographical and Historical Sketch*. Bombay, 1939; reprinted, New Delhi, 2008.

Elisséeff, Serge. 'Stael-Holstein's Contributions to Asiatic Studies', *Harvard Journal of Asiatic Studies*, 3 (1938), pp. 1-8.

Encyclopaedia Iranica, ed. E. Yarshater. London and New York, 1982-.

Encyclopaedia Islamica, ed. W. Madelung and F. Daftary. Leiden, 2008-.

The Encyclopaedia of Islam, ed. M. H. Houtsma et al. 1st ed., Leiden and London, 1913-1938; reprinted, Leiden, 1987.

The Encyclopaedia of Islam, ed. H. A. R. Gibb et al. New ed., Leiden, 1954-2004.

Entner, Marvin L. *Russo-Persian Commercial Relations, 1828-1914*. Gainesville, FL, 1965.

Ethé, Hermann. *Catalogue of the Persian, Turkish, Hindustani and Pashtu Manuscripts in the Bodleian Library*, vol. I. Oxford, 1889.

Falconet, Camille. 'Dissertation sur les Assassins, peuple d'Asie', in *Mémoires de Littérature, tirés des registres de l'Académie Royale des Inscriptions et Belles Lettres*, 17 (1751), pp. 127-170. English trans., 'A Dissertation on the Assassins, a People of Asia', as an appendix in John of Joinville, *Memoirs of John Lord de Joinville*, tr. T. Johnes. Hafod, 1807, vol. 2, pp. 287-328.

Fedorov-Davydov, German A. *Obshchestvennyi stroi Zolotoi Ordy* [The Social Structure of the Golden Horde]. Moscow, 1973.

Fida'i Khurasani, Muhammad b. Zayn al-Abidin. *Kitab-i hidayat al-mu'minin al-talibin*, ed. A. A. Semenov. Moscow, 1959.

Firro, Kais M. *A History of the Druzes*. Leiden, 1992.

Fyzee, Asaf A. A. 'Materials for an Ismaili Bibliography: 1920-1934', *Journal of the Bombay Branch of the Royal Asiatic Society*, New Series, 11 (1935), pp. 59-65.

—— 'The Study of the Literature of the Fatimid Daʿwa', in G. Makdisi, ed., *Arabic and Islamic Studies in Honor of Hamilton A. R. Gibb*. Leiden, 1965, pp. 232–249.

—— *Compendium of Fatimid Law*. Simla, 1969.

—— 'Wladimir Ivanow (1886–1970)', *Journal of the Asiatic Society of Bombay*, New Series, 45–46 (1970–1971), pp. 92–97.

—— 'A Collection of Fatimid Manuscripts', in N. N. Gidwani, ed., *Comparative Librarianship: Essays in Honour of Professor D. N. Marshall*. Delhi, 1973, pp. 209–220.

—— 'Bohoras', *EI2*, vol. 1, pp. 1254–1255.

Gacek, Adam. 'Library Resources at The Institute of Ismaili Studies, London', *British Society for Middle Eastern Studies Bulletin*, 11 (1984), pp. 63–64.

—— *Catalogue of Arabic Manuscripts in the Library of The Institute of Ismaili Studies*, vol. 1. London, 1984.

—— *Arabic Manuscripts in the Libraries of McGill University. Union Catalogue*. Montreal, 1991.

Ghani, Ghasem. *A Man of Many Worlds: The Memoirs and Diaries of Dr. Ghasem Ghani*, ed. C. Ghani. Washington DC, 2006.

al-Ghazali, Abu Hamid Muhammad b. Muhammad. *Fadaʾih al-Batiniyya*, ed. A. Badawi. Cairo, 1964. Partial English trans. in Richard J. McCarthy, *Freedom and Fulfillment*. Boston, 1980, pp. 175–286.

—— *Tahafut al-falasifa*, ed. M. Bouges. Beirut, 1927; ed. and tr. M. E. Marmura as *The Incoherence of the Philosophers*. Provo, UT, 1997.

Gnosis-Texte der Ismailiten, ed. R. Strothmann. Göttingen, 1943.

Goriawala, Muʿizz. *A Descriptive Catalogue of the Fyzee Collection of Ismaili Manuscripts*. Bombay, 1965.

Griffini, Eugenio. 'Die jüngste ambrosianische Sammlung arabischer Handschriften', *Zeitschrift der Deutschen Morgenländischen Gesellschaft*, 69 (1915), pp. 63–88.

Guyard, Stanislas (ed. and tr.). *Fragments relatifs à la doctrine des Ismaélis*, in *Notices et Extraits des Manuscrits de la Bibliothèque Nationale*, 22 (1874), pp. 177–428.

Haft bab-i Baba Sayyidna, ed. W. Ivanow, in his *Two Early Ismaili Treatises*. Bombay, 1933, pp. 4–44. English trans. as *The Popular Appeal of the Qiyama*, in Hodgson, *The Order of Assassins*, pp. 279–324.

Haj Manouchehri, Faramarz et al. 'Ali b. Abi Talib', *EIS*, vol. 3, pp. 477–583.

Halm, Heinz. *Kosmologie und Heilslehre der frühen Ismaʿiliya: Eine Studie zur islamischen Gnosis*. Wiesbaden, 1978.

—— *Die islamische Gnosis: Die extreme Schia und die Alawiten*. Zurich and Munich, 1982.

—— 'Les Fatimides à Salamya', in *Mélanges offerts au Professeur Dominique Sourdel*; being, *Revue d'Études Islamiques*, 54 (1986), pp. 133–149.
—— *The Fatimids and their Traditions of Learning*. London, 1997.
—— *Kalifen und Assassinen. Ägypten und der Vordere Orient zur Zeit der ersten Kreuzzüge 1074–1171*. Munich, 2014.
—— 'Nusayriyya', *EI2*, vol. 8, pp. 145–148.
Hamdani, Abbas. *The Beginnings of the Ismaʿili Daʿwa in Northern India*. Cairo, 1956.
al-Hamdani, Husayn F. 'Some Unknown Ismaʿili Authors and their Works', *Journal of the Royal Asiatic Society* (1933), pp. 359–378.
Hammer-Purgstall, Joseph von. *Die Geschichte der Assassinen aus Morgenländischen Quellen*. Stuttgart and Tübingen, 1818. French trans., *Histoire de l'ordre des Assassins*, tr. J. J. Hellert and P. A. de la Nourais. Paris, 1833; reprinted, Paris, 1961. English trans., *The History of the Assassins, derived from Oriental Sources*, tr. O. C. Wood. London, 1835; reprinted, New York, 1968. Italian trans., *Origine, potenza e caduta degli Assassini*, tr. S. Romanini. Padua, 1838; reprinted, San Donato, 2006.
Haneda, Masashi and Rudi Matthee. 'Isfahan. vii. Safavid Period', *EIR*, vol. 13, pp. 650–657.
Hasan, Maytham. 'Introduction to the Citadel of Masyaf', in S. Bianca, ed., *Syria: Medieval Citadels Between East and West*. Geneva, 2007, pp. 181–214.
Hinnells, John R. 'Bombay. i. The Zoroastrian Community', *EIR*, vol. 4, pp. 339–346.
—— 'Parsis', *EI2*, vol. 8, pp. 273–275.
Hitchins, Keith. 'Ayni', *EIR*, vol. 3, pp. 144–149.
Hodgson, Marshall G. S. *The Order of Assassins: The Struggle of the Early Nizari Ismaʿilis against the Islamic World*. The Hague, 1955; reprinted, New York, 1980; reprinted, Philadelphia, 2005.
—— 'The Ismaʿili State', in *The Cambridge History of Iran: Volume 5, The Saljuq and Mongol Periods*, ed. John A. Boyle. Cambridge, 1968, pp. 422–482.
Hollister, John N. *The Shiʿa of India*. London, 1953; reprinted, New Delhi, 1979.
Holzwarth, Wolfgang. *Die Ismailiten in Nordpakistan*. Berlin, 1994.
Huart, Clément. 'Ismaʿiliya', *EI*, vol. 2, pp. 549–552.
Hunsberger, Alice C. *Nasir Khusraw, The Ruby of Badakhshan: A Portrait of the Persian Poet, Traveller and Philosopher*. London, 2000.

Husain, M. Hidayat. *List of Arabic and Persian Mss. Acquired on Behalf of the Government of India by the Asiatic Society of Bengal, 1903–1907.* Calcutta, 1908.

Husayn, Muhammad Kamil. *Ta'ifat al-Ismaʿiliyya.* Cairo, 1959.

Ianin, Vladimir L. 'Numizmatika', in Nechkina et al., ed., *Ocherki istorii,* vol. 2, pp. 672–676.

Ibn Hani, Abu'l-Qasim Muhammad. *Tabyin al-maʿani fi sharh diwan Ibn Hani al-Andalusi al-Maghribi,* ed. Zahid Ali. Cairo, 1933.

Irvine, William and Mohammad Habib. 'Awrangzib', *EI2,* vol. 1, pp. 768–769.

Ivanov (Ivanow), Vladimir (Wladimir). 'Ismailitskie rukopisi Aziatskogo Muzeia. Sobranie I. Zarubina, 1916g.', *Izvestiia Rossiiskoi Akademii Nauk,* 6 Series, 11 (1917), pp. 359–386.

—— 'Notes on the Ismailis in Persia', in his *Ismailitica,* in *Memoirs of the Asiatic Society of Bengal,* 8 (1922), pp. 50–76.

—— 'Notes sur l'Ummu'l-kitab des Ismaëliens de l'Asie Centrale', *Revue des Études Islamiques,* 6 (1932), pp. 419–481.

—— *A Guide to Ismaili Literature.* London, 1933.

—— 'A Forgotten Branch of the Ismailis', *Journal of the Royal Asiatic Society* (1938), pp. 57–79.

—— *Catalogue of the Arabic Manuscripts in the Collection of the Royal Asiatic Society of Bengal,* revised and edited by M. Hidayat Husain. Vol. I. Calcutta, 1939.

—— *Ismaili Tradition Concerning the Rise of the Fatimids.* Bombay, 1942.

—— *The Alleged Founder of Ismailism.* Bombay, 1946; 2nd ed. as *Ibn al-Qaddah.* Bombay, 1957.

—— *Brief Survey of the Evolution of Ismailism.* Leiden, 1952.

—— 'Shums Tabrez of Multan', in S. M. Abdullah, ed., *Professor Muḥammad Shafi Presentation Volume.* Lahore, 1955, pp. 109–118.

——. *Alamut and Lamasar: Two Mediaeval Ismaili Strongholds in Iran – An Archaeological Study.* Tehran, 1960.

—— *Ismaili Literature: A Bibliographical Survey.* Tehran, 1963.

—— 'Spiski rukopisei Bukharskoi kollektsii (Predislovie i primechaniia Yurii E. Borshevskogo)' [List of the Manuscripts from the Bukhara Collection. Introduction and Notes by Yurii E. Borshchevskii], *Pis'mennye pamyatniki Vostoka. Istoriko-filologicheskoe issledovaniia, Ezhegodnik 1970.* Moscow, 1974, pp. 407–436.

—— 'Ismaʿiliya', *Shorter Encyclopaedia of Islam,* ed. H. A. R. Gibb and J. H. Kramers. Leiden, 1953, pp. 179–183.

Jackson, Peter. 'The Dissolution of the Mongol Empire', *Central Asiatic Journal,* 22 (1978), pp. 186–243.

Jafri, S. Husain M. *Origins and Early Development of Shiʿa Islam*. London, 1979.
Jalali-Moqaddam, Masoud and D. Safvat. 'Ahl-i Haqq', *EIS*, vol. 3, pp. 193–205.
Jambet, Christian (ed.). *Henry Corbin*. Paris, 1981.
Juwayni, Ata-Malik b. Muhammad. *Tarikh-i jahan-gusha*, ed. M. Qazwini. Leiden and London, 1912–1937. English trans., *The History of the World-Conqueror*, tr. John A. Boyle. Manchester, 1958.
Kashani, Abu'l-Qasim Abd Allah b. Ali. *Zubdat al-tawarikh: bakhsh-i Fatimiyan va Nizariyan*, ed. M. T. Danishpazhuh. 2nd ed., Tehran, 1987.
Kassam, Tazim R. *Songs of Wisdom and Circles of Dance: Hymns of the Satpanth Ismaʿili Muslim Saint, Pir Shams*. Albany, NY, 1995.
Kemper, Michal and Stephan Connermann (ed.). *The Heritage of Soviet Oriental Studies*. London, 2011.
Khams rasaʾil Ismaʿiliyya, ed. Arif Tamir. Salamiyya, 1956.
Khan, Ansar Z. 'Ismaʿilism in Multan and Sind', *Journal of the Pakistan Historical Society*, 23 (1975), pp. 36–57.
Khan, Dominique-Sila. *Crossing the Threshold: Understanding Religious Identities in South Asia*. London, 2004.
—— and Z. Moir. 'Coexistence and Communalism, the Shrine of Pirana in Gujarat', *South Asia*, Special Issue, 22 (1999), pp. 133–154.
Khayrkhwah-i Harati, Muhammad Rida b. Khwaja Sultan Husayn. *Tasnifat*, ed. W. Ivanow. Tehran, 1961.
Kireeva, Raisa A. 'K. N. Bestuzhev-Riumin i istoricheskaia nauka vtoroi Poloviny XIX v' [K. N. Bestuzhev-Riumin and Historical Science in the Second Half of the 19th Century]. Moscow, 1990.
—— 'Bestuzhev-Riumin, Konstantin N.', in A. A. Chernobaev, ed., *Istoriki Rosii: Biografii* [Russian Historians: Biographies]. Moscow, 2001, pp. 237–244.
al-Kirmani, Hamid al-Din Ahmad b. Abd Allah. *Rahat al-aql*, ed. Muhammad Kamil Husayn and M. Mustafa Hilmi. Leiden and Cairo, 1953.
Kohlberg, Etan. 'Some Imami-Shiʿi Views on *taqiyya*', *Journal of the American Oriental Society*, 95 (1975), pp. 395–402; reprinted in his *Belief and Law in Imami Shiʿism*. Aldershot, 1991, article III.
Krachkovskii (Kratchovsky), Ignatii Iu. (Y.). 'F. A. Rozenberg (1867–1937)', *Izvestiia Akademii Nauk SSSR*, 7 (1935), pp. 895–918.
—— *Among Arabic Manuscripts: Memoirs of Libraries and Men*, tr. T. Minorksy. Leiden, 1953.

—— (ed.). *Pamiati akademika Viktor R. Rozena: stat'i i materialy k sorokaletiiu so dnia ego smerti (1908-1948)* [In Memoriam Academician V. R. Rozen: Articles and Material on the Fortieth Anniversary of his Death (1908-1948)]. Moscow, 1947.

Kraemer, Joel L. 'The Death of an Orientalist: Paul Kraus from Prague to Cairo', in Martin Kramer, ed., *The Jewish Discovery of Islam: Studies in Honor of Bernard Lewis*. Tel Aviv, 1999, pp. 181-223.

Kramers, J. H. and F. Daftary. 'Salamiyya', *EI2*, vol. 8, pp. 921-923.

Kraus, Paul. 'La bibliographie Ismaëlienne de W. Ivanow', *Revue des Études Islamiques*, 6 (1932), pp. 483-490.

—— *Alchemie, Ketzerei, Apokryphen im frühen Islam*, ed. R. Brague. Hildesheim and New York, 1994.

Kuentz, Charles. 'Paul Kraus (1904-1944)', *Bulletin de l'Institut d'Égypte*, 27 (1944-1945), pp. 431-441.

Latham, John D. and Helen W. Mitchell. 'The Bibliography of S. M. Stern', *Journal of Semitic Studies*, 15 (1970), pp. 226-238; reprinted, with additions, in S. M. Stern, *Hispano-Arabic Strophic Poetry: Studies by Samuel Miklos Stern*, ed. L. P. Harvey. Oxford, 1974, pp. 231-245.

Lenhoff, Gail and Janet Martin. 'The Commercial and Cultural Context of Afanasij Nikitin's Journey Beyond Three Seas', *Jahrbücher für Geschichte Osteuropas*, 37 (1989), pp. 321-344.

Lewis, Bernard. *The Origins of Ismaʿilism: A Study of the Historical Background of the Fatimid Caliphate*. Cambridge, 1940; reprinted, New York, 1975.

—— *The Assassins: A Radical Sect in Islam*. London, 1967.

Litvinskii, Boris A. and N. M. Akramov. *Aleksandr Aleksandrovich Semenov (Nauchno-biograficheskii ocherk)*. Moscow, 1971.

Lokhandwalla, Shamoon T. 'The Bohras, a Muslim Community of Gujarat', *Studia Islamica*, 3 (1955), pp. 117-135.

Losensky, Paul et al. 'Jami', *EIR*, vol. 14, pp. 469-482.

Lunin, Boris V. *Zhizn' i deiatel'nost' akademika V. V. Bartol'da* [Life and Works of the Academician V. V. Bartol'd]. Tashkent, 1981.

McChesney, Robert D. 'Central Asia. vi. In the 10th-12th/16th-18th Centuries', *EIR*, vol. 5, pp. 176-193.

Maclean, Derryl N. *Religion and Society in Arab Sind*. Leiden, 1989.

Madelung, Wilferd. 'Fatimiden und Bahrainqarmaten', *Der Islam*, 34 (1959), pp. 34-88; English trans. (slightly revised), 'The Fatimids and the Qarmatis of Bahrayn', in Daftary, ed., *Mediaeval Ismaʿili History and Thought*, pp. 21-73.

—— 'Das Imamat in der frühen ismailitischen Lehre', *Der Islam*, 37 (1961), pp. 43–135.

—— *Studies in Medieval Shiʿism*, ed. S. Schmidtke. Farnham, UK, 2012.

—— 'Ismaʿiliyya', *EI2*, vol. 4, pp. 198–206.

—— 'Ḡazali. vii. Ḡazali and the Batenis', *EIR*, vol. 10, pp. 376–377.

—— 'Hasan b. Ali', *EIR*, vol. 12, pp. 26–28.

—— 'Hosayn b. Ali', *EIR*, vol. 12, pp. 493–498.

al-Majdu, Ismaʿil b. Abd al-Rasul. *Fahrasat al-kutub*, ed. A. N. Munzavi. Tehran, 1966.

Marefat, Mina. 'The Protagonists who Shaped Modern Tehran', in Chahryar Adle and Bernard Hourcade, ed., *Téhéran, capitale bicentenaire*. Paris and Tehran, 1992, pp. 95–125.

—— 'Guevrekian, Gabriel', *EIR*, vol. 11, pp. 382–383.

Massignon, Louis. *La passion d'al-Hosayn Ibn Mansour al-Hallaj, martyr mystique de l'Islam*. Paris, 1922; 2nd ed., Paris, 1975. English trans., *The Passion of al-Hallaj: Mystic and Martyr of Islam*, tr. H. Mason. Princeton, 1982.

—— 'Esquisse d'une bibliographie Qarmate', in Thomas W. Arnold and R. A. Nicholson, ed., *A Volume of Oriental Studies Presented to Edward G. Browne on his 60th Birthday (7 February 1922)*. Cambridge, 1922, pp. 329–338; reprinted in L. Massignon, *Opera Minora*, ed. Y. Moubarac. Paris, 1969, vol. 1, pp. 627–639.

Maxwell, Mary Jane. 'Afanasii Nikitin: An Orthodox Russian's Spiritual Voyage in the Dar al-Islam, 1468-1475', *Journal of World History*, 17 (2006), pp. 243–266.

Mehrvash, Farhang. 'Ashura', *EIS*, vol. 3, pp. 883–892.

Mélanges Louis Massignon. Damascus, 1956–1957.

Melville, Charles. 'Jame al-Tawarik̲', *EIR*, vol. 14, pp. 462–468.

Mikaberidze, Alexander (ed.). *Conflict and Conquest in the Islamic World: A Historical Encyclopedia*. Santa Barbara, CA, 2011.

Mikoulski, Dimitrii. 'The Study of Islam in Russia and the Former Soviet Union', in Azim Nanji, ed., *Mapping Islamic Studies: Genealogy, Continuity and Change*. New York, 1997, pp. 95–107.

Milani, Abbas. 'Ḡani, Qasem', *EIR*, vol. 10, pp. 276–278.

Miliband, Sofia D. (ed.). *Biobibliograficheskii slovar' otechestvennykh vostokovedov s 1917 g* [Biobibliographical Dictionary of Native Orientalists from 1917]. Moscow, 1995.

Minorsky, Vladimir F. 'Ahl-i Hakk', *EI2*, vol. 1, pp. 260–263.

Mitchell, Robert. 'The Regions of the Upper Oxus', *Proceedings of the Royal Geographical Society*, 6 (1884), pp. 489–512.

Mitra, Sisir K. *The Asiatic Society*. Calcutta, 1974.

Moir, Zawahir. 'The Life and Legends of Pir Shams as Reflected in the Ismaili Ginans: A Critical Review', in F. Mallison, ed., *Constructions hagiographiques dans le monde Indien. Entre mythe et histoire*. Paris, 2001, pp. 365–384.

Mustansir bi'llah. *Pandiyat-i jawanmardi*, ed. and tr. W. Ivanow. Leiden, 1953.

Nabokov, Konstantin D. *The Ordeal of a Diplomat*. London, 1921.

Nanji, Azim. *The Nizari Ismaʿili Tradition in the Indo-Pakistan Subcontinent*. Delmar, NY, 1978.

—— (ed.). *Mapping Islamic Studies: Genealogy, Continuity and Change*. New York, 1997.

Napier, Priscilla. *I Have Sind: Charles Napier in India, 1841–1844*. Salisbury, Wiltshire, 1990.

Napier, William F. P. *The Conquest of Scinde*. London, 1845.

—— *The History of General Sir Charles Napier's Conquest of Scinde*. 2nd ed., London, 1857.

Nasir-i Khusraw. *Shish fasl*, ed. and tr. W. Ivanow. Leiden, 1949.

Nasr, S. Hossein and M. Aminrazavi (ed.). *An Anthology of Philosophy in Persia*: Volume 2, *Ismaili Thought in the Classical Age, From Jabir ibn Hayyan to Nasir al-Din Tusi*. London, 2008.

Nechkina, Militsa V. et al. (ed.). *Ocherki istorii istoricheskoi nauki v SSSR* [Essays on the History of the Historical Sciences in the USSR]. Moscow, 1960–1963.

Nicholson, Reynold A. *A Literary History of the Arabs*. London, 1907.

Nikitin, Afanasii. *Khozhdenie za tri moria* [A Journey Beyond Three Seas]. Moscow, 1948.

Nizami, Farhan A. 'Fyzee, Asaf Ali Asghar', in *The Oxford Encyclopedia of the Islamic World*, ed. John L. Esposito. Oxford, 2009, vol. 2, pp. 281–282.

Nizami, Khaliq A. 'The Qadiriyyah Order', in S. H. Nasr, ed., *Islamic Spirituality: Manifestations*. New York, 1991, pp. 6–25.

—— *The Life and Times of Shaykh Nizam al-Din Awliya*. Delhi, 1991.

—— 'Nizam al-Din Awliya', *EI2*, vol. 8, p. 68.

Nizam al-Mulk, Hasan b. Ali. *The Book of Government, or Rules for Kings*, tr. H. Darke. 2nd ed., London, 1978.

al-Nuʿman b. Muhammad, al-Qadi Abu Hanifa. *Daʿaʾim al-Islam*, ed. Asaf A. A. Fyzee. Cairo, 1951–1961. English trans., *The Pillars of Islam*, tr. A. A. A. Fyzee, completely revised by Ismail K. Poonawala. Delhi, 2002–2004.

Oldenburg, Sergei F. 'Valentin Alekseevich Zhukovskii (1858–1918)', *Izvestiia Rossiiskoi Akademii Nauk*, 2 (1919), pp. 2039–2068.

—— *Aziatskii Muzei Rossiiskoi Akademii Nauk 1818-1918* [The Asiatic Museum of the Russian Academy of Sciences 1818-1918]. Petrograd, 1919.

—— 'Zapiska ob uchenykh trudakh F. A. Rozenberga' [Notes on the Academic Works of F. A. Rozenberg], *Izvestiia Rossiiskoi Akademii Nauk*, 6 (1923), pp. 369-371.

Osipov, Yurii S. *Akademiia nauk v istorii Rossiikogo gosudarstva* [The Academy of Sciences in the History of the Russian State]. Moscow, 1999.

The Oxford Encyclopedia of the Islamic World, ed. John L. Esposito. Oxford, 2009.

The Oxford Encyclopedia of the Modern Islamic World, ed. John L. Esposito. Oxford, 1995.

Paret, R. 'Rudolf Strothmann (4.9.1877-15.5.1960)', *Zeitschrift der Deutschen Morgenländischen Gesellschaft*, 111 (1961), pp. 13-15.

Pellat, Charles. 'Kurd Ali', *EI2*, vol. 5, pp. 437-438.

Penati, Batrice. 'The Reconquest of East Bukhara: The Struggle against the Basmachi as a Prelude to Sovietization', *Central Asian Survey*, 26 (2007), pp. 521-538.

Petrosyan, Yuri A. et al. *Pages of Perfection: Islamic Paintings and Calligraphy from the Russian Academy of Sciences, St Petersburg*. Lugano, 1995.

Pirunek, Éve and Y. Richard (ed.). *Louis Massignon et l'Iran*. Paris, 2000.

Polo, Marco. *The Book of Ser Marco Polo, the Venetian, Concerning the Kingdoms and Marvels of the East*, ed. and tr. H. Yule; 3rd ed. by H. Cordier. London, 1929.

Poonawala, Ismail K. *Biobibliography of Ismaʿili Literature*. Malibu, CA, 1977.

—— 'Al-Qadi al-Nuʿman and Ismaʿili Jurisprudence', in Daftary, ed., *Mediaeval Ismaʿili History and Thought*, pp. 117-143.

—— 'Nur Satgur', *EI2*, vol. 8, pp. 125-126.

—— 'Pir Shams or Shams al-Din', *EI2*, vol. 8, p. 307.

—— 'Sulaymanis', *EI2*, vol. 9, p. 829.

—— and E. Kohlberg. 'Ali b. Abi Taleb', *EIR*, vol. 1, pp. 838-848.

Prozorov, Stanislav and Hakim Elnazarov (ed.). *Russkie uchënye ob Ismailizme/Russian Scholars on Ismailism*. St Petersburg, 2014.

Qutbuddin, Tahera. 'The Daʾudi Bohra Tayyibis: Ideology, Literature, Learning and Social Practice', in Daftary, ed., *A Modern History of the Ismailis*, pp. 331-354.

Rabino, Hyacinth L. *Great Britain and Iran: Diplomatic and Consular Affairs*. London, 1946.

Rahimov, Rahmat R. 'Ivan Ivanovich Zarubin (1887–1964)', *Sovestkaia Etnografiia*, 1 (1989), pp. 111–121.

Rao, C. Hayavadano. *Indian Biographical Dictionary*. Madras, 1915.

Rashid al-Din Fadl Allah. *Fasli az Jami al-tawarikh: tarikh-i firqa-yi rafiqan va Isma'iliyan-i Alamut*, ed. Muhammad Dabir Siyaqi. Tehran, 1958.

—— *Jami al-tawarikh: qismat-i Isma'iliyan va Fatimiyan va Nizariyan va da'iyan va rafiqan*, ed. Muhammad Taqi Danishpazhuh and M. Mudarrisi Zanjani. Tehran, 1959; ed. M. Rawshan. Tehran, 2008.

Rastorgueva, Vera S. 'I. I. Zarubin (Nekrolog)', *Narody Azii i Afrika*, 4 (1964), pp. 273–275.

Rizvi, S. Athar A. 'The Chishtiyyah', in S. H. Nasr, ed., *Islamic Spirituality: Manifestations*. New York, 1991, pp. 127–143.

Ross, Edward Denison. 'W. Ivanow, Ismaili MSS in the Asiatic Museum, Petrograd 1917', *Journal of the Royal Asiatic Society* (1919), pp. 429–435.

—— *Both Ends of the Candle: The Autobiography of Sir E. Denison Ross*. London, 1943.

Rousseau, Jean Baptiste L. J. 'Mémoire sur les Ismaélis et les Nosaïris de Syrie, adressé à M. Silvestre de Sacy', *Annales des Voyages*, 14 (1811), pp. 271–303.

—— 'Extraits d'un Livre qui contient la doctrine des Ismaélis', *Annales des Voyages*, 18 (1812), pp. 222–249.

Ruthchild, Rochelle G. *Equality and Revolution: Women's Rights in the Russian Empire, 1905–1917*. Pittsburgh, PA, 2010.

Ruthven, Malise. 'Aga Khan III and the Isma'ili Renaissance', in Peter B. Clarke, ed., *New Trends and Developments in the World of Islam*. London, 1998, pp. 371–395.

—— 'The Aga Khan Development Network', in Daftary, ed., *A Modern History of the Ismailis*, pp. 189–220.

Sajjadi, Sadeq and E. Majidi (revised by F. Daftary). 'Alamut', *EIS*, vol. 3, pp. 449–461.

Samoilovich, Aleksandr N. 'V. V. Radlov kak turkolog' [V. V. Radlov as a Turkologist], *Novyi Vostok*, 2 (1922), pp. 707–712.

Schimmel, Annemarie. *Gabriel's Wing: A Study into the Religious Ideas of Sir Muhammad Iqbal*. Leiden, 1963.

—— 'Shams-i Tabriz', *EI2*, vol. 9, p. 298.

—— 'Iqbal', *EIR*, vol. 13, pp. 197–200.

Schimmelpenninck van der Oye, David. 'The Imperial Roots of Soviet Orientology', in Kemper and Conermann, ed., *The Heritage of Soviet Oriental Studies*, pp. 29–46.

Schoeberlein-Engel, John S. 'Basmachis', in *The Oxford Encyclopedia of the Islamic World*, ed. John L. Esposito. Oxford, 2009, vol. 1, pp. 317–318.

Semenov, Aleksandr A. 'Opisanie ismailitskikh rukopisei, sobrannykh A. A. Semyonovym' [Description of the Ismaili Manuscripts, A. A. Semenov's Collection], *Izvestiia Rossiiskoi Akademii Nauk/Bulletin de l'Académie des Sciences de Russie*, 6 Series, 12 (1918), pp. 2171–2202.

Sen Gupta, D. P. 'Sir Ashutosh Mookerjee – Educationist, Leader and Institution-Builder', *Current Science*, 78 (2000), pp. 1566–1573.

Shastri, Haraprasad. *A Descriptive Catalogue of Sanskrit Manuscripts in the Government Collection under the Care of the Asiatic Society of Bengal*. Calcutta, 1917.

Shayegan, Daryush. *Henry Corbin. La topographie spirituelle de l'Islam Iranien*. Paris, 1990.

—— 'Corbin, Henry', *EIR*, vol. 6, pp. 268–272.

Silvestre de Sacy, Antoine Isaac. 'Mémoire sur la dynastie des Assassins, et sur l'étymologie de leur nom', *Mémoires de l'Institut Royal de France*, 4 (1818), pp. 1–84; reprinted in Bryan S. Turner, ed., *Orientalism: Early Sources*, vol. I, *Readings in Orientalism*. London, 2000, pp. 118–169; reprinted also in F. Daftary, *Légendes des Assassins*, tr. Z. Rajan-Badouraly. Paris, 2007, pp. 139–181. English trans., 'Memoir on the Dynasty of the Assassins, and on the Etymology of their Name', in Daftary, *Assassin Legends*, pp. 131–188.

—— *Exposé de la religion des Druzes*. Paris, 1838; reprinted, Paris and Amsterdam, 1964.

Six, Jean-François (ed.). *Louis Massignon*. Paris, 1970.

Skachkov, Peter E. and Ksenia L. Chizhikova. *Bibliografiia trudov S. F. Ol'denburg*. Moscow, 1986.

Smoor, Pieter. 'al-Maʿarri', *EI2*, vol. 5, pp. 927–935.

Sorokina, Marina Iu. *Rossiiskoe nauchnoe zarubezh'e: materialy dlia biobibliograficheskogo slovaria* [The Russian Academic Frontier: Material for a Bibliographic Dictionary], vol. 3. Moscow, 2010.

Sprenger, Aloys. *A Catalogue of the Arabic, Persian and Hindustany Manuscripts of the Libraries of the King of Oudh*, vol. I. Calcutta, 1854.

Spuler, Bertold. *Die Goldene Horde: Die Mongolen in Russland 1223–1502*. 2nd ed., Wiesbaden, 1965.

—— 'Amu Darya', *EI2*, vol. 1, pp. 454–457.

—— 'Djanids', *EI2*, vol. 2, p. 446.

Stark, Freya M. *The Valleys of the Assassins and other Persian Travels*. London, 1934.

Stern, Samuel Miklos. 'Isma'ili Propaganda and Fatimid Rule in Sind', *Islamic Culture*, 23 (1949), pp. 298–307.

—— 'Isma'ilis and Qarmatians', in *L'Élaboration de l'Islam*. Colloque de Strasbourg 12–14 juin 1959. Paris, 1961, pp. 99–108.

—— *Studies in Early Isma'ilism*. Jerusalem and Leiden, 1983.

Stroeva, Liudmila V. *Gosudarstvo ismailitov v Irane v XI–XIII vv.* [The Ismaili State in Iran in the 11–13th Centuries]. Moscow, 1978.

Subtelny, Maria Eva. 'Mir Ali Shir Nawāʾi', *EI2*, vol. 7, pp. 90–93.

Tailleu, Dieter (ed.). *A Descriptive Bibliography of Allama Muhammad Iqbal (1877–1938)*. Louvain, 2000.

Talukdar, Mohammad. *Memoirs of Husayn Shaheed Suhrawardy, with a Brief Account of his Life and Work*. Oxford, 2009.

Tolz, Vera. *Russia's Own Orient: The Politics of Identity and Oriental Studies in the Late Imperial and Early Soviet Periods*. Oxford, 2011.

Turner, Ralph L. 'Obituary: Sir Edward Denison Ross', *Bulletin of the School of Oriental and African Studies*, 10 (1940), pp. 832–836.

al-Tusi, Nasir al-Din Muhammad b. Muhammad. *Rawdat al-taslim*, ed. and tr. W. Ivanow. Leiden, 1950; ed. and tr. S. Jalal Badakhchani as *Paradise of Submission: A Medieval Treatise on Ismaili Thought*. London, 2005. French trans., *La convocation d'Alamût. Somme de philosophie Ismaélienne*, tr. Christian Jambet. Lagrasse, 1996.

—— *Sayr va suluk*, ed. and tr. S. J. Badakhchani as *Contemplation and Action: The Spiritual Autobiography of a Muslim Scholar*. London, 1998.

Umm al-Kitab, ed. W. Ivanow, in *Der Islam*, 23 (1936), pp. 1–132. Italian trans., *Ummu'l-Kitab*, tr. Pio Filippani-Ronconi. Naples, 1966. Partial German trans., in Halm, *Die islamische Gnosis*, pp. 113–198. Turkish trans., in İsmail Kaygusuz, *Bir Proto-Alevi Kaynağı, Ummü'l-Kitab*, tr. A. Selman. Istanbul, 2009, pp. 121–258.

Vucinich, Wayne S. 'The Structure of Soviet Orientology: Fifty Years of Change and Accomplishment', in W. S. Vucinich, ed., *Russia and Asia*. Stanford, 1972, pp. 52–134.

Walker, Annabel. *Aurel Stein: Pioneer of the Silk Road*. London, 1995.

Walker, Paul E. *Abu Ya'qub al-Sijistani: Intellectual Missionary*. London, 1996.

—— 'Fatimid Institutions of Learning', *Journal of the American Research Center in Egypt*, 34 (1997), pp. 179–200.

—— *Hamid al-Din al-Kirmani: Ismaili Thought in the Age of al-Hakim*. London, 1999.

—— *Exploring an Islamic Empire: Fatimid History and its Sources*. London, 2002.

—— 'The Isma'ilis', in P. Adamson and Richard C. Taylor, ed., *The Cambridge Companion to Arabic Philosophy*. Cambridge, 2005, pp. 72–91.

—— *Fatimid History and Ismaili Doctrine*. Aldershot, 2008.

—— 'Institute of Ismaili Studies', *EIR*, vol. 12, pp. 164–166.

Whitehead, Clive. *Colonial Education: The British Indian and Colonial Education Service 1858–1983*. London, 2003.

Whitfield, Roderick. *The Art of Central Asia: The Stein Collection in the British Museum*. Tokyo, 1982.

Wickens, George M. 'Browne', *EIR*, vol. 4, pp. 483–485.

Willey, Peter. *The Castles of the Assassins*. London, 1963.

—— *Eagle's Nest: Ismaili Castles in Iran and Syria*. London, 2005.

Zahid Ali. *Tarikh-i Fatimiyyin-i Misr*. Hyderabad, 1948; reprinted, Karachi, 1963.

Zoeggeler, Bianca Marabini et al. *Il Conte Bobrinskoj. Il lungo cammino dal Pamir alle Dolomiti*. Bozen, Italy, 2012.

Index

Abbas I (Safawid shah, r. 1587–1629) 104
Abbasids 9–10, 12, 13, 133n35
Abd Allah b. Maymun al-Qaddah 13, 27, 28n43, 93, 93n94
Abu Ishaq Quhistani (Nizari author, d. after 1498) 28
Achaemenians 99, 110, 110n13
Afghanistan, Afghans 3, 9, 11, 20, 23, 66, 67, 82n76, 86n84, 87n86, 91n89, 106, 118n17, 150, 167n72
Aga Khan I, Hasan Ali Shah (Nizari Imam, 1804–1881) 31, 86, 86n84, 87, 89n87
Aga Khan II, Aqa Ali Shah (Nizari Imam, 1830–1885) 29
Aga Khan III, Sultan Muhammad (Mahomed) Shah (Nizari Imam, 1877–1957)
   history 86
   Islamic Research Association (Bombay) 24, 27, 92n93
   Ivanow, Wladimir (1886–1970) 1, 5, 83n80, 86, 88, 89
   Nizaris 74n60
   Persian Nizaris 90n89
   photograph 84
   reforms 165n69
   research 165
   Salamiyya (Syria) 133n35
   travel 83
Aga Khan IV, Prince Karim (current Nizari Imam) 1, 5, 6, 20, 35, 36

Aga Khans 12, 20, 74n60, 85, 90n89
Agra (northern India) 59, 158, 172, 172n82
Ahl-i Haqq 29
Ahmadabad (Gujarat) 175
Ajmer 59
Akimushkin, Oleg F. (1929–2010) 5–6, 60n38, 81n75
Aksakolov, Sultonbek 7
Alamut (fortress in northern Persia)
   history 95n103
   Hodgson, Marshall G. S. (American orientalist, 1922–1968) 34
   Ivanow, Wladimir (1886–1970) 31, 95
   Lamasar (fortress, northern Persia) 96n104
   Masyaf (castle in Syria) 136
   Nizam al-Mulk (Saljuq vizier, d. 1092) 13
   Nizari history 18, 25, 28
   Nizari literature 20, 29
   Nizaris 11, 18, 133n34
   photograph 37, 38
   Rashid al-Din Sinan (Nizari da'i in Syria, d. 1193) 32n59
Aleppo (Halab, in northern Syria) 81n75, 138
Alexander the Great 99
Ali, Abid 27
Ali b. Abi Talib (First Shi'i Imam and Fourth Caliph d. 661) 12, 121n19, 169n75
Alids 12–13, 27, 93n94

Alledged Founder of Ismailism, The 28
Ambrosiana Library (Milan) 19
American University of
    Beirut 130n31
American University of Cairo 129
Americans 85, 129
Amritsar (India) 59, 160
Andreyev, Sergei 7
Anjudan (village in central
    Persia) 25, 28–9
Arabs 95, 120, 128, 130, 132n32,
    133n35, 145n50
    Bukhara (now in Uzbekistan) 120
    Ismaili texts 95
    Kurd Ali, Muhammad (Syrian
        scholar, 1876–1953) 132n32
    Nicholson, Reynold A. (British
        orientalist, 1868–
        1945) 145n50
    physical characteristics 128
    Salamiyya (Syria) 133n35
    Umm Kulthum (Egyptian singer,
        d. 1975) 130n30
Armenia, Armenians 50, 50n26, 56,
    65, 103, 110
Asafiyya Library (Hyderabad) 76,
    76n66
Asani, Ali 35, 87n86, 166n71
Ashkabad 59
Asia 175n84, 175n85
    Aga Khan III, Sultan
        Muhammad (Mahomed)
        Shah (Nizari Imam, 1877–
        1957) 83n80
    Asiatic Museum (Aziatskii
        Muzei, Rossiiskoi Akademii
        Nauk, St Petersburg) 47n22
    Badakhshan 150n54
    Barthold (Bartol'd), Vasilii V.
        (Russian orientalist, 1869–
        1930) 43n12, 46
    Basmachi movement 64n44
    Cairo (al-Qahira) 129
    Central Asia 2

ceramics 117
Damascus (Dimashq) 131
Gonds 146n52
Institute of the Peoples of Asia
    and Africa 48
Ismaili studies 19, 20
Ismaili texts 23
Ismailis 74n60
Loan and Discount Bank of
    Persia (Uchetno-ssudni
    Bank Persii) 54
manuscript sources 9–11, 60n38,
    62n42
Minaev, Ivan P. (Russian
    orientalist, 1840–
    1890) 154n61
Mir Ali Shir Nawa'i (Central
    Asian poet, 1441–
    1501) 144n48
Nizaris 87n86
Pamir (region in Central
    Asia) 90n88
Parsis (Zoroastrians of
    India) 151n57
Persia (Iran) 63
Qaderi (Sufi order) 167n72
Radlov, Vasilii V. (Russian
    orientalist, 1837–
    1918) 60n39
Satpanth 166n71
Semenov, Aleksandr, A. (Russian
    orientalist, 1873–1958) 21,
    89n88
Stein, Sir Aurel (Hungarian
    archaeologist and explorer,
    1862–1943) 75n63
Sufism 166n72
Tayyibis (branch of
    Ismailism) 76n65
Tehran 109
Upper Oxus 82n76
Zaleman (Salemann), Karl (Carl)
    G. (H.) (Russian orientalist,
    1849–1916) 49n25

Asiatic Museum (Aziatskii Muzei, Rossiiskoi Akademii Nauk, St Petersburg)
   atmosphere 143
   Bukharan Collection 2, 119
   employment 56
   founded 47n22
   Ismaili texts 81–2
   Ivanow, Wladimir (1886–1970) 22, 51, 61, 62, 73
   manuscript sources 48, 49n25, 50, 59, 81, 114
   Oriental studies 42n11
   photograph 50
   Rousseau, Jean Baptiste (French diplomat, 1780–1831) 81n75
   Russian Academy of Sciences 47–54
   Semenov, Aleksandr, A. (Russian orientalist, 1873–1958) 90n88
   Zarubin, Ivan I. (Russian orientalist, 1887–1964) 20–1
Asiatic Society of Bengal
   Calcutta 91
   Catalogue of the Arabic Manuscripts in the Collection of the Royal Asiatic Society of Bengal 75n61
   description 140
   difficulties 82, 146
   founded 70n50
   Ivanow, Wladimir (1886–1970) 3, 4n4, 58, 70, 144–5
   Journal of the Royal Asiatic Society 140
   lectures 143
   library 142–3
   management 3–4
   manuscript sources 58, 71–2, 79
   Mukherjee, Ashutosh (educator, 1864–1924) 70, 70n53
   Ross, Sir Edward D. (British orientalist, 1871–1940) 73n57, 75n62
   Royal Asiatic Society (Bombay Branch) 91
   Shastri, Haraprasad (1853–1931) 74n59
   Stein, Sir Aurel (Hungarian archaeologist and explorer, 1862–1943) 82
   tensions 74–5
Assassin legends
   Aga Khan III, Sultan Muhammad (Mahomed) Shah (Nizari Imam, 1877–1957) 92
   Central Intelligence Agency (CIA) 89
   Crusaders 15n11, 18n16
   Defrémery, Charles F. (French orientalist, 1822–1883) 19n17
   Europeans 17n13
   Hodgson, Marshall G. S. (American orientalist, 1922–1968) 34n64
   Lamasar (fortress, northern Persia) 96n104
   Masyaf (castle in Syria) 135, 136n40, 136n41
   Nizaris 15–19
   Polo, Marco (Venetian traveller, 1254–1324) 16, 135n39
   Rashid al-Din Sinan (Nizari *daʻi* in Syria, d. 1193) 135n38
   Silvestre de Sacy, Antoine I. (French orientalist, 1758–1838) 17n14
   Sunni chronicles 18
Astrakhanids (dynasty of Transoxania) 118–19
Avicenna (Ibn Sina, philosopher and physician, 980–1037) 95, 95n102
Ayni, Kamol (1928–2010) 6, 6n5

Ayni, Sadr al-Din (poet and novelist, 1878–1954) 6
Ayyubids 11
Aziatskii Muzei *see* Asiatic Museum (Aziatskii Muzei, Rossiiskoi Akademii Nauk, St Petersburg)

baboo 67, 67n49, 142, 143, 145, 181
Babylon 57, 57n33, 121
Bacon, Sir Francis (1561–1626) 165
Badakhshan 165
  see also Central Asia; Upper Oxus
  Bombay 150
  description 150n54
  Fida'i Khorasani, Muhammad b. Zayn al-Abidin (Nizari author, ca. 1850–1923) 91n89
  Nizaris 6, 20
  Pamir (region in Central Asia) 62n42
  Semenov, Aleksandr, A. (Russian orientalist, 1873–1958) 21, 89n88
  Umm al-kitab 24
  Upper Oxus 82n76
Baffin, William (navigator, 1584–1622) 124
Baghdad
  Abd al-Qadir al-Jilani (Sufi, d. 1166) 167n72
  development 123
  Ibn Rizam (Sunni polemicist, 10th century) 12, 93n94
  Ivanow, Wladimir (1886–1970) 56–7
  Mashmeer-Patrik, P. I. (Russian engineer) 78
  Popov, E. K. (Russian diplomat) 121
  Rousseau, Jean Baptiste (French diplomat, 1780–1831) 81n75
  travel 122, 139

al-Baghdadi, Abd al-Qahir (Sunni theologian, d. 1037) 13, 13n6
Bahrain 25n33, 122–3, 125
Baku (Caucasus) 65
Balaklava (Crimea) 41, 41n9
Baluchis 55, 66, 67, 86, 86n84
Baluchistan 55, 66, 67, 86, 86n84
Bandar-i Abbas(i) 58, 123n23, 124–5
Banque d'Escompe de Perse *see* Loan and Discount Bank of Persia (Uchetno-ssudni Bank Persii)
Barthold (Bartol'd), Vasilii V. (Russian orientalist, 1869–1930)
  background 43n12
  history 44n12
  Ivanow, Wladimir (1886–1970) 46–7, 53
  Loan and Discount Bank of Persia (Uchetno-ssudni Bank Persii) 54
  photograph 45
  Rozen, Victor R. (Russian orientalist, 1849–1908) 46n17
  St Petersburg University (Faculty of Oriental Languages) 43
Basil Bolgar-Machos (Byzantine emperor) 118
Basmachi movement 3, 63, 64n44, 115
Basra (southern Iraq) 122
Batinis (Esotericists) 14, 93n94
Bedouins 124, 139
Beirut 130n31, 138–9
Belarussia 41
Benares (India) 59, 154–5
Berlin 58, 126n25
Bertel's (Bertels), Andrei E. (Russian orientalist, 1926–1995) 34

Bestuzhev, Konstantin N. (Russian educator and historian, 1829–1897) 39n3
Bhutan 150n56, 164
Bibliotheca Indica Series 3
Catalogue of the Arabic Manuscripts in the Collection of the Royal Asiatic Society of Bengal 75n61
Bibliothèque Nationale (Paris) 32
Bidukht (Khorasan) 102
Birjand (Khorasan)
  dervish (*darwish*) 102
  fieldwork 4
  gypsies 106–7
  Ismailis 81
  Journal of the Royal Asiatic Society 140
  Loan and Discount Bank of Persia (Uchetno-ssudni Bank Persii) 52n29, 54
  travel 104, 106, 113
Bobbili (Andhra Pradesh) 78, 78n69
Bobrinskoy, Count Aleksey A. (Russian scholar of the Pamir, 1861–1938) 20, 21, 89n88
Bodleian Library (Oxford) 82n78
Bogoiavlenskii, P. G. (Russian diplomat) 100n4
Bohras
  see also Ismailis; Tayyibis
  Fatimid texts 23
  Gujarat 175
  Hydari, Sir Mahomed Akbar Nazarally (Muslim politician and reformer, 1869–1942) 76
  Ismaili texts 84, 86, 89
  research 166
  scholars 24
  Sulaymanis (branch of Tayyibis) 152
  Tayyibis (Tayyibi branch of Ismailism) 11, 175n85
Bombay
  Aga Khan I, Hasan Ali Shah (Nizari Imam, 1804–1881) 86n84
  black panthers 149
  Da'udis (branch of Tayyibis) 175n85
  Fyzee, Asaf A. A. (Bohra scholar and educator, 1899–1981) 91n91
  Ismaili studies 89
  Ismailis 74, 84
  Ivanow, Wladimir (1886–1970) 4, 5, 22, 80–96, 153
  location 151
  Parsis (Zoroastrians of India) 152
  people 149–50
  photograph 57
  Royal Asiatic Society 90–1
  spiritual literature 166
  Sulaymanis (branch of Tayyibis) 76n65
  travel 122, 123, 140
Bombay Branch of the Royal Asiatic Society *see* Royal Asiatic Society
Bombay University 23, 91n91
Both Ends of the Candle: The Autobiography of Sir E. Dennison Ross 73n57
Brockelmann, Carl (German orientalist, 1868–1956)
  Geschichte der arabischen Litteratur 143
Browne, Edward G. (British orientalist, 1862–1926) 19, 144n49
Bukhara (now in Uzbekistan)
  Ayni, Sadr al-Din (poet and novelist, 1878–1954) 6
  Basmachi movement 64

bazaar (photograph) 116
experiences 114-21
feast days 117
history 115
Ivanow, Wladimir (1886-
    1970) 2-3, 47, 54, 59-60
manuscript sources 2, 114, 116
Panj River 20
Russian protectorate 64
Bushir (Bushihr, southern
    Persia) 58, 59, 80, 162
Byzantines 10, 118

Cairo (al-Qahira) 10, 33, 126n25,
    127, 128-9
Calcutta
    Asiatic Society of Bengal 3, 91,
        140
    British viceroys 159
    Eurasians 142
    Ivanow, Wladimir (1886-
        1970) 58, 70-8, 80, 162-3
    Mashmeer-Patrik, P. I. (Russian
        engineer) 77
    people 150
    photograph 71
    Stein, Sir Aurel (Hungarian
        archaeologist and explorer,
        1862-1943) 76
    travel 154
Calcutta Madrasah 73
Calcutta University 70
Cambay (port in Gujarat) 175
Canard, Marius (French orientalist,
    1888-1982) 35
Caprotti, Guiseppe (Italian
    merchant, 1869-1919) 19
Caspian Sea 63, 163
*Catalogue of the Arabic Manuscripts
in the Collection of the Royal
Asiatic Society of Bengal* 75n61
Catholic University, Beirut 139
Central Asia

see also Badakhshan; Pamir;
    Tajikistan; Upper Oxus
da'i (summoner) 10
Ismaili texts 23, 87n86
Ismailis 20
Ivanow, Wladimir (1886-
    1970) 2, 63, 117
manuscript sources 9, 19, 49n25
map 8
Nizaris 11
Semenov, Aleksandr, A. (Russian
    orientalist, 1873-1958) 21,
    89n88
Stein, Sir Aurel (Hungarian
    archaeologist and explorer,
    1862-1943) 75-6
Umm al-kitab 62n42
Upper Oxus 82n76
Central Desert (Dasht-i Kavir,
    Persia) 55, 104
Central Intelligence Agency
    (CIA) 88-9
ceramics 11
chador (veil) 156
Chaghatai language 120
chaprasi 142
*charwadar*s (muleteers) 114, 120-1
chay-khana (tea house) 100, 101,
    116
China 153n60, 164
Chinese 150
Chishti (Sufi order) 167n73, 168,
    169, 170-1
Christians 14, 17
Christmas 43, 50
Chuguev (Ukraine) 41, 41n8
Colombo 59
Congress of Orientalists 95, 127
Corbin, Henry (French orientalist,
    1903-1978) 33, 85n82
Cossacks 60, 66, 110
Cowley, Arthur E. (British scholar,
    1861-1931) 82, 82n78
Crimea 43

Crusaders
   Assassin legends 16, 18n16
   Fatimids 10
   Ismailis 14
   Masyaf (castle in Syria) 135
   misrepresentation 22
   Nizaris 11, 15
Cyprus 136

Da'a'im al-Islam, of al-Qadi al-Nu'man 23
da'i (summoner) 9–10, 13
Damascus (Dimashq) 100, 128, 131, 139
Darius (Achaemenid king of Persia) 99
Darjeeling (India) 117, 159, 164
Da'udis (branch of Tayyibis) 27, 76n65, 175n85
   see also Bohras; Ismailis
De Smet, Daniel 35
Deccan, The 128
Defrémery, Charles F. (French orientalist, 1822–1883) 19
Delhi 59, 159–60
dervish (*darwish*)
   analysis 172
   Isfahan (Central Persia) 101–3
   Ivanow, Wladimir (1886–1970) 55, 65
   letter by Ivanow, Wladimir (1886–1970) 66
   Multan (now in Pakistan) 161
   qalandar 172
Dickson, William E. (1871–1957) 67
   East Persia: A Backwater of the Great War 67n48
Diwan of Khaki Khorasani 24, 26
Dizbad (village in northern Khorasan) 90n89
Dobrokhotov, Vladimir A. 59, 59n37, 64
Druzes 17, 114, 127, 132

Duzdap see Zahidan (Persia)

East Africa 83n80, 96
East Persia: A Backwater of the Great War 67n48
Echmiadzin (Ejmiatsin, Armenia) 50, 50n26
Egypt
   British rule 127
   Crusaders 14
   experiences 126–31
   Fatimid caliphate 10
   Fyzee, Asaf A. A. (Bohra scholar and educator, 1899–1981) 91n91, 152
   Ghani, Ghasem (Iranian scholar, 1893–1952) 130n31
   Ismaili Society (Bombay) 94
   Kraus, Paul (Czech orientalist, 1904–1944) 126n25
   Sufism 166n72
Egyptians 94
Elburz (Alborz) mountains (Persia) 111
Encyclopaedia of Islam 22, 26, 35
England 54, 85
Enzeli (Anzali), formerly Bandar-i Pahlavi (port) 97n1
Ethé, Hermann (1844–1917)
   Catalogue of the Persian, Turkish, Hindustani and Pushtu Manuscripts in the Bodleian Library 82n79
Euphrates River 122, 138
Europe 14, 16, 21, 166n72
Europeans 15, 17, 142
Exposé de la religion des Druzes 133

Faculty of Oriental Languages (St Petersburg University) 2, 41–2
Faizi see Fyzee, Asaf A. A.
Fatimids
   see also Ismailis

Cairo (al-Qahira) 10
Caliphate 10, 12, 93n94
Crusaders 14
Husayn, Muhammad K.
   (Egyptian scholar of Ismaili studies, 1901–1961) 33
   Ismaili history 34
   Ismaili texts 86n85
   Nasir-i Khusraw (Ismaili *da'i* and poet, d. after 1070) 22
   al-Nu'man b. Muhammad, al-Qadi Abu Hanifa (Ismaili jurist and author, d. 974) 91n91
   texts 23
Fida'i Khorasani, Muhammad b. Zayn al-Abidin (Nizari author, ca. 1850–1923) 90
   Kitab-i hidayat al-mu'minin al-talibin 90n89
*fida'i*s (self-sacrificing devotees) 15
First World War
   Afghanistan 66
   British Government 80
   Ivanow, Wladimir (1886–1970) 2, 50, 59
   Kermanshah (western Persia) 56
   Malmisa Force 3
Fraehn, Christian M. D. (German scholar and numismatist, 1782–1851) 48, 48n24
Fyzee, Asaf A. A. (Bohra scholar and educator, 1899–1981)
   Islamic Research Association (Bombay) 24, 92n93, 152–3
   Journal of the Royal Asiatic Society 34n63
   photograph 22
   Royal Asiatic Society 91–2
   Sulaymanis (branch of Tayyibis) 23

Ganges River 154

Gankovskii, Yuri V. (Russian orientalist) 5
Ghani, Ghasem (Iranian scholar, 1893–1952) 130n31
Gharibi *see* Khayrkhwah-i Harati, Muhammad Rida (Nizari *da'i* and author, d. after 1553)
ghat 154n62
al-Ghazali, Abu Hamid Muhammad (Sunni theologian, d. 1111) 14
   Tahafut al-falasifa 119–20
Gibb, Sir Hamilton A. R. (British orientalist, 1895–1971) 26, 43n12
Gibb Memorial Series 32, 43n12, 144n49, 145n50
Golden Horde 53n30, 53n31, 54
Golenishchev-Kutuzov, N. (Russian diplomat) 122
Golpayegan (Persia) 113–14
Gonds 146, 146n52, 147, 180
Grammar of the Persian Language, A 70n52
Griffini, Eugenio (Italian orientalist, 1878–1925) 19–20
Guide to Ismaili Literature 23
Gujarat
   Bohras 175
   Da'udis (branch of Tayyibis) 175n85
   Imam-Shahis 171
   Ismaili persecution 155n63
   Ismaili texts 86n85
   Parsis (Zoroastrians of India) 151n57
   Sulaymanis (branch of Tayyibis) 76n65
Gulbarga (India) 154
Gulf of Finland 41
Gunabadi (Sufi order) 102
Gushchin, Sergei E. 68
Guyard, Stanislas (orientalist, 1846–1884) 19
gypsies 2, 102, 106–8

Haft bab-i Baba Sayyidna 29–30
Halm, Heinz (German scholar, b. 1942) 35
Hama (Syria) 133, 134
Hamadan (Persia) 52n29, 55, 95, 104, 113
Hamburg University 85n83
Hamdani, Abbas (Bohra scholar of Ismaili studies, b. 1926) 27, 34
al-Hamdani, Fayd Allah (Bohra scholar of Ismaili studies, 1877–1969) 27
al-Hamdani, Husayn F. (Bohra scholar of Ismaili studies, 1901–1962) 25, 26, 27
Hammer-Purgstall, Joseph von (Austrian orientalist and diplomat, 1774–1856) 18, 18n16, 34
Harley, Alexander H. (British orientalist, 1882–1951) 72n56, 73
Hasan Kabir al-Din, Pir (d. ca. 1470) 171, 171n77
Hasan-i Mahmud-i Katib, Salah al-Din (Nizari poet and author, d. after 1243)
  Rawdat al-taslim 29–30
Hasan-i Sabbah (Nizari leader and founder of Nizari state, d. 1124) 11, 13, 31
  Haft bab-i Baba Sayyidna 30
hashishi 15, 17
hashishiyya 15
heretics *see malahida*
Hilla (Iraq) 121
Himalayas 163
Hinduism 146, 159, 165, 171, 173
Hindus 146, 149, 154–5, 165n68, 171n77
Hodgson, Marshall G. S. (American orientalist, 1922–1968) 34
  Order of Assassins: The Struggle of the Early Nizari Isma'ilis against the Islamic World, The 34n64
Holy Land 128
Homs (Syria) 133
Hormuz 123, 124, 163
Huart, Clément (French orientalist, 1854–1926) 22
Hunza (now in northern Pakistan) 150, 150n55
Husayn, Muhammad K. (Egyptian scholar of Ismaili studies, 1901–1961) 33, 129n29
Husayn, Taha (Egyptian educator, 1889–1973) 127, 127n26
Hydari, Sir Mahomed Akbar Nazarally (Muslim politician and reformer, 1869–1942) 76–7, 165–6
Hyderabad (Gujarat)
  Asafiyya Library (Hyderabad) 76–7
  British protectorate 64
  customs 163
  hospitality 162
  Hyderabad, Osman Ali Khan, Nizam of (1886–1967) 4, 77
  Hydari, Sir Mahomed Akbar Nazarally (Muslim politician and reformer, 1869–1942) 166
  Ivanow, Wladimir (1886–1970) 59, 83
  manuscript sources 74
  relics 128

Ibn Hani (Ismaili poet, d. 973)
Ibn Sina *see* Avicenna
Ibrat Afza 31, 86n84
Imam-Shah, Abd al-Rahman (eponym of Imam-Shahis) 86n84
Imam-Shahis 165n71, 171, 174, 175

India
    accident 176–81
    Aga Khan I, Hasan Ali Shah (Nizari Imam, 1804–1881) 86n84
    British Indian Army 66, 67
    Chishti (Sufi order) 167n72
    Eastern India 146–53
    elephants 178
    ethnography 151
    experiences 140–6
    hospitality 114
    Ismaili Society (Bombay) 94
    Ismaili studies 24
    Ismailis 80
    Ivanow, Wladimir (1886–1970) 3, 54, 56–60, 78, 79
    language 120
    Malmisa Force 69
    manuscript sources 74
    Mashmeer-Patrik, P. I. (Russian engineer) 78
    North-western India 158–65
    Northern India 153–8
    plagiarism 73
    Ross, Sir Edward D. (British orientalist, 1871–1914) 72n57
    Russian Revolution (1917) 80
    sects 171
    Sufism 166n72
    Tayyibis (branch of Ismailism) 11
    Western India 165–76
    xenophobia 74
Institut Franco-iranien 33
Institute of Ismaili Studies (London) 6, 7, 27, 36, 94n98
Institute of Oriental Manuscripts (Institut Vostochnikh Rukopisei, Rossiiskaia Akademiia Nauk, St Petersburg) 7, 21, 42n11, 47n22, 49, 63n42
Institute of Oriental Studies (Institut Vostokovedeniia Akademii Nauk SSSR) 5, 44n14, 47n22
Institute of the Peoples of Asia and Africa 47n22, 48
    see also Institute of Oriental Manuscripts (Institut Vostochnikh Rukopisei, Rossiiskaia Akademiia Nauk, St Petersburg)
Iqbal, Muhammad (poet, 1877–1938) 160n65
Iran
    see also Persia (Iran)
    Ayni, Kamol (1928–2010) 6
    dervish (*darwish*) 103
    Ghani, Ghasem (Iranian scholar, 1893–1952) 130n31
    Ivanow, Wladimir (1886–1970) 139
    Markov, Nikolai L. (Russian architect, 1882–1957) 110
    Nizaris 11
    Rozenberg, Fedor A. (Russian orientalist, 1867–1934) 51n27
    travel 122
    Zoroastrians 109
Iraq 75n63, 78, 121–6
Isfahan (Central Persia)
    dervish (*darwish*) 103
    Ivanow, Wladimir (1886–1970) 55, 99
    Khaju Bridge photograph 101
    Loan and Discount Bank of Persia (Uchetno-ssudni Bank Persii) 52n29
    Safawid (dynasty of Persia) 98n2
    travel 104, 113
Ishkashim (Badakhshan) 20
Islamic Research Association (Bombay)

Aga Khan III, Sultan
    Muhammad (Mahomed)
    Shah (Nizari Imam, 1877–
    1957) 24, 27
  founded 24, 92, 92n93
  Fyzee, Asaf A. A. (Bohra scholar
    and educator, 1899–
    1981) 91n91, 152
  Ismaili Society (Bombay) 27
  Ivanow, Wladimir (1886–
    1970) 93
Islamic studies 84, 88, 145n50, 165
Ismaili Society (Bombay)
  Abd Allah b. Maymun al-
    Qaddah 27, 28n43
  closure 94n98
  Congress of Orientalists 95
  founded 94
  Husayn, Muhammad K.
    (Egyptian scholar of Ismaili
    studies, 1901–1961) 33
  Islamic Research Association
    (Bombay) 27
  Ismaili texts 33
  Ivanow, Wladimir (1886–
    1970) 32
  Pandiyat-i jawanmardi 30
Ismaili studies
  biased 12, 18
  Christians 17
  Corbin, Henry (French
    orientalist, 1903–1978) 33
  evidence 25
  Fyzee, Asaf A. A. (Bohra scholar
    and educator, 1899–
    1981) 23, 91n91
  Ismaili Society (Bombay) 27
  Ivanow, Wladimir (1886–
    1970) 1, 5, 22, 34
  Kraus, Paul (Czech orientalist,
    1904–1944) 126n25
  manuscript sources 9
  Marxism 34
  misrepresentation 19
  progress 9, 32, 35–6
  scholarship 23–4
  Semenov, Aleksandr, A. (Russian
    orientalist, 1873–1958) 89
  Silvestre de Sacy, Antoine I.
    (French orientalist, 1758–
    1838) 133n34
  Strothmann, Rudolf (German
    orientalist, 1877–
    1960) 85n83
Ismaili texts
  access 23, 165
  availability 33
  Bobrinskoy, Count Aleksey A.
    (Russian scholar of the
    Pamir, 1861–1938) 20
  Bohras 24
  Bombay 22
  doctrine 20
  Fyzee, Asaf A. A. (Bohra scholar
    and educator, 1899–
    1981) 152
  al-Hamdani, Husayn F. (Bohra
    scholar of Ismaili studies) 27
  history 86n85
  Ismaili Society (Bombay) 94
  Ivanow, Wladimir (1886–
    1970) 21, 84, 119–20
  manuscript sources 59–60
  propaganda 88
  publication 92
  recovery 9, 19, 32, 34, 35
  Semenov, Aleksandr, A. (Russian
    orientalist, 1873–
    1958) 90n88
  Syria 35
*Ismaili Traditions Concerning the
  Rise of the Fatimids* 24–5
Ismailis
  Abd Allah b. Maymun al-
    Qaddah 93n94
  Assassin legends 15–19
  Badakhshan 90n88
  Birjand (Khorasan) 55

Central Asia 20
Europeans 17
Fatimids 10
history 9, 13, 86
Hydari, Sir Mahomed Akbar Nazarally (Muslim politician and reformer, 1869–1942) 76
Ivanow, Wladimir (1886–1970) 4n4, 74
Massignon, Louis (French orientalist, 1883–1962) 85n82
misrepresentation 19, 22
persecution 155n63
religion 63n42
research 165
Rousseau, Jean Baptiste (French diplomat, 1780–1831) 81n75
Salamiyya (Syria) 133n35
schism 134
Syria 127
Tajikistan 6
taqiyya (precautionary dissimulation) 80–1, 137
Ismailism
   Abd Allah b. Maymun al-Qaddah 13, 93
   Central Intelligence Agency (CIA) 89
   Hunza (now in northern Pakistan) 150n55
   lectures 129
   Nizaris 11
   propaganda 160–1
   relics 133
   research 83–5, 94
   Satpanth 165
   Shams-i Tabrizi (spiritual guide of Rumi) 162n67
   Sufism 103
Italy 16, 19
Ivanow, Wladimir (1886–1970)
   Abd Allah b. Maymun al-Qaddah 28n43, 93
   Alledged Founder of Ismailism, The 28
   Asiatic Society of Bengal 71–2
   background 39–40
   Bombay 22
   book buying 155–8
   British Indian Forces 67–9
   career aspirations 51–3
   exile 1
   Guide to Ismaili Literature 23
   Haft bab-i Baba Sayyidna 29
   India 56–60
   Islamic Research Association (Bombay) 92n93
   Ismaili studies 22, 118
   Ismaili texts 24, 32–3
   Ismaili Traditions Concerning the Rise of the Fatimids 24–5
   Loan and Discount Bank of Persia (Uchetno-ssudni Bank Persii) 54–6
   malaria 161
   Memoirs 27
   military service 60–3
   naturalisation as a British Subject 79–80
   photographs 4, 141
   salary 88
   travel 99–100

Jaʿfaris *see* Muhammad-Shahis (Muʾminis, branch of Nizaris)
Jafer, Ismail M. 90
Jami, Abd al-Rahman (Persian Sufi, d. 1492) 144
Jami al-tawarikh (of Rashid al-Din Fadl Allah, d. 1318) 31, 32
Jerusalem 14, 128, 131
Journal of the Royal Asiatic Society 31, 34n63, 140

Juwayni, Ata-Malik (historian and Mongol administrator, d. 1283) 31–2

Kabul (Afghanistan) 76
Kagan (Kogon) 64, 120
Kahak (village in central Persia) 25
Kalam-e Mawla 167
Kalimpong (India) 117, 163–5
Karachi 58, 59, 125, 162, 172
Karbala (Iraq) 121n20, 139
Kashani, Abu'l-Qasim Abd Allah (historian, d. ca. 1337) 31–2
Kashi (India) 154
Kashira (Russia) 40
Kashmir 128
Kassis, As'ad 65, 66
Kathiawar (Gujarat) 58
Kerman (city and province, Persia) 86n84, 102, 107, 109, 125
Kermanshah (western Persia) 52n29, 55, 56, 121
Kharkov (Ukraine) 39, 41
Khashshab, Anton F. (linguist, 1874–1920) 52n28, 53
Khayrkhwah-i Harati, Muhammad Rida (Nizari *da'i* and author, d. after 1553) 28–9
Tasnifat 94n98
Khojas
   Aga Khan III, Sultan Muhammad (Mahomed) Shah (Nizari Imam, 1877–1957) 165
   Ismaili texts 84, 89
   Ivanow, Wladimir (1886–1970) 5, 74n60, 83, 85–6, 96
   Nizaris 11
   Pirana 175
   Sadr al-Din, Pir 171n77
   Satpanth 165n71
   traditions 87n86
Khorasan 3, 66, 81n74, 130n31
Khorasanis 65
Khozhdenie za tri moria (Journey beyond Three Seas, A) 154
al-Kirmani, Hamid al-Din (Ismaili *da'i* and author, d. ca. 1020) 10, 33
Kitab-i hidayat al-mu'minin al-talibin 90n89
Kokeli, Khanum 55–6
Koldewey, Robert (German architect and archaeologist, 1855–1925) 57n33, 121
Koran (Qur'an) 132n32, 155, 156, 169
Kraus, Paul (Czech orientalist, 1904–1944) 26, 126, 126n25, 137
Krishna 159
Kumzari dialect 124
Kunstkamera (of Peter the Great) 48, 48n23
Kurd Ali, Muhammad (Syrian scholar, 1876–1953) 132, 132n32
Kurdistan 55, 59
Kurds 67
Kuwait 122–3

Lab-i Hauz Mosque (Bukhara) 116
Ladoga (lake) 41
Lahore 32, 59, 160
La'l Shahbaz Qalandar (Sufi saint) 172n81, 173
Lamasar (fortress, northern Persia) 96n104, 136
Laptevo (Russia) 40
Larak 123, 124
Lataqiyya (Latakia, Syria) 138, 138n42
Latin Orient 15
Lepchus 150n56, 164
Lewis, Bernard (British orientalist, b. 1916) 34

Loan and Discount Bank of Persia
    (Uchetno-ssudni Bank Persii)
  Birjand (Khorasan) 55
  history 52n29
  Ivanow, Wladimir (1886–
    1970) 53, 54–6, 121
  Kermanshah (western Persia) 56
  Khashshab, Anton F. (linguist,
    1874–1920) 52
Loiko, Ivan I. 59
Lucknow (northern India) 59, 74,
  155–6, 163

al-Ma'arri, Abu'l-Ala (Syrian poet
  and philosopher, 973–
  1058) 138
McGill University (Montreal) 3
Madelung, Wilferd (German
  scholar of Islamic studies, b.
  1930) 25, 34, 35, 85n83
Madras (India) 59
malahida (heretics) 12, 85
Malmisa Force 3, 67, 69, 70
Mangits (dynasty in Central
  Asia) 118–19
Marchenko, Maria P. (Ivanow's
  mother) 39–40, 80
Margoliouth, David S. (British
  orientalist, 1858–1940) 26
Markov, Nikolai L. (Russian
  architect, 1882–1957) 110
Mashhad *see* Meshhed (Mashhad,
  Khorasan)
Mashmeer-Patrik, P. I. (Russian
  engineer) 77, 139, 140, 146,
  176, 178–9
Masqat (Muscat, Oman) 123
Massignon, Louis (French
  orientalist, 1883–1962) 21, 26,
  85n82, 126n25
Masyaf (castle in Syria) 134, 135,
  136
Mecca (Makka)
Mecklai, Ali Mahomed 92n93, 93–4

Memoir 17, 17n14, 81n75
Memoirs 5, 27
Menjil (village in northern
  Persia) 98
Meshhed (Mashhad, Khorasan)
  dervish (*darwish*) 102
  Dickson, William E. (British
    General, 1871–1957) 67
  Ghani, Ghasem (Iranian scholar,
    1893–1952) 130n31
  haramat 112–13
  history 112
  holy sites 139
  Ivanow, Wladimir (1886–
    1970) 3, 65, 66, 79, 80, 121
  Loan and Discount Bank of
    Persia (Uchetno-ssudni
    Bank Persii) 52n29
  modernization 108, 111–12
  Shrine of Imam Reza 111
  travel 140
Mesopotamia 55, 108, 139
  see also Iraq
Middle East 76n63
  see also Holy Land; Near East
  Barthold (Bartol'd), Vasilii V.
    (Russian orientalist, 1869–
    1930) 43n12, 44n12
  Cairo (al-Qahira) 127
  Druzes 132n33
  Ismaili studies 23n27
  Nizaris 133n35
  Stein, Sir Aurel (Hungarian
    archaeologist and explorer,
    1862–1943) 76n63
Mihrijan 104–5
Minab (near Bandar-i Abbas(i)) 124
Minaev, Ivan P. (Russian orientalist,
  1840–1890) 154n61
Mir Ali Shir Nawa'i (Central Asian
  poet, 1441–1501) 144, 144n48
Mir Arab Mosque (Bukhara) 115
Mongols 11, 31, 96n104
Moscow 39, 40

Moti Masjid (Agra) 158–9
Mughals 155n63, 172, 172n82
Muhammad-Shahis (Mu'minis, branch of Nizaris) 25, 134, 137
Muhammad, the Prophet 169n75
Mukherjee, Ashutosh (Indian educator, 1864–1924) 70, 70n53
Multan (now in Pakistan) 59, 160–1, 162, 162n67, 166–9
Mumtaz Mahal 172
Musa Khan b. Muhammad Khorasani (d. 1937) 89n87
Kitab-i hidayat al-mu'minin al-talibin 90n89
Museum of Anthropology and Ethnography (Muzei antropologii i etnographii imeni Petra velikogo Rossiiskoi Akademii Nauk, St Petersburg) 60, 116, 117
Musta'lians (branch of Ismailism) 11, 134
Mustansir bi'llah (Nizari Imam, d. 1480)
Pandiyat-i jawanmardi 28
al-Mustansir (Fatimid Imam-caliph, d. 1094) 11
al-Mustazhir (Abbasid caliph, 1094–1118) 14
al-Mustazhiri (of al-Ghazali) 14

Nabokov, Konstantin D. (1872–1927) 58n34, 59
Nabokov, Vladimir D. (1870–1922) 58n35
Nagawali River 78, 147
Najaf (Iraq) 112–13, 121n19, 139
Nanji, Azim 35
Nasir-i Khusraw (Ismaili *da'i* and poet, d. after 1070) 10, 21–2, 108
Navsari (Gujarat) 173
Near East 8, 14
   see also Middle East

Nepal, Nepalese 150, 150n56, 154n61
Neva River 41, 47n22
New Delhi 159
Nicholson, Reynold A. (British orientalist, 1868–1945) 145n50
Nikitin, Afanasii (Russian traveller, d. 1475) 123n24, 175
Khozhdenie za tri moria (Journey Beyond Three Seas, A) 154
Ni'mat Allahi (Sufi order) 102
Nishapur (Nishabur, northern Khorasan) 65, 81, 103–4
Nizam al-Din Awliyya (Sufi saint, d. 1325) 159n64
Nizam al-Mulk (Saljuq vizier, d. 1092) 13–14
Siyasat-nama 14
Nizam of Hyderabad *see* Hyderabad
Nizar b. al-Mustansir (Nizari Imam, d. 1095) 11
Nizaris (branch of Ismailism)
Afghanistan 11, 87n86
Aga Khans 74n60
Ahl-i Haqq 29
Alamut (fortress in northern Persia) 11
Assassin legends 15–16
Badakhshan 150n54
Central Asia 20
Crusaders 14
Fatimids 134
Hasan Kabir al-Din, Pir (d. ca. 1470) 171n77
history 25, 28
Hunza (now in northern Pakistan) 150n55
Ismaili texts 87n86
Ismailism 11
Ivanow, Wladimir (1886–1970) 5, 34, 74n60
Khorasan 81n74
literature 20, 29, 87n86

Masyaf (castle in Syria) 136n40
misrepresentation 18, 19
Persia 11, 31
Salamiyya (Syria) 133n35
Satpanth 165n71
schism 25
Silvestre de Sacy, Antoine I. (French orientalist, 1758–1838) 133n34
Sufis 28
Tajikistan 6
Umm al-kitab 62n42
North Africa 10, 166n72
al-Nu'man b. Muhammad, al-Qadi Abu Hanifa (Ismaili jurist and author, d. 974) 91n91
Da'a'im al-Islam 23
Nusayris (Alawis) 85n83, 138n42

Odessa 59, 162
Old Man of the Mountain *see* Rashid al-Din Sinan
Oldenburg (Ol'denburg), Sergei F. (Russian orientalist, 1863–1934)
  Asiatic Museum (Aziatskii Muzei Rossiiskoi Akademii Nauk, St Petersburg) 61n41, 62
  Aziatskii Musei Rossiiskoi Akademii Nauk 1818–1918 47n22
  Ivanow, Wladimir (1886–1970) 63
  photograph 61
  Rozen, Victor R. (Russian orientalist, 1849–1908) 46n17
  Stein, Sir Aurel (Hungarian archaeologist and explorer, 1862–1943) 76
Omayyad Mosque (Damascus) 132
Omayyads 10, 121n20, 169n74

Order of Assassins: The Struggle of the Early Nizari Isma'ilis against the Islamic World, The 34n64
Oriental studies
  Barthold (Bartol'd), Vasilii V. (Russian orientalist, 1869–1930) 43n12
  Ivanow, Wladimir (1886–1970) 2, 42, 154
  manuscript sources 47n22
  Rousseau, Jean Baptiste (French diplomat, 1780–1831) 81n75
  Rozen, Victor R. (Russian orientalist, 1849–1908) 44n17
  Soghdian language 63
  Sprenger, Aloys (orientalist, 1813–1893) 143–4
  St Petersburg University (Faculty of Oriental Languages) 42n11
  University of Cambridge 144n49
  Zarubin, Ivan I. (Russian orientalist, 1887–1964) 63n42
Orientalism 19
Orissa 146
Ottomans 57, 81n75, 133n35
Oxus (Amu Darya) River 20, 82n76

Pakistan 150n55, 160n65
Palestine 126n25, 128
Pamir (region in Central Asia) 20, 21, 49n25, 63n42, 82n76, 90n88
Pandiyat-i jawanmardi 28, 30
Panj River 20
Paris 19, 33, 81n75, 126n25, 127n26, 130n31
Parsis (Zoroastrians of India) 151n57
Peking University 153n60
Persia (Iran)

archaeological evidence 25, 26
banditry 104–5
drought 65
experiences 97–114
gypsies 107
Hasan-i Sabbah (Nizari leader and founder of Nizari state, d. 1124) 13
hospitality 114
Ismaili Society (Bombay) 94
Ismaili texts 23, 87n86
Ismailis 80
Ivanow, Wladimir (1886–1970) 22, 47, 51, 54, 63–7
manuscript sources 9, 74, 79
Mashmeer-Patrik, P. I. (Russian engineer) 78
Nizari texts 34
Nizaris 11, 31
oil 122n21
punishments 118
Rozenberg, Fedor A. (Russian orientalist, 1867–1934) 51n27
rural life 113
Russian bank 2
Tehran 109
travel 121
travel route 59
Persian Gulf 122, 125, 151, 163
Persian literature 144n49
Persians 67
Peter the Great (1682–1725) 48, 116
Phoenicians 136
Polo, Marco (Venetian traveller, 1254–1324) 15–16, 18
Poonawala, Ismail K. (scholar of Ismaili studies, b. 1937) 35
Popov, E. K. (Russian diplomat) 121
Punjab 167n72, 168, 171
Punjabis 152

Qaderi (Sufi order) 166, 166n72, 168, 169, 170
Qadmus (castle in Syria) 136
qahwa-khana (coffee house) 99, 100
Qa'in (Khorasan) 4, 81
Qajar dynasty (Persia) 54, 86n84, 106, 109–10
qalandar 172, 173, 174
qalyan (water pipe) 106
Qarmatis (branch of early Ismailis) 25, 34, 126n25
Qasim-Shahis (branch of Nizaris) 25, 134
Qazwin (Persia) 52n29, 98, 132
Qazwini, Muhammad (Iranian scholar, 1877–1949) 32, 130n31
Qeshm 123, 124
Quchan (Khorasan) 59
Quetta 66, 69
Qum (central Persia) 139

Radlov, Vasilii V. (Russian orientalist, 1837–1918) 49n25, 60, 60n39, 116, 117
Raipur (India) 78n70
Ranking, George S. A. (British surgeon and scholar, 1852–1934) 70n51
Grammar of the Persian Language, A 70n52
Rashid al-Din Fadl Allah (historian, d. 1318) 31–2
Jami al-tawarikh 31, 32
Rashid al-Din Sinan (Nizari *daʿi* in Syria, d. 1193) 14–15, 16, 135
Rasht (northern Persia) 52n29, 97–8
Rawdat al-taslim 29, 83, 84
Rayagada (India) 78n70, 83, 140, 146–7, 147, 147–9, 176
Revel *see* Tallinn (Estonia)
Rey (Persia) 109

Ross, Edward D. (British orientalist, 1871–1940) 72, 72n57, 73n57, 75
Rousseau, Jean Baptiste (French diplomat, 1780–1831) 81n75
Royal Asiatic Society 58, 90–2
 Guide to Ismaili Literature 23, 24
 Ivanow, Wladimir (1886–1970) 92n93
Rozen, Victor R. (Russian orientalist, 1849–1908) 44, 45
Rozenberg, Fedor A. (Russian orientalist, 1867–1934) 51
Rushan (Badakhshan) 20, 63n42, 82n76
Russia 20, 42n11, 47n22, 52n29, 66
Russian Academy of Sciences
 Asiatic Museum (Aziatskii Muzei, Rossiiskoi Akademii Nauk, St Petersburg) 2, 20, 47–54
 Barthold (Bartol'd), Vasilii V. (Russian orientalist, 1869–1930) 47
 Institute of Oriental Manuscripts (Institut Vostochnikh Rukopisei Rossiiskaia Akademiia Nauk, St Petersburg) 7
 Ivanow, Wladimir (1886–1970) 64–5, 73
 parcels 116
 Shcherbatskoi (Scherbatsky), Fedor R. (Russian orientalist, 1866–1942) 153
 St Petersburg University (Faculty of Oriental Languages) 44
Russian Revolution (1917) 1, 2, 50, 61n40, 66, 80
Rustichello of Pisa 16

Sabzewar (Khorasan) 52n29, 59, 65, 102
Sadr al-Din, Pir 171n77
Safawid (dynasty of Persia) 98n2, 118
Saladin (Salah al-Din, founder of the Ayyubid dynasty) 10
Salamiyya (Syria) 133n35, 134
Saljuqs 11, 13, 14
Samarkand (now in Uzbekistan) 47, 54, 63
Sanaa (Yemen) 19
Sanskrit (language) 73–4, 153–4
Sasanians 110
Satgur Nur, Pir (d. ca. 1094) 173n83, 174
Satikona (India) 147
Satpanth
 see also Ismailis; Khojas; Nizaris
 Nizari Khojas 165n71
 Pirana 175
 religious ceremonies 173
 Satgur Nur, Pir (d. ca. 1094) 173n83
 tombs 171
 traditions 87n86
 Uchchh (now in Pakistan) 171n77
School of Oriental and African Studies (University of London) 26, 73n57
Sebastopol (Sevastopol, Crimea) 41, 41n10
Sedeh (village in southern Khorasan) 81
Sehwan (Sindh) 172, 173, 174–5
Semenov, Aleksandr, A. (Russian orientalist, 1873–1958) 21, 89, 89n88, 90n88
Semirechye Regiment (Russian Cossacks) 66, 68, 103
Senendaj (western Persia) 55
Shah Jahan (Mughal emperor, 1628–1659) 172, 173
Shams-i Tabrizi (spiritual guide of Rumi) 162n67

shari'a (sacred law of Islam) 14
Shastri, Haraprasad (1853–1931) 73n59, 74n59
Shatt al-Arab river 122
Shcherbatskoi (Scherbatsky), Fedor R. (Russian orientalist, 1866–1942) 43, 44, 46n17, 153
Shihab al-Din Shah al-Husayni (Nizari author, d. 1884) 29
Shi'i Islam
  al-Hasan b. Ali (625–669) 169n74
  Bedouins 124
  Christians 17
  holy sites 121–2, 139
  Ismaili studies 21
  Ismailis 17
  Ivanow, Wladimir (1886–1970) 1, 57
  Massignon, Louis (French orientalist, 1883–1962) 85n82
  persecution 155n63
  sects 171
  Strothmann, Rudolf (German orientalist, 1877–1960) 85n83
  Sufism 102
  taqiyya (precautionary dissimulation) 80n73
Shi'is 1, 9
Shiraz (southern Persia) 59, 80, 102, 108
Shughnan (Badakhshan) 20, 63n42, 82n76, 90n88
al-Sijistani, Abu Ya'qub (Ismaili *da'i* and author, d. after 971) 10
Sikkim 150n56, 164
Silvestre de Sacy, Antoine I. (French orientalist, 1758–1838) 17–18, 17n14, 81n75
  Exposé de la religion des Druzes 17, 133
  Memoir 17

Simla (northern India) 58
Sindh (now in Pakistan) 86n84
Sistan (Arabic, Sijistan) 54, 76, 106, 117
Siyasat-nama 14
Smirnov, Vasilii D. (Russian Turkologist, 1846–1922) 46, 46n19
Soghdian language 49n25, 51n27, 63
South Africa 142
South Asia 8, 9, 11, 165n71
Sprenger, Aloys (orientalist, 1813–1893) 143
St Petersburg
  Asiatic Museum (Aziatskii Muzei, Rossiiskoi Akademii Nauk, St Petersburg) 50
  conference 7
  Institute of Oriental Manuscripts (Institut Vostochnikh Rukopisei Rossiiskaia Akademiia Nauk, St Petersburg) 21, 47n22
  Ivanow, Wladimir (1886–1970) 1, 2, 40, 59, 162
  Loan and Discount Bank of Persia (Uchetno-ssudni Bank Persii) 56
  Marchenko, Maria P. (Ivanow's mother) 39
  Mashmeer-Patrik, P. I. (Russian engineer) 77
  Ross, Edward D. (British orientalist) 72n57
  Russian Academy of Sciences 20, 44n16
  Tsarskoe Selo (Pushkin, Russia) 41
St Petersburg University (Faculty of Oriental Languages) 2, 42n11, 43, 46n17, 48, 153n60

St Petersburg University (Faculty of Physics and Mathematics) 39, 77
Stael-Holstein, Alexander von (Russian scholar, 1877–1937) 153n60
Stein, Sir Aurel (Hungarian archaeologist and explorer, 1862–1943) 75–6, 82, 116, 117
Stern, Samuel M. (Hungarian-British scholar, 1920–1969) 25, 34
Stroeva, Liudmila V. (Russian orientalist, 1910–1993) 34
Strothmann, Rudolf (German orientalist, 1877–1960) 34–5, 85n83
Suez 128, 129
Sufis 28, 167n72, 172
Sufism
   analysis 172
   Iqbal, Muhammad (1877–1938) 160
   Ivanow, Wladimir (1886–1970) 2, 103
   Nizam al-Din Awliyya (Sufi saint, d. 1325) 159n64
   research 166
   Satpanth 165
   Shams-i Tabrizi (spiritual guide of Rumi) 162
   Uchchh (now in Pakistan) 170
Suhrawardy, Huseyn S. (Bengali politician and statesman, 1892–1963) 72n55
Suhrawardy, Ma'mun 72, 73
Sulaymanis (branch of Tayyibis) 23, 76, 91n91, 132n32, 152
Sunni Islam 10, 17
Sunnis
   Abbasids 9
   black legend 16, 18
   chronicles 18
   Ismailis 12–13, 22, 80

Larak 124
Nizaris 11
Satpanth 165n71
Shi'is 12
Suwayda (Syria) 114, 132–3
Syria
   Crusaders 14
   experiences 131–40
   Fatimids 10
   Ismaili Society (Bombay) 94
   Ismaili texts 35
   Ismailis 80
   Ivanow, Wladimir (1886–1970) 127
   Kassis, As'ad 65, 66
   manuscript sources 9, 19, 81
   Merje Square (photograph) 131
   Nizaris 11
   people 137, 138
   Sufism 166n72

Tabas (southern Khorasan) 59, 104
Tagore, Rabindranath (Bengali poet and Nobel laureate, 1861–1941) 152n58
Tahafut al-falasifa 119
Taj Mahal (Agra) 158, 172
Tajikistan 5, 20, 82n76, 90n88, 91n89
Tajiks 6
Tallinn (Estonia) 41, 49n25
Tamir, Arif (Syrian scholar of Ismaili studies, 1921–1988) 35
taqiyya (precautionary dissimulation) 80, 80n73, 165
Tartus 136–7, 138
Tasawwurat see Rawdat al-taslim
Tashkent (now in Uzbekistan) 54, 90n88, 160
Tasnifat 94n98
Tayyibis (branch of Ismailism)
   Bohras 175n85
   excommunication 27

Fyzee, Asaf A. A. (Bohra scholar and educator, 1899–1981) 23
al-Hamdani, Husayn F. (Bohra scholar of Ismaili studies, 1901–1962) 26
Ismailism 11
Strothmann, Rudolf (German orientalist, 1877–1960) 34–5
Sulaymanis (branch of Tayyibis) 76n65
texts 23
Yemen 86n85
Tehran
  altitude 164
  architecture 110–11
  Avicenna (Ibn Sina, philosopher and physician, 980–1037) 95
  Ayni, Kamol (1928–2010) 6
  Corbin, Henry (French orientalist, 1903–1978) 33
  description 98–9
  Dickson, William E. (1871–1957) 67n48
  Ivanow, Wladimir (1886–1970) 5, 80, 94n98, 162
  Jami al-tawarikh (of Rashid al-Din Fadl Allah) 32
  Khashshab, Anton F. (linguist, 1874–1920) 52n28
  modernization 108–10
  photograph 98, 107
  Qajar mosques 109–10
  Shams al-Imare (photograph) 109
  travel 131
  Tup-khane (Square in Tehran) 108
Tehran University 5
Telugu language 147
Tigris (Dajla) River 57, 122
Tizenhausen, Vladimir G. (Russian orientalist, 1825–1902) 53n30
Tolstoi, Count Lev N. (1828–1910) 46n20
Tsarskoe Selo (Pushkin, Russia) 41, 41n7, 51
Tula (Russia) 40, 40n6
Tup-khane (Square in Tehran) 107, 108, 109
Turaev, Boris A. (Russian scholar, 1868–1920) 44n15
Turbat Haydari (Persia) 128
Turgenev, Ivan (1818–1883) 153
Turkestan 54, 63, 68, 80, 120, 162
Turkestan Down to the Mongol Invasion 43n12
Turks 67
al-Tusi, Nasir al-Din (Shi'i scholar, d. 1274)
  Rawdat al-taslim 29
  Sayr va suluk 29n53
Twelver Shi'is 9, 80n73, 85n82, 85n83, 112n14, 165n71
Tyabji family (India) 91n91, 92n93

Uchchh (now in Pakistan) 166, 169, 170, 171n77
ulama (religious scholars) 12
Umayyads *see* Omayyads
Umm al-kitab 24, 62n42
Umm Kulthum (Egyptian singer, d. 1975) 129, 130
University of Cairo 126n25, 127, 129, 130–1
University of California, Berkeley 6
University of Cambridge 91n91, 144n49, 145n50, 152, 160n65
University of Kashmir and Jammu (Srinagar) 91n91, 152
University of Oxford 26, 82n78
Upper Oxus 82, 82n76
  see also Badakhshan; Central Asia; Pamir
Uqr Zayti (Syria) 137, 138
Urdu language 26

Vienna 18
Vitebsk (Belorussia) 41
Vladivostok 59, 162
Volga River 40, 63
Vyborg 41

Wakhan (Badakshan) 82n76
Walker, Paul E. (American scholar of Ismaili studies) 10n2, 129n28

Yaghnob (Central Asia) 63, 64
Yaroslavl (Russia) 40, 40n5
Yazd (Persia) 59, 109
Yemen 9, 11, 19, 26, 76n65, 86n85

Zahid Ali (Bohra scholar of Ismaili studies, 1888–1958) 26, 27
Zahidan (Persia) 69, 80, 140
Zaleman (Salemann), Karl (Carl) G. (H.) (Russian orientalist, 1849–1916)

Asiatic Museum (Aziatskii Muzei, Rossiiskoi Akademii Nauk, St Petersburg) 2, 49n25
death 61
Ivanow, Wladimir (1886–1970) 54, 59, 114
photograph 45
St Petersburg University (Faculty of Oriental Languages) 44
travel 56
Zangids (of Syria) 10
Zarubin, Ivan I. (Russian orientalist, 1887–1964) 20, 62n43, 81–2
Zayandeh-rud (river in Isfahan) 102
Zhukovskii, Valentin A. (Russian orientalist, 1858–1918) 45, 46n18, 101–2
zikr (dhikr) 169
Zoroastrians 109, 151n57